Webs of Reality

Webs of Reality

*Social Perspectives on
Science and Religion*

WILLIAM A. STAHL
ROBERT A. CAMPBELL
YVONNE PETRY
GARY DIVER

RUTGERS UNIVERSITY PRESS
New Brunswick, New Jersey, and London

Library of Congress Cataloging-in-Publication Data

Webs of reality : social perspectives on science and religion / William A.
Stahl . . . [et al.]
    p. cm.
    Includes bibliographical references and index.
    ISBN 0-8135-3106-3 (cloth : alk. paper)—ISBN 0-8135-3107-1 (pbk : alk.
paper)
    1. Religion and science—Social aspects. I. Stahl, William A. (William
Austin)

BL240.3 . W43 2002
306.6'9175—dc21

                                                                2001058686

British Cataloging-in-Publication information is available from the British Library.

Manufactured in the United States of America

Contents

Preface and Acknowledgments

In 1994 the John Templeton Foundation began the Science and Religion Course Program (SRCP) and turned what had been a small, sputtering discussion over the relationship between the natural sciences and religion into a large international debate. Our book aims to add a new dimension to that debate by bringing in the voice of the social sciences. It also is an expression of what has come to be known as the Toronto Approach to the science-religion dialogue.

Between 1996 and 1999 the SRCP workshop held annually in Toronto developed a distinctive style. Its approach was to be open, inclusive, and tolerant of differing points of view. The Toronto workshop welcomed more religions than Christianity, more sciences than physics and biology, and historians and social scientists as well. It had a much broader understanding of religion than just academic theology, and it saw ethics and technology as issues that must be addressed. In addition it was populist, believing that the dialogue between science and religion was as much for the scientists in the lab and the believers in the pew as it was for the academic elite. Its style was also playful and, at times, mischievous (taking an afternoon off to discuss science fiction, for instance). Although the Toronto workshops have been canceled as a result of policy changes within the Templeton organization, the international community that was formed in Toronto has become a voice in the science-religion dialogue in its own right.

As the subtitle of this book indicates, what we are offering here is a social perspective on the relationship between religion and science. Much of the present literature in the area reflects efforts by theologians to talk about science, or by scientists (particularly astronomers, physicists, and evolutionary biologists) to talk about religion. Tremendous advances in our understanding of our selves and of the structure of the universe have given rise to new perspectives on matters of intelligent design, creation, evolution, and the place of humankind in the overall order of things. Thus, the traditional division of labor between theologians and scientists has broken down, and the quest to answer some of the ultimate questions of existence has become an open arena for scholars from many disciplines. Historians like John Hedley Brooke have provided a great deal of contextual information and detail on the interactions between theologians and scientists as they confront these issues, while philosophers have provided insight into the nature of the arguments and evidence used by these scholars.[1] What the social sciences have to offer is a broader perspective on the relationship between religion and science, expanding beyond the realm of theory to include the practical questions of technology and ethics. The social sciences can explore both science and religion as practices, as ways of ordering our lives, as systems of meaning, and as institutions.

Our approach to the social sciences is itself interdisciplinary, drawing primarily from history, sociology, and science studies. The reader should be aware that there are a variety of schools of thought within science studies, including, for example, the strong program of David Bloor and Barry Barnes, the functionalism of Robert Merton, the actor-network theory of Bruno Latour, the social epistemology of Steve Fuller, the anthropology of science of Karin Knorr Cetina, and a variety of feminist approaches, such as those of Evelyn Fox Keller, Sandra Harding, and Donna Haraway.[2] Each school approaches the study of science in its own way, and it would be a mistake to make one speak for the others. We will call upon the various insights of a number of these perspectives.

The unifying theme of the book is the metaphor of the seamless web of science, technology, religion, and ethics. We will look for the subtle relationships, tacit understandings, unrecognized assumptions, forgotten history, symbols, and implicit myths that tie all four elements together. We will redraw the usual disciplinary boundaries, analyzing science through religious categories. This will expose some of the images and assumptions that have constructed walls and will allow the dialogue to begin to develop a dialectical understanding of science and religion that is both more holistic and more oriented toward ethical action than could arise from just another discussion of natural science theories and academic theology. To the extent that we can do this, we hope to embody the Toronto Approach.

Our book is a fully collaborative effort that tries to embody the science-religion dialogue in the discussions among the four of us. In addition to our primary disciplinary foundations—religious history, the sociology of religion, science and technology studies, physics—all of us are cross-trained in other disciplines. All of us teach classes that are Templeton Foundation Course award winners. Three of us have seminary training. We each gain insight from a different faith tradition: Roman Catholic, Lutheran, Presbyterian, and Anglican. While we all acknowledge and strongly affirm that the science-religion dialogue does and should encompass more religions than Christianity, we also realize our own limitations and have no desire to try to appropriate the voice of others.

The Plan of the Book

The structure of the book will look at science and religion by borrowing, rather playfully and metaphorically, from Max Weber's categories of religious thought: soteriology, saintliness, magical causation, theodicy, and mystery (with due recognition to Steve Fuller's *Science*, which pioneered this technique).[3] Since Weber was one of the originators of "value-free" science, which emphasized the importance of the researcher's remaining objective, the final section combines mystery and objectivity in an appropriately Weberian manner. While the bulk of each chapter has its origins in the disciplinary perspective and research interests of one or another of the authors, in the end, we have tried through discussion and debate to ensure that the whole represents a collaborative effort on our parts.

The introduction makes the argument that the social sciences belong in the science-religion dialogue. Over the past century and a half, thick boundaries have been drawn between science and religion, which has led most people to think that there is either an automatic conflict between them or that they have nothing to say to each other. Fortunately, those boundaries are beginning to break down as the science-religion dialogue grows, but the social sciences have largely been left out of the discussion. We examine three models of the relationship between science and religion, arguing for an inclusive model that sees a seamless web between science, religion, technology, and ethics. We then briefly look at some of the potential contributions that the social sciences could make to the dialogue, and we elaborate on Max Weber's categories of religious thought.

Soteriology, Weber's first category, is the term used to describe ideas about salvation. Part 1 looks at science as salvation. When social scientists step back from the content and theories of science and examine its functions and discourse, science is revealed as implicitly religious. The sacred myth of science proclaims science as salvation. This "scientific worldview" portrays science as progress toward knowledge and rationality that will liberate us ("the truth will make you free"). By "demy-thologizing" science, the social sciences open up the science-religion dialogue by allowing us to understand the origins, as well as the internal and external consequences, of this worldview.

Chapter 1 takes the view that if it is legitimate to examine religion scientifically, it should also be possible to examine science religiously. Science and religion are both elaborate systems of meaning, with immense institutional frameworks to support them. Yet, both rely on communities of faith to support them, whether that faith is in God or in the power of the scientific method. What truth may lie at the heart of either science or religion is of less importance than how each of them provides answers to the pressing questions of existence. It is common in contemporary society, with all of its scientific and technological marvels, to link our freedom to our own abilities, but just as with religion, it takes a leap of faith.

Chapter 2 is an examination of the history of science as a discipline and a study of its evolution from the late nineteenth century to the present. Specifically, this chapter suggests that the way that the Scientific Revolution has been understood as a historic event has both shaped and been shaped by the role of science in the twentieth century. If one views science as an ever-increasing body of knowledge, then the history of science becomes a history of success stories. If, on the other hand, one views science as a human activity, the history of science becomes the story of both the successes and the failures, and the contexts in which they unfolded. It is suggested that the current debates around the Scientific Revolution as a meaningful historical concept reflect ambivalence about the role of science in contemporary society.

Part 2 looks at saintliness, Weber's second category of religious thought, in science. Saintliness refers to the idea that there are always special individuals who stand out because of their dedication, genius, or both, and who demonstrate that religion—and science—when taken seriously, are a vocation or calling. Saints provide exemplars for the community. The saint is a potent image. But here ambiguity enters in. First, the image is always different from the reality. Images of science create a gap between how it is portrayed and how it is practiced. Second, images have power, and we often accept them unconsciously. Images of scientific saints serve to establish science as authority and as an alternative to religion. The social sciences can make important contributions to the science-religion dialogue by analyzing science as an active practice of discovery and debate engaged in by a community. As a practice, science becomes a process of knowing rather than a corpus of truths about the natural world, divorced from any context, which the nonexpert must accept on faith.

Chapter 3 examines the images that introductory biology textbooks project of scientists and the scientific method, and pictorial representations of scientific models. One of these images is the scientific genius as a secular saint. It concludes with a few reflections on what these images mean for the science-religion dialogue.

Chapter 4 examines the greatest of scientific saints, Isaac Newton, and finds him to be more of a Faust figure. On the one hand, Newton's genius was the culmination of the Scientific Revolution, and his physics still has great importance for our understanding of the world. On the other hand, Newton was a mystic who wrote voluminously on alchemy and biblical prophecy. The chapter concludes with some reflections on what the philosophy of naturalism, derived from Newton's science, means for the dialogue with religion.

Part 3 examines Weber's third category of religious thought, magical causation. The Scientific Revolution drew boundaries that separated science from its earlier association with magic. In spite of a strong and continuing rhetorical rejection of magic, a social scientific analysis of scientific practice reveals that in scientific discussion of causation and in technology, these boundaries are not so clear. This has ethical and political implications that the science-religion dialogue needs to address. We approach science and technology as magic through three different lenses: the substantive, the functional, and the symbolic.

Chapter 5 takes a historical perspective and looks at the definitions of magic, religion, and science as they evolved over time in Western society. In order to understand the distinctions that we make, it is valuable to examine how each of these categories was understood prior to the modern period. The chapter shows how prescientific Western culture understood the interaction of the material and spiritual realms and suggests that what really changed with the rise of science was the attitude that scientists began to take toward the inexplicable and the invisible.

Chapter 6 employs a functional analysis of magic in an exploration of the healing power of prayer and the controversy over the source of the AIDS epidemic. Both of these phenomena demonstrate the tenuous relationship that can exist between cause and effect. We do not understand how prayer heals, and yet, with the growing amount of evidence to support the fact that it can and does cure, it is increasingly difficult for medical science and the public to ignore. Similarly, the AIDS epidemic is having a frightening and all too real impact on the people of every country, but especially on those in several African nations. What causes AIDS? Where did it come from? We simply do not know. Like the mechanism through which prayer heals, AIDS appears to have just come into existence, as if by magic.

Chapter 7 uses a symbolic perspective in seeing technology as magic.

The chapter is built around a case study of the recent "magic box" advertising campaign by IBM. Why, in our supposedly secular society, would one of the world's largest technology companies want to refer to its products as magic? The search for an answer to that question reveals some of the symbols and myths underlying our discourse about technology, and a few of their spiritual, ethical, and political implications.

Theodicy, Weber's fourth category of religious thought and the subject of part 4, is usually explained as the answers religion gives to the questions of suffering and death. The notion of theodicy is closely related to ideas about salvation and centers on the concept of justice, whether God-given or emerging out of the scientific enterprise. Chapter 8 raises the problem that mass extinction poses for theodicy. This chapter is a case study of the controversy surrounding the discovery that sixty-five million years ago a comet or asteroid struck the Earth, exterminating the dinosaurs and 70 percent of all the other species on the planet. A sociological analysis of this controversy reveals the workings of scientific practice. The more we understand about how scientists work, the richer our dialogue can become. Also, the history of the controversy reveals some of the implicitly religious ideas embedded in scientific theory. And finally, the content of the discovery itself both challenges many assumptions in the science-religion dialogue and raises in a particularly strong form the question of theodicy.

Mystery, that which is unknown, was the final category of religious thought, according to Weber. What is the relationship between mystery and objectivity, and does it mean that conflict between science and religion is inevitable? The so-called science wars that raged throughout the nineties answered that it does and raised in dramatic form many questions that also lie at the heart of the science-religion dialogue. Using the science wars as a foil, in part 5 we argue that there is a necessary tension between the poles of mystery and objectivity. Truth is found in the tension between them and is lost when the tension is abandoned for one pole or the other. The social sciences bring a crucial means of understanding and retaining this tension to the science-religion dialogue.

Chapter 9 provides an analysis of the science wars in order to demonstrate that philosophical and metaphysical squabbles often detract from the more important tasks of actually doing science and studying the part that it plays in the construction of contemporary society.

Chapter 10 combats the mystification of science by describing how working scientists, particularly physicists, approach the creation and validation of scientific knowledge and the relationship between different ways of knowing reality. It concludes that there is nothing in science that necessarily excludes religion.

The tensions between mystery and objectivity are not new. Using history as an exemplar of interpretive social science, chapter 11 shows that the natural sciences are now facing challenges that the social sciences have had to face over the past century and a half. In particular, the understanding of language developed by interpretive social science may be of value in understanding the relationship between objectivity and mystery.

Chapter 12 looks at two contrasting ways of knowing: the quest for certainty, as exemplified by the science wars, and an understanding of truth as dialogue. After criticizing the quest for certainty and its fear of relativism, the chapter explores the work of Alfred Schutz on the nature of symbols and multiple realities to demonstrate the centrality of dialogue. This approach can ground the science-religion debate.

We would like to take this opportunity to recognize the efforts of Thaddeus Trenn, Don MacNally, and Gordon Baker in creating and sustaining, for at least four years, the formal and informal environment that allowed the Toronto workshop to thrive.

Chapter 1 is adapted from Robert A. Campbell, "The Truth Will Set You Free: Towards a Religious Study of Science," *Journal of Contemporary Religion* 16 (2001): 29–43. Used with permission.

Webs of Reality

Introduction

Finding a Place at the Table

Science and religion have different purposes, different limitations, different modes of action. But they are both part, and I would argue a necessary part, of every culture and every person. They need to exist in some vital and healthy whole in which each is integral. This means not simply a tacit agreement to ignore each other but open inter-change between them with all the possibilities of mutual growth and transformation that that entails.

—Robert Bellah, *Beyond Belief*

Good fences make good neighbors. That may be sound advice for the open range or the backyard, but it leaves something to be desired as a formula for academic life. Modern universities are all too often characterized by the barricades separating departments and disciplines. Nowhere is this more apparent than between science and religion.

One belief common today is that science and religion are mutually exclusive. Some self-appointed spokespeople, for either science or religion, proclaim that the more there is of one, the less there will be of the other. They profess that either science or religion has a monopoly on truth. Even more frequent is the belief that science and religion have nothing to say to each other at all. Millions of people live their lives with their faith and their knowledge of the world securely stored in separate compartments.

This has not always been the case. For most of Western history, religious faith and knowledge of the natural world walked hand in hand. Indeed, as we will see in chapter 2, until the nineteenth century most people did not see a necessary opposition between the two. The process of drawing boundaries between what today we call science and religion has been long, complicated, and at times painful.

Fortunately, over the past half century a number of individuals and small groups dedicated themselves to continuing a dialogue between religion and science. Then in 1994 the John Templeton Foundation began offering substantial monetary awards for classes on religion and science. This input of resources transformed what had been since the 1950s a relatively small discussion among a few scholars and church people into a large international debate. While the volume and pace of work in this area has increased, a peculiarity of the current debate between religion and science is that, with the notable exception of the history of science, the social sciences are usually ignored. They have not been invited to the table.

In this book we argue that without the inclusion of the social sciences the science-religion dialogue is incomplete. Much of the dialogue to date has been an effort either by theologians to talk about science or by scientists (particularly astronomers, physicists, and evolutionary biologists) to talk about religion. This is fine, as far as it goes, but the dialogue so far has tended to be very theoretical and, quite frankly, abstract. All too often, the focus of discussion has been the impact of scientific theories on religious beliefs. What the social sciences have to offer is a broader perspective on the relationship between religion and science, expanding beyond the realm of theory to include other, more practical, issues like those of technology, ethics, and politics. The social sciences are uniquely equipped with analytical tools to explore both science and religion as practices, as ways of ordering our lives, and as institutions.

In this book we will redraw the usual disciplinary boundaries, analyzing science through religious categories. This will expose and demystify some of the images and assumptions that have constructed walls between them. We will argue for the importance of maintaining a creative tension between science and religion, between objectivity and mystery, between Creation and the Word. This, we believe, will allow the dialogue to begin to develop an understanding of science and religion that is both more holistic and oriented toward ethical action.

In this introduction we will first look at some of the reasons the social sciences have been ignored. This involves examining the nature of the process of drawing identity boundaries and the models used to guide the debate. Once we have found a model that invites the social sciences to the table, we will show some of the benefits that they can bring to the game. We conclude the introduction by setting out the framework that we will use for our own exploration of the seamless web of science, religion, technology, and ethics.

Left out of the Game

Why the social sciences have not been major players in the science-religion debate in recent years is not clear. In the past, the social sciences were deeply involved. The founders of modern social science played a prominent role in drawing the boundaries between science and religion in the nineteenth century. For example, August Comte, the founder of sociology, postulated a "Law of Three Stages" that claimed science would replace religion. Historians John Draper and Andrew White first articulated what today would be called the "conflict approach" to the relationship between religion and science later in the century. Karl Marx, Emile Durkheim, Max Weber, and Sigmund Freud, all argued, each in his own way, that science would supplant traditional religion.

In the twentieth century, active involvement in the debate by the social sciences continued. The sociology of religion, in particular, had long discussions on the relationship between science and religion, usually under the rubric of secularization. As the modern science-religion dialogue developed in the 1950s, Ralph Burhoe, the founder of the Institute for Religion in an Age of Science and the journal *Zygon*—and the person who has perhaps done more than any other to shape the current form of the debate—was also prominent in the early years of the Society for the Scientific Study of Religion, the largest group of sociologists of religion.[1] But today, for whatever reason, those drawing the boundaries for the dialogue have left social science outside.

This can be demonstrated by a content analysis of *Zygon*, regarded as the premier journal in the field by many. The content of articles published between 1994 and the first half of 2000 were analyzed, including review essays but excluding editorial material and book reviews. This period covers the massive increase in the debate due to the John Templeton Foundation's financial support. Of 281 articles, only 34 (12.10 percent) referred to social science, and of these sociology was mentioned in only 12 (4.27 percent) and psychology in 13 (4.63 percent). Another 13 articles (4.63 percent) mentioned feminism. By contrast, sociobiology was discussed in 42 articles (14.95 percent) and neuropsychology in 29 (10.32 percent). These were articles that mentioned social science, not that necessarily were about social science or were presented from a social science perspective. Some were critical of the social sciences.

If social scientists want to find a place at the table, they will have to redraw the boundaries of the debate. This may not be easy. Drawing boundaries has always been a difficult social task. It is a process of definition and demarcation in which criteria of inclusion and exclusion are applied to both define one's own identity and separate that identity from others. Identities are fluid, and their boundaries are never simply "given" but are constructed as the need arises in specific historical situations.[2]

For example, what it means to be a scientist is not automatically bestowed by granting a degree. Astronomers are a good illustration. On one occasion (while trying to recruit prospective science majors, for instance), they may need to distinguish their work from that of chemists or biologists and draw lines of distinction between the sciences by appealing to such things as subject matter, specialized techniques, and so on. Studying the stars is what distinguishes them from other scientists. At another time (during, say, a television interview about astrology), they may identify with chemists and biologists as fellow scientists by calling upon a shared scientific method in opposition to "pseudoscience." Studying the stars, in this case, neither makes them different from other scientists nor establishes any kinship with astrology based on a common "subject matter."

Because so much energy is expended in boundary work, it is not surprising that the results would be strongly defended. Indeed, challenges to established boundaries are often perceived as threatening. One way of protecting them is to see them as "natural" and "the way things are." However, problems may result if boundary walls become too high or impermeable.

This, we believe, is to a large extent what has happened to science and religion in modern society. The process of demarcating science and religion as separate realms tends to both reify and fragment our systems of meaning. The science-religion dialogue has gone a long way in breaking down the walls, but, we argue, it has not gone quite far enough.

In order to make the science-religion dialogue more inclusive of the social sciences, it would be useful to examine how its boundaries have been constructed by analyzing the models of the debate itself. In the current debate there are three models that illustrate ways of relating science and religion. One, that of Ian Barbour, has clearly been dominant and has structured much of the dialogue that has taken place over the past decade. It has recently been challenged by the models of Stephen Jay Gould and of Ronald Cole-Turner.

Ian Barbour's Models

Ian Barbour actually has two models, one of the relationship between science and religion and another for science, technology, and society. We will look at both (see figs. I.1 and I.2). His model of science and religion has been the dominant one in the debate.[3] It is widely copied in textbooks and has been institutionalized in the John Templeton Foundation's approach to the dialogue.[4] A few other scholars have developed models that are variations on Barbour's.[5] Most of what we say about Barbour applies equally to these variants. Barbour's ap-

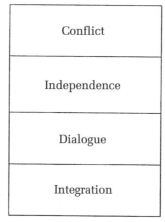

Figure I.1 Ian Barbour's Model of Ways to Relate Science and Religion

proach is typological, listing four types of relationship between science and religion.

The first type is *conflict,* which sees science and religion as mutually exclusive and inherently incompatible. This approach creates strong and thick boundaries between science and religion. Conflict arises because proponents of either science or religion claim a monopoly on truth. Scientific materialists, such as Richard Dawkins, Stephen Weinberg, or Jacques Monod, believe that science is the only valid form of knowledge and that it can explain all of reality. Religion is therefore false. Biblical literalists are examples from the side of religion, arguing that the first two chapters of Genesis give a full and accurate account of the formation of the universe. Scientific theories are therefore false.

The second type is *independence.* Here the boundaries are also strong and thick, but science and religion are seen as separate spheres that do not make claims upon each other. For theologians and philosophers, such as Karl Barth, Rudolf Bultmann, George Lindbeck, and the early Langdon Gilkey (interestingly, Barbour does not mention any practicing scientists), science and religion have contrasting methodologies, subject matter, and languages that simply do not compete. This approach has been institutionalized in the "mainstream" churches and is probably the position most commonly held by the public.

The third type, *dialogue,* sees that the spheres of science and religion are separate but do indeed impinge on each other, requiring dialogue between them. There are a wide variety of positions here. Typical kinds of questions include: What are the presuppositions and limits of science? Are there methodological parallels between science and religion? Is there a nature-centered spirituality? A few examples of people working from this position are Wolfhardt Pannenberg, Karl Rahner, David Tracy, and Michael Polanyi.

The fourth and final type is *integration*, "a more systematic and extensive kind of partnership between science and religion [which] occurs among those who seek a closer integration of the two disciplines."[6] This usually takes one of three forms. Natural theology, as exemplified by William Paley or Richard Swineborne, sees God's design revealed in scientific findings, or, as it is usually put, the book of nature reveals God as much as does the book of Scripture. The theology of nature argues that specific scientific theories may affect the content of theology. This approach includes Arthur Peacocke, Pierre Teilhard de Chardin, and Barbour himself. Finally, a systematic synthesis, as argued by process theologians such as John Cobb and Charles Hartshorne, tries to build an inclusive metaphysics that unites religion and science.

There is great value in Barbour's model, and it has shaped most of the debate over the past decade. Nevertheless it has a number of limitations. We think it has three problems in particular.

First, while Barbour's model has considerable merit as a typology of the science-religion debate as it exists at present, it lacks both dynamics and historical agency. It is static and ahistorical.[7] Positions are categorized without explanation of how those categories arose or of the dynamics of the debate within or between positions. Each position is defined by its essence, rather than seen as the result of boundary work. In other words, Barbour presents us with boundaries but does not let us watch how those boundaries were constructed. But unless we can understand the dynamics and trajectories of a debate, we cannot fully comprehend it.

Second, Barbour presents a model of dialogue between academic theology and a rather surprisingly narrow range of scientific theories rather than between a full spectrum of science and religion. He discusses what the content of science means for theology, instead of seeing both as processes or practices. It is a very abstract, intellectual, and circumscribed model. Other than a few incidental references, social dimensions are left out. The experiential and community aspects of science are notably absent, while those of religion are brief and abstract. There is no meaningful discussion of institutions and power relationships. As a consequence, there is little room for the social sciences. In Barbour's expanded Gifford Lectures, for instance, the sociology of science is dismissed in less than two pages, while the sociology of religion is ignored altogether.[8] Feminism does slightly better, meriting four pages and scattered references elsewhere.[9] This volume does acknowledge the importance of history, but these chapters are quite clearly "added on" and are not the center of his analysis.

Finally, Barbour sharply separates theory and practice. He writes extensively on technology and ethics, but these are in separate volumes

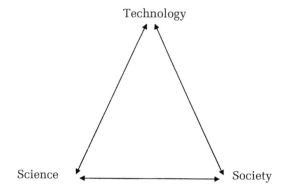

Figure I.2 Ian Barbour's Model of Science, Technology, and Society

from his work on science and religion, in which technology is barely mentioned. Barbour maintains the distinction between "pure" science and the "applied" science of technology, and he generally exempts the former from criticisms aimed at the latter.[10]

This final criticism is well illustrated by Barbour's second model, developed in his second series of Gifford Lectures.[11] In this volume, Barbour discusses the social dimension so conspicuously absent from the first. He presents three models of the relationship between science, technology, and society. The first is linear development, which sees science leading directly to technology, which in turn impacts upon society. He rejects this model. The second is technological determinism, which sees technology as the causative factor in both science and society. He rejects this as well. Both of these models portray one-way relationships and neither allows for interplay between the three elements. His own position he calls contextual interaction, which sees mutual interactions between science, technology, and society (see fig. I.2).

In doing this, however, Barbour reveals a flaw in his second model. He talks about science, technology, and society as three separate entities that, while they may influence each other, remain essentially distinct. Science and technology are portrayed as apart from, albeit influenced by, society, not as integral elements of society. So in spite of his extensive discussion of science and values, lurking in his model are the separation of science from society and the theoretical from the practical. In this second work he presents a magisterial overview of ethical issues involving technology, but its connection to his model of the science-religion dialogue is unclear and indistinct.[12]

As a consequence, Barbour may have a useful model of the science-religion debate, but it is deficient as a guide for the debate. Given the dominance of Barbour's model, it is perhaps not surprising that social scientists have rarely found a place at the table. But recently two new

Non-Overlapping Magisteria (NOMA)

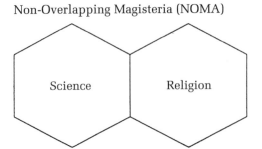

Figure I.3 Stephen Jay Gould's Model

models of the relationship between religion and science have appeared.

Stephen Jay Gould's Model

Stephen Jay Gould has articulated a model of the science-religion dialogue that is deliberately at variance with that of Barbour. Gould calls his model NOMA, for Non-Overlapping Magisteria (see fig. I.3).

Gould defines a *magisterium* as "a domain where one form of teaching holds the appropriate tools for meaningful discourse and resolution."[13] Science and religion are each magisteria. Each holds sway over its own domain, science over the empirical realm of fact and theory, and religion over the domain of ultimate meaning and moral value.[14] The two domains do not overlap, but their boundaries are not permanently fixed. "A magisterium," he says, "is a site for dialogue and debate, not a set of eternal and invariable rules."[15]

Gould is sharply critical of those who step over the boundary into the other domain. Creationists are lambasted for trespassing into the magisterium of science, but he is equally harsh with those scientists who dismiss religion or pronounce on matters of faith or morals. He singles out for criticism some papers presented at a conference, "Science and the Spirit," sponsored by the John Templeton Foundation for their syncretism, the blending of the two domains.

Perhaps because of that, Gould has been sharply attacked for advocating an "independence" position in which science and religion have nothing to say to each other.[16] Such criticism seriously misrepresents Gould's argument. While the two domains are separate, he argues, "the contact between magisteria could not be more intimate and pressing."[17] He explains: "The two magisteria bump right against each other, interdigitating in wondrously complex ways along their joint border. Many of our deepest questions call upon aspects of both magisteria for different parts of a full answer—the sorting of legitimate domains can become quite complex and difficult."[18] This means dialogue is essential between the two, because "any interesting problem, at any scale . . . must call upon the separate contributions of both magisteria for any adequate illumination."[19] On some questions, such as the composition of the periodic table, theology has nothing to say. Others, such as the doctrine of the atonement, are beyond the scope of science. But for most of the important issues of the day—Gould uses the example of genetic engineering—debate is necessary to determine where the proper boundaries lie.

Gould consciously patterns his position after that of the nineteenth-century Darwinist Thomas Huxley, but the philosophy behind it is the trifurcation of reason developed by Immanuel Kant during the Enlightenment. Science, for Gould as it was for Kant, is the domain of the cognitive-instrumental, religion that of the practical-moral. And while the aesthetic-expressive is not formally part of Gould's model, he recognizes its domain as well.[20] Gould maintains that as magisteria, science and religion are different in their essence. However much they may need demarcation at the frontier, each is characterized at its core by unique, necessary, and invariant qualities that distinguish them from each other.[21] So Gould is not presenting anything radically new—his separation of fact from value, of science from ethics, is part of the mainstream of modern thought. His model does, however, create a few problems.

First, while separate magisteria may be clear so long as one remains in the realm of pure theory, their separation becomes problematic as soon as one moves to the practical. Since Gould wants to promote dialogue, not compartmentalized solitudes, he cannot escape the dilemmas that occur as soon as an individual or group tries to resolve a real problem. Inevitably, when one becomes practical, the empirical and moral are intermixed. Technology, in particular, becomes problematical. Because technology is instrumental, questions of both how and should are inherent in its practice. Technology crosses the boundaries between the realms of facts and values and defies separation into distinct domains.

Lying just beneath this first problem is a second. Since the magisteria are nonoverlapping, is either complete in and of itself? If religion is denied claim upon "factual" reality, is it left without a foundation? Can one meaningfully discuss either morals or ultimate meaning without making claims upon empirical reality? Conversely, if separated from value, is science merely instrumental and scientists no more than amoral technicians? If so, how can one account for the norms and values that scientists themselves use to demarcate the scientific community? This challenges Kant's separation of fact from value. Philosophers may want to disconnect values and facts, but historians and sociologists testify that people blend the two in their practice every day. Perhaps a model should account for that.

Finally, while Gould does not rule out the social sciences in prin-

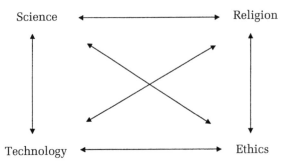

Figure I.4 Ronald Cole-Turner's Model

ciple, he does not bring them into the dialogue either. It is not easy to see where they fit into his conception of NOMA. So while Gould's model is more dynamic than Barbour's and is clearly intended to be a model for the science-religion dialogue and not just of it, it goes no further in creating a place at the table for the social sciences.

Ronald Cole-Turner's Model

A third way of talking about the relationship between science and religion was developed by Ronald Cole-Turner.[22] Compared to the previous two models, Cole-Turner's is much more comprehensive. He includes technology and ethics, defines science as more than just theory, and goes beyond theology to explicitly include all aspects of religion (see fig. I.4). He is concerned not only with finding meaning but also with transforming society.[23]

We have to be careful in building models not to reify abstractions but to see all elements as moments in the practices of actual people. Cole-Turner begins by insisting on the communal and experiential dimensions of all four elements in his model. Religion is not reduced to theology nor science to theory. Both are the practices of communities, and as such, each is an interweaving of experiences, norms, values, symbols, and rituals, as well as beliefs. This is equally true of technology and ethics. Theory is important, but it is not given the privileged position given it by the other models. Notice that *society* is not a term in the model. All four elements are fully social. Scientists can no more step outside of society when they step into the lab than clergy can when they step into the pulpit.

Around the "outside" of Cole-Turner's model are the pair linkages familiar from other discourses: science-technology, religion-ethics, science-religion, and technology-ethics. His model can therefore encompass and bring into the debate several discourses (and not just science-religion). There are three virtues in doing that. The first, of course, is simply that it includes more people and perspectives. The more this happens, the

less the debate can become hived off into just another compartmentalized academic discipline of a small group of specialists who speak only
to one another, and the richer the discussion is likely to become. Second, his model tends to counteract the tendency of pair-linkages to produce essentialist definitions. It is much harder to make the dialogue into
a discussion of "this versus that" when other practices are continually
in play. Third, unlike Barbour, who develops separate models for science-religion and technology-ethics and deliberately weakens the "vertical" connections between the theoretical and practical, Cole-Turner
integrates all four elements into a common model. The practical is given
equal standing with the theoretical, and both are encompassed within a
common discourse.

The heart of his model is "all the fuzzy stuff in the middle," the
center where all four elements meet. Here we find a plait of interrelationships. Where the other models are concerned with maintaining
boundaries, Cole-Turner refuses to reify categories and recognizes that
neat boundaries are rarely found in the lab or in the pew. Because they
are concerned with practice, all four elements are inherently relationships or networks, which means that far from being autonomous, each
is a form of social action. One simply cannot understand any of them
apart from the actions of people. If we may use a metaphor Cole-Turner
does not, in the center of his model we find a seamless web that unites
the theoretical and the practical, the technical, scientific, ethical, and
religious dimensions. All four elements are interwoven, influencing and
shaping each other. Together they spin a web of reality that may begin
to allow us to understand our world and permit us to begin to effectively engage in dialogue. As Cole-Turner concludes: "We need not to
just think abstractly about science and theology, but soberly and criti-
cally, with a four-fold matrix of understanding involving theology/eth-
ics/science/technology. We are asking not merely about Jerusalem and
Athens, faith and knowledge, but faith and *techne*, faith and novelty,
creatio nova and new stuff."[24]

Cole-Turner's model not only offers the social sciences a place in
the science-religion dialogue, but also moves them into the very heart
of the debate. His model is fully transdisciplinary. But if, in the Cole-
Turner model, social scientists have finally been offered a place at the
table, they still have to accept the invitation.

Why the Science-Religion Dialogue Needs
the Social Sciences

So the social sciences have finally been offered a
place at the table, but what do they bring to the game? It is time to ante
up. Fortunately, they do not come to the table empty-handed—they have

theories and tools that can be of great value in the debate. There are at least three reasons why the science-religion dialogue needs the social sciences.

First, the social sciences can give a better understanding of many of the issues that have been at the center of the debate. For example, one of the most contentious issues in recent years has been the attack on evolution by creationists, including attempts either to limit the teaching of evolution in public schools in the United States or to have "creation science" given equal time. Efforts by scientists and philosophers to refute creationism have focused on their beliefs, showing that Darwin's theory is well supported by evidence and that creation science is not. However, denouncing those one disagrees with as mistaken, or even as frauds, neither leads to much understanding nor provides an adequate basis for ethics and politics.[25] Contrast the usual approach with the rather different set of issues that emerges when historical and sociological perspectives are brought to the controversy.

Historians point out that the idea that religion went to war with science over Darwin is largely a later construction built around a mythologized recollection of Thomas Huxley's famous debate with Bishop Wilberforce.[26] In the nineteenth century and first years of the twentieth, religious people approached Darwin in a variety of ways—from outright rejection to enthusiastic support—varying a great deal from country to country. In the United States, those Protestants who would eventually become known as fundamentalists were not particularly concerned with evolution. A few were even open to theistic interpretations of Darwin.[27] In the 1920s William Jennings Bryan, a distinguished "elder statesman" in U.S. politics (and not the ignorant boob he is portrayed as in the unhistorical play and film *Inherit the Wind*), raised the cry against evolution over two issues. First, he equated evolution with social Darwinism, which he believed—with considerable justification—to be one of the intellectual causes of the First World War. As a philosophy based on competition and conflict, Bryan charged, evolutionary theory was detrimental to society. Second, as a populist, Bryan was concerned that ordinary people were losing control of knowledge (particularly in terms of what would be taught in the public schools) to a remote intellectual elite. In 1924 Bryan even joined the American Association for the Advancement of Science to make the point that science should belong to the people.[28]

Those who followed Bryan were primarily lower-middle- and working-class people and those professionals (especially clergy) whose status and way of life were being threatened by the expansion of industrial capitalism.[29] To overlook social class as an aspect of creationism is therefore to miss much of its dynamics. Fundamentalism was, and still is, an antimodernist movement. So instead of dismissing creationism out of hand, we need to understand its roots as a social protest movement. As historian George Marsden observes, creationists "have correctly identified some important trends in twentieth century American life and see that these trends have profound cultural implications."[30] However inadequate creationists' solutions may be, we cannot lightly dismiss the social causes of creationism. The social sciences give us a means to understand and engage in the debate over evolution in a way that concentrating only on theories and beliefs cannot.

The second way the social sciences are needed is that they can give a better understanding of the science-religion dialogue itself. Because the dialogue overemphasizes theories, it is frequently abstract. People often talk about science and religion as if these were entities instead of practices. Science is often portrayed as an epistemologically unified entity (the scientific method) that can be compared and contrasted with the way that religion knows. Sociological research gives a very different picture, however.

For example, the implication is not infrequent that scientists are nontheistic, if not atheistic. However, few in the dialogue pay attention to the stratification of scientists or the corporate culture of scientific organizations. In 1914 and again in 1933, James H. Leuba asked scientists in the United States whether they believed in a God who could be influenced by worship and whether they believed in an afterlife. Even with the evangelical slant to his question, in both surveys 40 percent of scientists believed in God as defined. Fifty percent believed in an afterlife. Edward Larson and Larry Witham recently replicated this study, using the same questions, and found remarkably similar results—40 percent of scientists still believed in a personal God who answers prayer, and 40 percent believed in an afterlife. Larger numbers accepted a more mystical understanding of God. On the other hand, both sets of surveys found that elite scientists have very different beliefs. Larson and Witham discovered that up to 95 percent of members of the National Academy of Sciences claimed to be atheists or agnostics.[31] Thus we might ask, Is religion opposed by science, or by only certain groups of scientists? It would seem that there is a corporate culture in elite scientific organizations that is much more hostile to religion than is the case among scientists as a whole. So science is perhaps not as unified as some would paint it, and, at least in regard to issues involving religion, the social sciences raise the question, who speaks for science?

A third way the social sciences can aid the debate is in helping to inform ethical reflection. It is difficult to do ethics well without the insights of the social sciences. For instance, the ethical issues surrounding technology are a place where the public most needs the guidance that the science-religion dialogue could provide. A persistent feature of debates about science and technology are what sociologist Thomas Gieryn calls "credibility contests." These are disputes about allocating "epistemic authority," which he defines as "the legitimate power to define, describe, and explain bounded domains of reality."[32] In other words, when scientists are on both sides of an argument, whom should the public believe? The media are full of both the extravagant claims by advocates for this or that technology and the apocalyptic fears of their opponents (see chapter 7). Each side claims to know objective truth while charging that its adversaries propagate "junk science." Are genetically modified crops really safe? Is HIV the sole cause of AIDS? Does global warming necessitate curbing greenhouse gas emissions? Now, if natural scientists cannot answer these questions (or, more accurately, cannot agree on an answer), social scientists cannot either. But they can help us to understand how the issues get framed, how the boundaries between "good" and "bad" science are drawn, and how each side maneuvers to gain epistemic authority. And most of all they can ask, Qui bono? Whose good is being served? Without answers to these questions the science-religion dialogue either must remain silent on crucial issues or, if it does speak, risk getting hijacked by those with an agenda who wrap themselves in the mantle of "science." With the insights of the social sciences, however, those informed by the science-religion dialogue will be in a better position to act with moral and political responsibility.

A Weberian Framework

Our approach to the dialogue will be to analyze science through religious categories. This will expose and demystify some of the images and assumptions that have constructed walls between science and religion and reveal the creative tensions between them. In order to do this, we will adopt a framework built of the methods and categories of religious thought developed by Max Weber.

Max Weber (1864–1920) is generally considered to be one of the most important figures in the development of social theory, and his work has had a tremendous influence on developments in the fields of economics, history, law, political science, and sociology.[33] Trained in law and history, Weber wrote extensively on religion, the economy, bureaucracy, and many other topics. Of particular interest to us here, however, is the fact that he was very concerned with the methods used by scholars to investigate social phenomena and the ways in which they developed their theories. Thus, Weber's ideas provide a very useful framework within which we can explore and present various aspects of the relationship between religion and science. It is important to recognize, though, that we are not necessarily taking a Weberian perspective on these issues, as opposed to a Marxist or a social constructionist perspective. Rather, we are using a Weberian structure as a starting point for discussion and as an organizing principle.

One of the primary reasons for selecting a Weberian framework is Weber's insistence that social science be carried out through a historical-comparative method. In Weber's time, historians were engaged in a heated debate over methodology, with one group arguing for a *nomothetic* view, and the other advocating an *idiographic* approach. According to the nomothetic view, certain types of events happen regularly in all societies, and the task of the historian is to observe how these types of events manifest themselves in various cultures at various periods in history. By contrast, the idiographic view emphasizes the uniqueness of societies, and thus the task of historians is to document the particularistic courses of historical cultures. Weber adopted a middle position, suggesting that historians gather as much specific information as possible about distinct cultures at various periods, while sociologists, or social historians, look for patterns and trends. This middle position required a change in the way that data were gathered and in the way that conceptual development, based on the data, took place.

With respect to the gathering of data, Weber suggested that, as much as possible, historians and social scientists attempt to place themselves in the situations that they are trying to explore, rather than stand outside of them. This method of *Verstehen*, or understanding, aimed at striking a balance between an objective or detached approach and a subjective or engaged approach. For Weber, objectivity, or true detachment, was an ideal that could not be attained, while subjectivity, or taking too personal a stance, was certainly possible but extremely undesirable. Weber's method of Verstehen was based on the study of texts, known as hermeneutics, that was being developed in Germany at the time by scholars like Wilhelm Dilthey.[34] This method, which was used primarily to explore the meaning of Scripture, was predicated on an effort to get at the author's thoughts as well as at the meaning and structure of the text itself. More recently, hermeneutics and the method of Verstehen have formed the basis for many of the popular qualitative research methods, such as participant observation, employed in the social sciences.[35]

On the issue of conceptual development and theory building, Weber developed a device known as an "ideal type," which is designed as a heuristic device, or a tool to help us explore and understand something. The word *ideal* here is not meant to imply a value judgment that some type is better than another or that one type is preferred to another. Rather, the implication is that the ideal type is an idea (image) of what a typical object might be, but there is no real (concrete) example of that type to be found. Thus there may be an ideal type of university, or baseball team, or poem, but actual universities, teams, and poems only approximate these ideal types; we can then speak about certain characteristics that all examples seem to share. The fact that some examples may lack one characteristic or another does not exclude them from the category but shows that historically concrete phenomena are likely to have unique features representative of their own circumstances. Weber devoted a great deal of time to studying religion, and yet he did not suggest that there was an ideal type of religion. Rather, he suggested that there might be an ideal type of Calvinism, Confucianism, and so on, because these represent concrete, historically situated manifestations of religion. Similarly, in spite of what many philosophers and scientists might argue, Weber would not likely consider it rational to speak of an ideal type of science. More likely, he would suggest that there might be an ideal evolutionary biology or quantum physics that represents particular historical and cultural cases of the development of scholarly disciplines. The utility of the ideal type is in helping us to identify specific examples and in providing a mechanism to delineate the similarities and differences among these particular cases.

Another important aspect of Weber's method is his notion of causality. In explorations of social phenomena, Weber thought that researchers should look to see if somehow two or more events are related probabilistically. In other words, Weber was concerned to discover the likelihood that one event would follow another. So, for example, in one of his most famous works, *The Protestant Ethic and the Spirit of Capitalism*, Weber suggests that the Protestant ethic was one of many possible factors that contributed to the emergence of capitalism in Europe.[36] Later, Robert K. Merton would suggest that similar conditions provided fertile ground for the rise of modern science.[37] Neither Weber nor Merton were suggesting that the rise of capitalism or science could be explained completely by Protestantism, but both authors did demonstrate that, through an examination of the historical record, it was possible to identify specific factors that likely played a significant role in later developments. Again, Weber can be viewed as taking the middle road between the extremes of billiard-ball causality typical of Newtonian science, for example, and the randomness that some would argue is characteristic of all events, physical and historical, in the universe.

Values were also important to Weber, inasmuch as he thought that academics should present their findings in as objective a manner as possible. However, he also argued that subjective elements could not be ignored in our study of historical phenomena, as these provide insight into what various events might have meant to the participants at the time. As for those phenomena that scholars choose to study, Weber observed that these are likely to be value relevant. In other words, scholars are likely to study those things that are of value to them. Certainly, in today's world, religion and science, and the relationship between them, are extremely relevant topics for study.

One of the concepts that Weber developed at some length through his studies is that of rationalization, or rationality. Following his own advice, Weber did not try to offer some definitive position on rationality. Instead, the details of the concept emerged through the exploration of concrete historical examples. As Stephen Kalberg suggests, Weber appears to have used the notion of rationality in four relatively distinct manners.[38] First, the notion of practical rationality refers to the attitude of accepting things as they are and figuring out how best to function within those parameters. Thus, rather than seeking magical, supernatural, or even scientific explanations for events and conditions, most people just focus their attention on the practicalities of getting on with life. Second, theoretical rationality refers to the cognitive schemes that people develop as a way of providing logical and conceptual explanations and frameworks to describe the world. Today philosophers and scientists have come to represent the major practitioners of this form of rationality, once the realm of sorcerers and priests. Third, substantive rationality refers to the way in which values shape actions. So, for example, our collective reverence for human life manifests itself in behaviors and laws that reflect respect for personal property and for the rights of all people to have access to the basic needs of existence (food and shelter). Fourth, formal rationality, or means-end rationality, is similar to practical rationality except that it reflects adherence to a broader system of justification. For example, industrial capitalism and bureaucratic administration follow well-established rules of operation in order to achieve their goals. Anyone who has ever filled out an income tax form or registered at a university knows that the inherent logic of the system, rarely apparent to the individual taxpayer or student, dictates what must be done and how it will be done. Rationality is often held up as the distinguishing characteristic of science, while religion is equally likely to be seen as irrational. Weber's multifaceted conceptualization of rationality can help us to understand more precisely what critics and supporters of these positions have in mind and how they attempt to support their views.

On a substantive level, Weber devoted a great deal of attention to the study of religion, and in so doing he provided us with an extremely useful scheme through which we can explore the relationship between religion and science. In his *Sociology of Religion*, Weber identifies five traditional categories of religious thought: mystery, soteriology, saintliness, magical causation, and theodicy.[39] Following Weber, Steve Fuller attempts to analyze science in terms of these five categories, in an effort to determine whether humanity's faith in science is superstitious.[40] In other words, he tries to determine in what ways the foundations for our belief in science differ from those that support our belief in religion. What we attempt to do throughout this book is use these five categories to see if they can help us understand the relationship between religion and science as it has manifested itself in a variety of concrete historical instances. As a starting point, the rest of this introduction is devoted to an initial exploration of Weber's five categories, as further developed in Fuller's work.

At the simplest level, the notion of mystery has to do with the unknown. Those things that we cannot or do not know are by definition mysterious. Within the context of the social sciences, the notion of mystery can be used to determine whether knowledge is an integral part of everyday life, or whether it is somehow limited to elite or esoteric groups within society. In this respect, Fuller observes that the proliferation of scientific publications and the intrusion of science into more and more aspects of daily life contrasts starkly with the more esoteric pursuit of truth. In fact, he argues that "*accelerating* the rate at which scientific publications are produced is perfectly compatible with *decelerating* the rate at which agreement is reached on the solutions to a field's fundamental problems" (emphasis in original).[41] In other words, it would appear that the more vigorously science is pursued, the more scientific understanding recedes from the grasp of those pursuing it. There are at least two factors to consider here. First, as in many other areas, the "law of diminishing returns" comes into effect, inasmuch as each additional dollar spent on scientific research appears to contribute less to the advancement of science than dollars previously spent. Second, with increased specialization and fragmentation of scientific exploration, very few scientists are in a position to reflect on what is happening in their field as a whole. Increased detail does not necessarily equal increased understanding.

Saintliness refers to the idea that there are always special individuals who stand out because of their dedication, genius, or both, and who demonstrate that religion and science, when taken seriously, are vocations. In Christendom at least, Newton, Darwin, and Einstein are as familiar as Augustine, Aquinas, and Luther. In his work on religion, Weber identified certain charismatic individuals who, because of their personal presence, were able to influence large numbers of people to carry out certain actions or adhere to certain beliefs. It is not uncommon for us to attribute almost superhuman capabilities to such individuals, and we tend to defer to their opinions on diverse matters, well beyond their areas of expertise. So, for example, celebrities are regularly asked for their views on issues relating to politics, psychology, and medicine, as if they somehow know more than politicians and doctors. At the same time, it is difficult to deny the power of these individuals to raise awareness and money around causes they elect to champion (for example, Elizabeth Taylor and AIDS, Michael J. Fox and Parkinson's disease, Princess Diana and land mines).

Magical causation concerns the relationship between correlation and causation and refers to the link between understanding something theoretically and applying that knowledge to practical problems. Using airplanes as an example, Fuller argues that "to reduce the airborne capabilities of such a craft to the 'application of science' is as much wishful thinking and hand-waving as claiming that an 'infusion of the Holy Spirit' is responsible for airworthiness . . . the fact that humans appeal to science to justify their beliefs is not sufficient to render those beliefs rational."[42] When the Wright brothers managed to get a plane to fly, for however brief a period, they may have thanked God, but it is unlikely that they attributed their success to an act of God. Similarly, their theoretical knowledge of the scientific principles of aerodynamics was rudimentary at best, and they would not have used science to explain how they finally managed to get their craft off the ground. Rather, their success falls into the realm of what Weber referred to as practical rationality, that is, craft knowledge built up through experience. The Wright brothers accepted the world as it was and learned, largely through trial and error, how to accomplish their goal. The fact that the science of aerodynamics can be used to explain their success is not the same as saying that they succeeded on account of that science. Correlation is not causation. Just because two things are related to each other does not mean that one can be used to account for the other.

The notion of theodicy is closely related to ideas about salvation and centers on the concept of justice, whether God-given or emerging out of the scientific enterprise. Basically, the idea of theodicy in a religious context is that the evil and destruction that are everywhere in the world must ultimately be there for some good purpose. We may never learn or understand that purpose, but we believe that God or some ultimate power does. Alternatively, from a scientific perspective, explanations of natural disasters and disease are often framed in terms of the hostility of the natural world and the "survival of the fittest." Within both religious and scientific contexts, then, theodicies provide us with a way to focus on our daily existence without having to constantly attempt to understand the challenges that confront us. Fuller observes that within the scientific enterprise this notion is regularly interpreted as a justification for leaving scientists alone to pursue whatever they think is appropriate, provided they do so within parameters set by their peers (other scientists).[43] In other words, scientists argue that the more we understand and ultimately control the world we live in, the more our fate will be self-determined and less prone to the whims of a god or the randomness of natural events.

Soteriology is the term used to describe ideas about salvation. Religious systems often provide a rationale for personal suffering in this life by indicating that there will be a reward in the next life, or lives. A big part of these systems is identifying what we need to be saved from and how we should go about ensuring that we will be saved. In Christianity, belief in Jesus Christ ensures that we will be freed from the bondage of sin and live for eternity in heaven. Science, especially modern medical science, holds out the promise of a long and good life, free of hunger and disease, in the here and now. It is easy to make the argument that scientific worldviews are replacing religious ones because they offer a more immediate, this-worldly liberation from those things that we believe are constraining us. Whether this is in fact the case is an open question. However, the human need or desire for a path to salvation is undeniable, and an exploration of this issue is surely an excellent way to gain a better understanding of the relationship between religion and science.

So, with this framework, and equipped with Weber's tools, we will examine science through the categories of religious thought. In the following chapters we will analyze science as soteriology, as saintliness, as magic, and as theodicy and conclude by exploring the tension between objectivity and mystery.

PART

I

Soteriology

1 | The Sacred Myth of Science

If you remain in my word, you will truly be my disciples, and you will know the truth, and the truth will set you free.

—John 8: 31–32

Science and scientific thinking have become such a dominant part of our everyday life, it is difficult to imagine, in a general sense, instances where the scientific worldview may be an overly narrow or even inappropriate approach to the problem at hand. We look to science for a better life, characterized by freedom from disease, protection from the elements, abundant food, and so on. At one time, it was more common to look to religion for the satisfaction of these same needs, and, as we will show in the next chapter, it has been only in the last couple of centuries that most people have even thought of religion and science as distinct. The most common understanding today, though, is to assume that science and religion are two separate entities, that is, things that are essentially distinct, based on their content or substance.

In this section we challenge that assumption. We explore some of the similarities between religion and science that stand out when they are treated as social structures and as systems of meaning. As a means of challenging the taken-for-grantedness of the scientific perspective, in this chapter we ask whether science can be studied as a religion. In other words, we apply some of the tools of the sociology of religion to the study of science. Here we use a functionalist approach, that is, rather than examining what science and religion supposedly are, we analyze what they do. What we find is that the so-called scientific worldview is itself implicitly religious.

Science, Religion, and Salvation

Words like *salvation, redemption, freedom, emanci- pation, purification, absolution, illumination*, and *enlightenment* are often used interchangeably to express the concept of liberation.[1] While all of these terms can be used to indicate some notion of release, the social practices and ideological convictions behind their use can be very dif- ferent. In this regard, some people quickly point out that some concept or other may not mean the same thing to adherents of one religion as it does to adherents of some other religion. So, for example, the notion of salvation that is central to this chapter means very different things to Christians, Buddhists, and Jews. For Christians, salvation is generally equated with eternal life granted through faith in the grace of Jesus Christ. For Buddhists, salvation means liberation from the drudgery of mun- dane existence achieved through a life of contemplation and disciplined coexistence with other forms of life. For Jews, salvation is viewed as the continuing existence and growth in numbers of the Jewish people that will result from a life of obedience to God's law and the performance of good works. Of course, common sense would tell us that these state- ments are simplifications that would be subject to much further varia- tion in interpretation within the many communities of faith and practice that constitute each of these religious traditions. What is puzzling, how- ever, is that those same people who would be quick to criticize gener- alizations with respect to religious concepts are quite likely to assume that scientists share a much more unified interpretation of the concepts they work with.

So, for example, a term like *Earth* will generally be assumed to mean the same thing to biologists, chemists, geologists, and cosmologists, and its use, unlike the use of the word *salvation*, is unlikely to be seen as contextual, let alone controversial. However, we would suggest that a biological notion of the Earth as the global environment within which life forms exist is of little or no concern to cosmologists, who view the Earth as the third rock traveling in an elliptical orbit around a minor star in a fairly unspectacular galaxy. Of course, the reverse situation also holds true. We think it unlikely that, in the absence of a certain popu- lar television show, the majority of biologists would care that Mercury and Venus are in closer proximity to the sun than Earth is. In the cases of notions of both Earth and salvation, there are common elements that justify the use of a single term to express a variety of interpretations, regardless of scientific or religious context, respectively. At the same time, it is very common for researchers within a specific discipline, or within a particular community of scholars, to share certain interpretations of these terms. Such shared meanings serve to facilitate internal commu- nication, and it is perhaps unfortunate that these same shared meanings

Bernal and geneticist J. B. S. Haldane, both of whom were heavily influenced by Karl Marx's condemnation of religion, sanctification of science, and advocacy of revolutionary change.[9] For his part, Bernal argued that the human species would no longer be content to live on the less than perfect Earth and would move to the other planets and eventually the whole universe. Haldane, who is, of course, well known for his quip that God displayed an inordinate fondness for beetles, went so far as to outline a plan for space colonization in his 1927 essay "The Last Judgment."

More recently, physicist Freeman Dyson extended this other-worldly trend by positing that humans will in fact shed their bodies and exist as intelligent quanta, everywhere and nowhere at the same time. As he states: "It is impossible to set any limit to the variety of physical forms that life may assume. . . . It is conceivable that in another 10^{10} years life could evolve away from flesh and blood and become embodied in an interstellar black cloud or in a sentient computer."[10] Similarly, some researchers in the field of artificial intelligence assume that, as Bryan Appleyard points out, "We will download our personalities on to machines and become immortal by making any number of back-up copies of ourselves."[11] It is difficult to see how statements like these are any less metaphysical than the speculations put forth over the centuries by any number of saints, mystics, or theologians. In fact, Stephen Hawking appears to conflate the roles of scientist and theologian in his statement that "we shall all—philosophers, scientists, and just ordinary people—be able to take part in the discussion of the question of why it is that we and the universe exist. If we find the answer to that, it would be the ultimate triumph of human reason—for then we would know the mind of God."[12]

Perhaps the most extreme version of this implicit religion of science is to be found in the notion of the *anthropic cosmological principle* posited by physicists John Barrow and Frank Tipler.[13] This principle is based on the notion that "the physical universe can in some ways be explained by assuming that it must be such as to contain people."[14] They argue that if there were even slight differences from natural laws as they currently are, then life could not exist in the universe. One version of this notion, generally referred to as the *participatory anthropic principle* (PAP), can be interpreted to mean that in the absence of observers, the universe would not exist. This position is consistent with the kind of psychological reductionism that started with Descartes and is enjoying a new lease on life in the form of the so-called cognitive sciences. Barrow and Tipler even go so far as to posit what they call a *final anthropic principle* (FAP), which states that intelligent information processing must come into existence in the universe and that, once it has, it will never die out.

We would stop short of suggesting that all scientists buy into these kinds of speculations. However, the fact remains that those making them continue to receive financial and intellectual support within the scientific community and continue to have their musings published in peer-reviewed journals.

Speculations of this kind are based on a notion of evolution to something, rather than evolution from something. Contrary to the position generally associated with modern science, these ideas are fundamentally teleological in nature. That is, they betray a sense of purpose or design in the universe. Yet, whether we look to cosmology, with its emphasis on stochastic processes, chaos, and complexity, or to biology, with its advocacy of variational evolution, the abandonment of the design argument is one of the primary factors that differentiate the scientific enterprise from natural theology. Not only is there no need for a designer, but, as Darwin demonstrated, life evolved through a process of natural selection, that is, the struggle for existence among genetic variants. It is, however, an integral part of what it means to be human to join together concern for finding the order and meaning of phenomena with trying to find out the intention or plan underlying that order, as Mary Midgley points out.[15] Similarly, she argues that teleological thought is not limited to such means-end patterns, and that rather than centering on questions like "What later thing is this leading to?" questions like "What is this for? What is the point of it?" and "What part does it play in a wider whole?" are more appropriate to science.[16] We would suggest that, in confusing these senses of purposive thinking, scientists construct and institutionalize a soteriology, while engaging in a sort of denial. That is, a great part of the myth of science that scientists fail to recognize, or perhaps fail to acknowledge, is that in their efforts to escape from metaphysics they are entrenching themselves as firmly in speculative dogma as any religion ever has.

Weber on Salvation

In his exploration of historical examples of soteriologies in the religions of the world, Weber speaks of "institutional grace" and indicates that wherever it operates, it has three characteristics.

> The first is *extra ecclesiam nulla salus:* salvation cannot be obtained apart from membership in a particular institution or church vested with the control of grace. The second principle is that it is not the personal charismatic qualification of the priest which determines the effectiveness of his distribution of divine grace. Third, the personal religious qualification of the individual in need of salvation is altogether a matter of indifference to the institution which has the power to distribute religious grace. That is, religion is universal.[17]

Each of these three principles can be found in the scientific enterprise.

Weber's first principle implies that there is no salvation outside of science. Midgley argues that this is precisely what most people mean when they use the word *scientism*. Mikael Stenmark refers to two types of scientism. The first is redemptive scientism, which he defines as "the view that science alone is sufficient for dealing with our existential questions or for creating a world view by which we could live."[18] A good example of this is found in sociobiologist E. O. Wilson's comparison of religion and science:

> I consider the scientific ethos superior to religion: its repeated triumphs in explaining and controlling the physical world; its self-correcting nature open to all competent to devise and conduct the tests; its readiness to examine all subjects sacred and profane; and now the possibility of explaining traditional religion by the mechanistic models of evolutionary biology. The last achievement will be crucial. If religion, including the dogmatic secular ideologies, can be systematically analyzed as a product of the brain's evolution, its power as an external source of morality will be gone forever.[19]

Wilson's view is consistent with the participatory anthropic principle discussed earlier, and it also betrays a means-end type of teleological thought, in that the purpose of science is to free humankind from the bondage of ignorance and false ideologies. Stenmark's second type of scientism, comprehensive scientism, takes into account the more exclusive views of scientists like Dyson, Barrow, and Tipler. Stenmark defines it as the view that "science alone can and will eventually solve all, or almost all, of our genuine problems."[20] Here, the sacred myth of science reaches its peak: Not only is science the key to salvation, but science alone can define those things from which we need to be saved.

Weber's second principle, which focuses on the priesthood, refers to notions of apostolic succession and the idea that the right to perform the sacred rituals—and thus provide the key to salvation—is passed on through the laying on of hands. In other words, the kind of esoteric knowledge needed to function at the core of a scientific community is passed on to the initiates through special training and apprenticeship. Either through the acquisition of this special knowledge or through a rite of passage, scientists and priests are placed in a position of authority as distributors of grace (truth), irrespective of individual merit. Sharon Traweek, in her examination of the high-energy physics community, provides an insightful analysis of the way in which physicists gain the kind of tacit knowledge required to join the elite. As she indicates, in making the transition from student to full-fledged scientist, individuals "must learn how to rely on oral rather than written information."[21] In other words, there are aspects of being a scientist that are not to be found in textbooks and laboratory manuals, and that can be learned only through social interaction with existing members of the scientific community.

The point to be made here is that in a process parallel to the way in which the institution of science becomes revered, scientists, as the living manifestations of that institution, become equally revered. Evidence for this phenomenon can be found at every turn in daily affairs. Scientists are continually consulted as generic experts to hold forth on matters about which they have little or no direct knowledge or experience, while priests and other academics are mocked or ignored whenever they proffer an observation concerning a scientific matter.

The third principle is that science is all for all. In other words, it is all things to all people. Nothing outside of science matters. If in fact there is anything outside of science, and in the absence of science, continued existence is in doubt. Fuller speaks of an "autonomous science" that "transforms all things in the course of subserving them to its own imperatives."[22] This concept is built on Weber's insight that "institutional grace, by its very nature, ultimately and notably tends to make obedience a cardinal virtue and a decisive precondition of salvation. This of course entails subjection to authority."[23] This condition leads to a situation in which it is not necessary for the believer to fully understand the dogma, but simply to accept a general framework of meaning (worldview) provided by the institution. So, for example, while one might ask how much Catholicism the average Roman Catholic parishioner understands, the point is that it does not really matter. Even in their ignorance, parishioners will be saved if they accept as part of their faith that there are experts whose job it is to know the finer details of Catholic doctrine. As Weber indicates, "Every prophetic religion has based religious faith upon something other than real understanding of theology."[24] In other words, in place of a *fides explicita*, an explicit faith, a *fides implicita*, defined as a "general readiness to subject one's own convictions to religious authority," is considered to be sufficient. Thus, for the laity, a profession of faith is tantamount to a "declaration of confidence in and dedication to a prophet or to the authority of a structured institution." On the other hand, a *fides explicita* is limited to priests and theologians; that is, all those who have been "trained in dogmatics." As Weber goes on to argue, at some point this situation leads to a "sacrifice of the intellect," because faith requires an absolute trust, best expressed in the formula "Credo quia absurdum est" (I believe because it is absurd).[25] We would suggest that, certainly for the average citizen, but also for the majority of initiates, trust in science requires no less a leap of faith than trust in religion does, and for the same reason.

By way of concluding this section and further illustrating our argument, we want to look briefly at the New Testament saying that serves as the epigraph of this chapter. In the Gospel of John (8:31–32), Jesus is reported to have said: "If you remain in my word, you will truly be my disciples, and you will know the truth, and the truth will set you free." Most people are familiar with at least the final portion of this saying, which has often been used as a political slogan, but in fact it is crucial to examine all four segments of this saying to understand its importance. The first phrase is particularly noteworthy, because it establishes a condition for salvation. The Gospel story continues by indicating that those around Jesus objected by saying that as descendants of Abraham, they were not in a state of slavery or bondage and therefore had no need of salvation. Jesus responded by indicating that their existence in a state of sin left them in need of salvation that only he could provide. All four phrases can be viewed as forming a causal chain, a peculiar conditional logic. Freedom is derived from knowledge that is gained through membership in an elite group made up of those willing to accept a particular worldview, as expressed in the message of a certain charismatic leader. The individual merit of the disciples is irrelevant, as is their real understanding of their condition. Jesus is aware of their condition, and he also possesses the means for their salvation from that condition. All that they need do is remain in his word. In other words, if they take a leap of faith and trust in the worldview presented by Jesus, they will be counted among the saved. Not only is it clear that the grace of Jesus Christ is in fact an institutional grace, as defined by Weber, but the parallels to modern science are obvious. To quote a piece of popular pseudo-scripture by Alexander Pope by way of illustration: "Nature and Nature's laws lay hid in night: God said, Let Newton be! and all was Light."

Analytical Biases

Scientism is not unique to the natural sciences. Many social scientists are just as ensnared in the sacred myth of science. If the social sciences are to play a meaningful role in the science-religion dialogue, we will have to remove the beam from our own eyes first. We need to reexamine some of the assumptions behind the social scientific approach to religion. When we do, we will find that, as much as they may differ in other things, many social and natural scientists share the same biases about religion.

In a recent historical analysis of scientific approaches to the study of religion, U.S. sociologist Rodney Stark found that the scientific paradigm dominated as the proper method of inquiry. It was assumed that the only proper way to study religion was "scientifically." This dominance has emerged out of two distinct, but often overlapping, strands in the study of religion, which he calls the anthropological and the psychological.[26] The combined effect of these strands creates biases that lead to treating science and religion asymmetrically and help erect walls between them.

The first strand is the anthropological, which argues that religion is contextual, that is, a product of culture. Since all cultures have a religion of some kind, all are equivalent. This is the argument for cultural relativism. Therefore some would claim that Christianity, for example, is just another manifestation of stories about gods procreating with humans. What anthropologists were trying to accomplish was, as Stark indicates, "to link all religion to primitive irrationality and thus to bring contemporary religion into intellectual disrepute."[27] Stewart Guthrie suggests that the comparative study of religion and efforts to explain religion can all be categorized as anthropomorphism, or as Midgley would phrase it, "the apotheosis of man."[28] Religion in this view is very much a case of society worshiping itself. It is believed that in time scientific analyses will demonstrate that those phenomena that we associate with religion are merely collectively agreed-upon products of the human mind.

Efforts to apply this kind of anthropological approach to studying science have met with strong and bitter criticism. A few scientists have lashed out in the so-called science wars (see chapter 9). This demonstrates not only the powerful hold that science has over social institutions like education, government, and industry, but also the very limited nature of some scientists' appreciation of what goes on outside of the scientific enterprise. This narrow worldview is particularly evident, for example, in comments like one made by physicist Steven Weinberg: "No one would give a book about mountain climbing the title *Constructing Everest*."[29] The science wars are predicated on the assumption that people—whether laypersons, other academics, or government officials— do not understand what goes on in science and therefore are in no position to analyze or criticize it. A perceptive statement of what is really going on is provided by Fuller: "I believe that most of what non-scientists need to know in order to make informed public judgments about science falls under the rubric of history, philosophy, and sociology of science, rather than the technical content of scientific subjects."[30] In other words, part of the myth of science is that its methods and the knowledge produced through their application are beyond scrutiny and untainted by subjectivity, when in fact science is no more or less a human practice than is religion. Further, just as people can question religion based on what they see happening in the world around them, this is also a perfectly legitimate basis for questioning science.

The second strand Stark identified in the study of religion is the psychological and centers on the notion that religion is an irrational product of the mind. In the words of anthropologist Weston LaBarre, "A god is only a shaman's dream about his father." Stark notes that this Freudian construct is repeated without comment or criticism in several books that claim to analyze theories of religion. In a more extreme version of this argument, as part of his examination of Catholic folk religion, Michael Carroll contends that praying the rosary is "a disguised gratification of repressed anal-erotic desires," a substitute for "playing with one's feces." The psychological approach has been important to science and the implicit and often denied metaphysics that undergirds it, because science is seen as the supreme exercise of rational behavior in a world where the human species is distinguished by its rationality. Hence, it is very difficult to do the scientific study of religion, because religion has been characterized, in Stark's words, as "a sign of stupidity, neurosis, poverty, ignorance, false consciousness, or a flight from modernity."[31] Fortunately, some scholars brave the storm, but biases remain.

The combined effect of these two strands leads to three particular biases. An examination of these might help us to understand the reluctance among scientists even to consider what religion might be able to tell them.[32] The first of these biases is that empirical studies of religions tend to focus on obscure and marginal groups, particularly if they exhibit what might be considered exotic or abnormal characteristics. In other words, we are more likely to read accounts of secret enclaves that practice aberrant sexual acts than we are to learn about the several hundred thousands of parishioners attending Baptist churches around the world on Sunday morning.

If studies of religion overreport the exotic and marginal, the same cannot be said for reporting on science. How many molecular biologists around the world are engaged in mapping the genomes of various plants and animals? What we tend to hear about are those scientists who, however mundane and highly repetitive the activities are that they engage in on a daily basis, discover some genetic marker for a disease of concern to the broader population that directly or indirectly finances their efforts. It is interesting to note in this regard that the vast majority of social studies of science have focused on Nobel Prize–winning scientists.

The second bias is antagonism to high levels of religious commitment. To those whose own commitment is to scientism, the commitment found among adherents of various religious beliefs and practices seems irrational. In other words, atheism, or nonbelief, is assumed to be a virtue, and some scientists feel they must work extra hard to expose those groups that demonstrate the most unshakable faith. This kind of "organized skepticism" or "detached scrutiny of beliefs" is considered to be a hallmark of the scientific method.[33] This approach is well illustrated by the continued attention journalists, scholars, and anticult networks pay to Scientology. All find it incredible that high-profile public figures (mostly actors), who should know better, pour millions of dollars into supporting the personal illusions of a now-dead eccentric charismatic leader.

However, commitment to scientific beliefs is not treated the same way. As Thomas Kuhn found in several historical and contemporary controversies in science, hanging on to one set of beliefs (paradigms) in the face of substantial amounts of evidence to the contrary (anomalies) is considered a normal part of scientific progress.[34] This ability to explain away or ignore empirical evidence that goes against established theories is one of the reasons scientific controversies are not infrequently protracted and bitter, as we will see in chapter 8. So, we are presented with the paradox that while some scientists attack religion on the basis of its irrationality and reliance on blind faith, science institutionalizes these very phenomena to its own benefit. Yet, as Fuller argues, there is more to this issue. The vast amount of resources invested in some types of scientific research make questions about their validity and direct benefit to humanity virtually irrelevant. In other words, there might be criteria outside of, for example, rationality, objectivity, and truth that can readily account for the perpetuation of certain scientific traditions. Clearly, this is not very different from arguments that link religious vitality to political involvement and personal gain.

The third bias differs in that it is most often found among those who do have religious commitments. This is the fear of eroding faith. That is, some would argue that if religion is true, then it must be exempt from scientific analysis, because any weaknesses that could be demonstrated through exploration would raise doubts among the faithful. By the same token, some scientists argue that if science is true, it must be exempt from external scrutiny, whether by historians, philosophers, sociologists, or scholars of religion. This position ignores the distinctly human side of religion that in actuality forms the evidential base through which religion can be studied, as Stark points out. In other words, it is only as a social phenomenon that we can study religion, and we would suggest that the same holds for studying science. Any absolute truth that may be at the heart of either religion or science is beyond our ken and therefore irrelevant as an object of study, religious or scientific. However, just as some religious institutions have fallen into the trap of claiming absolute authority at some point in history, the success of modern science has led some scientists to adopt a decidedly absolutist stance. As Appleyard states: "Science now answers questions as if it were a religion and its obvious effectiveness means that these answers are believed to be the Truth—again as if it were a religion. But it confronts none of the spiritual issues of purpose and meaning. And, meanwhile, its growing power enables it to drive the very systems that did confront those issues to the margins of our concern and, ultimately, out of existence. As I have said before, our science, whatever it may pretend, is incapable of co-existence."[35] This reluctance to tolerate alternative worldviews or systems of meaning gets us to the core of what a religious study of science can offer us.

Esteeming Science the Right Way

All this has direct bearing on the science-religion dialogue. While a creative tension will always exist between science and religion, our hope is that boundaries and barriers can be taken down and religion and science can join in a common pursuit of the answers to the questions of concern to humanity. The absolutist position taken by some scientists means that we can never move out of what Ian Barbour calls the conflict position. As long as scientific exploration is predicated on the notion that given enough time and resources, all of the questions that we can ask will be answered, the scientific worldview will remain a religion, blinded by faith in its own methods and accomplishments.

Following Ronald Cole-Turner, we would suggest that by broadening the terms of the debate beyond religion and science to include technology and ethics, and by recognizing the social basis of all of these terms, scholars can probe the common ground that is shared by all four. However, the transition toward exploration of the seamless web at the core of our existence will require learning to see things initially from a fresh perspective and then from more than one perspective, as individuals come to the realization that their faith emerges more out of the importance they attach to the issues than it does out of any supremacy that they perceive to reside in the approach.

In this chapter we have tried to suggest that our understanding of the scientific worldview will increase dramatically if we examine it as implicitly religious. By this point, some readers may be ready to accuse us of blatant and easily dismissed science bashing. That is certainly not our intention, for as Mary Midgley says, "We do not need to esteem science less. What we need is to esteem it in the right way. Especially we need to stop isolating it artificially from the rest of our mental life."[36] We are not saying that science has not been successful in providing technological and conceptual means for coming to terms with many of the problems that we face, or that scientists are all living in a fanciful world, blinded by a myth of truth seeking and knowledge making. Nor are we suggesting that science is another form of religion. We are saying, however, that in order to sustain their daily activities in the style to which they have become accustomed and to maintain the level of commitment required to carry on their work, scientists have managed to convince themselves, and most of the public, that what they do is essential to the long-term survival of the human species. The level of devotion that they exhibit toward this belief and the zeal with which they defend it, not to mention the unprecedented degree of deference to authority afforded them by the public, would be the envy of members of any religious community. By using religion to study science, we can come to understand the origins, as well as the internal and external consequences, of this scientific worldview in ways not otherwise open to us. While this exercise will amount to a demythologization of science, in the long run it will help us to gain a deeper understanding of the scientific enterprise.

2 Writing the History of Science

The so-called "scientific revolution" ... outshines everything since the rise of Christianity.
—Herbert Butterfield,
The Origins of Modern Science

Historians can be active players in the dialogue between science and religion. Taking a historical approach to the relationship of science and religion allows us to examine the origins of our attitudes toward science. Moreover, by looking at the context in which those attitudes were created, we are in a better position to evaluate their worth. The purpose of this chapter is not to provide a comprehensive discussion of the history of science, or of the history of science and religion. Both topics would require entire books.[1] Rather, it is to examine some of the most important developments in the writing of the history of science, and to discuss what this reveals about the role of science in society and the relationships between religion and science that underscore these historical interpretations.

The value in studying the history of historical writing, or historiography, is that it enables us to uncover some of the assumptions of past generations and to examine how those assumptions affected their interpretations. To understand a historical interpretation requires an understanding of the time in which it was formulated. However, as the writers of the story, historians also influence future generations and shape what will become common perceptions, even after the immediate context in which the historian was writing has changed. There is therefore a continual process of reinterpretation at work. Each generation inherits the conclusions of previous generations. However, these conclusions were the result of the battles fought by that generation and the particular issues its members faced in their own time. It is for this reason that, as is commonly stated, each generation writes its own history. One of the best ways to see this mechanism at work is to look at a specific example. In this chapter we will focus primarily on how historians have defined and understood what is commonly referred to as the Scientific Revolution.

The Scientific Revolution has been, since the beginning of the twentieth century, one of the most powerful and enduring concepts in the history of Western society. It informs our notions of modern science, of Western culture, and of the relationship between religion and science. It is used to explain how Europe became a world power. Most importantly, it has become part of our identity as a modern society that places its faith in science rather than in religion. However, it is worth remembering that the term *Scientific Revolution* is a historical construct; individuals in the seventeenth century did not simply wake up one day to discover that they were living during the Scientific Revolution. Such terms are invented after the fact as analytical tools to make sense of the past. In this case, the term came into use in the early twentieth century. It was popularized by Herbert Butterfield in his book *The Origins of Modern Science*, delivered as a series of lectures at Cambridge in 1948. Since that time, historians have debated the usefulness of the term, since it implies a single event or phenomenon that can be named. The concept of the Scientific Revolution has been routinely dissected, analyzed, questioned, rejected, and reaffirmed by historians of science. Recent scholarly books have been titled *Reappraisals of the Scientific Revolution* and *Rethinking the Scientific Revolution*.[2] A recently published bibliography of the Scientific Revolution comprises more than 350 pages.[3] It clearly remains a useful, if controversial, concept, as Steven Shapin suggests in the ironic opening line of one of his recent works: "There was no such thing as the Scientific Revolution, and this is a book about it."[4] Its persistent use also implies that historians continue to try to find some way to acknowledge that something important happened to the Western worldview between 1500 and 1800.

The Traditional Narrative

To understand the ways in which historians have viewed this period, it is useful to begin with what might be called a textbook summary of the Scientific Revolution. The traditional narrative goes something like this: After the fall of the Roman Empire in Western Europe, civilization was dominated by the Christian Church for a period of about one thousand years, a period called the Middle Ages, or as earlier historians had labeled it, the Dark Ages. By the end of this period, Christian theology had been wedded to Aristotelian philosophy in a system of thought called scholasticism, which included the incorporation of Aristotelian physics and cosmology into a Christian framework. During this period, it was believed that the Earth was the center of the universe, around which the moon, planets, sun, and stars moved in circular orbits. Around 1400, Europe began to "awaken" from this period of presumed darkness. Renaissance writers, artists, and philosophers began to look to Greco-Roman sources for inspiration and knowledge. Moreover, by the early 1500s, religious reformers began to purge Christianity of elements considered magical or superstitious; this resulted in the permanent rupture known as the Protestant Reformation. In 1543, Nicholas Copernicus published *On the Revolution of the Heavenly Spheres*, challenging the traditional notion of the Earth-centered universe by proposing that the Earth revolved around the sun. A few decades later, Johannes Kepler discovered his three laws of planetary motion, refuting the Aristotelian notion that the heavenly orbits were spherical. Meanwhile, Galileo used evidence collected from turning his telescope on the heavens to prove that the Aristotelian cosmology was incorrect. Because of his challenge to the prevailing system, he was brought before the Inquisition and forbidden to write or teach about astronomy. In spite of the Church's opposition, a new breed of scientists began to emerge by the middle of the seventeenth century. Francis Bacon helped to develop scientific method with his emphasis on the use of empirical evidence. Finally, Sir Isaac Newton came along and synthesized the new astronomy of Kepler and the new physics of Galileo and developed a universal law of gravity. Thus was born modern science.

This is a powerful story full of drama, peopled with heroes and villains, a story of the triumph of truth over superstition and of science over religion. The problem with this story is that many aspects have either been modified or questioned by many historians. Such is the case because embedded in almost every statement are important assumptions—assumptions about how science works, what is important in the history of science, what drives scientific progress, and how religion and science are related. Before proceeding further, it is worthwhile to make explicit the ways in which historians' assumptions affect their interpretation of the past, and, in particular, how these assumptions inform their understanding of the Scientific Revolution.

First, all historians work with some assumptions regarding the practice of science in general. Most are concerned with change over time, in particular, the way science changes over time. Some view it as a process of evolution, that is, the slow accretion of knowledge, while others emphasize change as revolution, or the overturning of entire frameworks for others.[5] Did the Scientific Revolution actually occur as a revolution, and is it even a useful historical term? Some historians suggest not. Second, historians disagree over what a history of science ought to look like. Is it the story of successes and discoveries, or ought one also include in the narrative the failures and sidetracks? A historian who assumes the former will write a history that differs greatly from one who assumes the latter. Those who focus only on the progressive nature of scientific discovery are sometimes accused of Whiggism by their opponents, that is, of writing history in a way that implies that the present was the ultimate goal naturally embedded in the past. Third, historians disagree as to what drives scientific development, and what are the most important factors to emphasize. For example, some historians focus on the scientific ideas themselves, while others look at the individuals who created them. Yet others, informed by the methods and insights of social science, focus on external factors, such as the cultural, social, political, or economic context in which science is done. For example, a historian may look at how scientific research was funded in a particular time and place. Finally, and most importantly for our present purposes, historians work with a variety of assumptions about the historical interaction between religion and science. There are two aspects of this last issue that are relevant. The first has to do with the relationship of the Western Church as an institution to the rise of science. Did the Church hamper the development of science in the West, or nurture it? The second has to do with the contrast between a religious view of the world and a naturalistic one. What role did belief in the supernatural world have in the beginnings of the Scientific Revolution? Was it something to be discarded, or was it the context in which modern science originated? Each of these issues has informed debates among generations of historians and complicated the "textbook history" just outlined.

The Rise of Conflict Interpretations of the History of Science

The conflict thesis in the history of science originated in the nineteenth century with the publication of two important books: J. W. Draper's *History of the Conflict Between Religion and Science* in 1875 and A. D. White's *History of the Warfare of Science with Theology in Christendom* in 1896. The titles of the works are self-explanatory. Both works highlighted the Galileo affair (the conflict between Galileo and the Inquisition in the seventeenth century) as one of the key moments in the history of science.[6] Draper's work in particular typifies the anticlerical reaction of the nineteenth-century scientific community. Draper clearly stated his position: "The history of Science . . . is a narrative of the conflict of two contending powers, the expansive force of the human intellect on one side, and the compression arising from traditionary faith and human interests on the other."[7] To understand such writing, we need to consider the period in which it was written.

In our time, generally thought of as a secular age, we are unaware

of the religious tensions of the Victorian age, tensions that fueled a belief that religion and science were necessarily in conflict. The impact
of Darwinism in the late nineteenth century created a growing conflict
between science and religion. Christianity had already come under criticism in the eighteenth century with the skepticism of the Scottish philosopher David Hume (1711–1776) and the anticlericalism of the French
philosophes.[8] In the nineteenth century, devout Christians had to work
increasingly hard to integrate new scientific information into their belief system. By the end of the eighteenth century, the study of geology
had developed into a distinct discipline, setting up challenges to religious understandings of the history of creation.[9] In 1830, Charles Lyell
published his *Principles of Geology*, which refuted traditional dating
methods and showed the Earth to be much older than the six thousand
years as calculated from the biblical genealogies. While some scientists
looked at the natural world, others examined human societies in scientific terms, most notably Herbert Spencer and Thomas Malthus, who had
developed theories of population, or demography. Further challenges
were presented by biblical criticism, which emphasized the historical
origins of the Scriptures and questioned the concept of the Bible as written by the direct hand of God.

In 1859, Darwin's *Origin of Species* was published and immediately
created a furor that has not yet subsided. The first real debate of the issue occurred at a meeting of the British Association for the Advancement of Science in 1860. The "conflict" mentality was typified at that
meeting by an exchange between Thomas Huxley, one of Darwin's strongest advocates, and Bishop Wilberforce. The debate reached its peak when
Bishop Wilberforce asked Huxley whether he considered himself descended from an ape on his grandmother's or grandfather's side. Huxley's
supposed retort—that he would prefer to be descended from an ape than
from someone who obscured the truth—epitomized the conflict between
science and religion.[10] William Draper also spoke at this historic conference at some length.

The battle lines were drawn on both sides by individuals who considered the new scientific theories incompatible with Christianity. An
important event was the first Vatican Council called by Pope Pius IX in
1868. High on the agenda items was the discussion of a statement of
faith opposing "rationalism, naturalism, materialism, pantheism, and
kindred errors."[11] Moreover, it was this council that ultimately declared
papal infallibility in matters of doctrine to be church dogma.

Most significant, for our purposes, is that William Draper's book was
written in direct response to the first Vatican Council. Draper discusses
the matter at length in the last chapter of his book. By the 1870s, as
A. N. Wilson tells us, "in some circles, men of science felt it was their

duty not merely to express doubt about religion, but actively to promote atheism."[12] The hostile climate of religion and science in the Victorian age shaped the interpretation of the history of the Scientific Revolution. The Victorians read their own struggles into the past. Today we interpret Draper's book as a polemical work that grew out of a specific political climate. However, such polemics were passed on to subsequent generations as history.

These attitudes, developed in the climate of late Victorian society, were supported by a more subtle development as well. One of the most important intellectual influences on the writing of history in the late nineteenth and early twentieth centuries was positivism. Positivism can be briefly defined as the claim that true knowledge is derived by empirical inquiry and is subject to verification. Knowledge that cannot be verified is "merely subjective." These ideas were most fully developed by the nineteenth-century founder of sociology, Auguste Comte (1798–1857). As discussed earlier, Comte believed that each area of human knowledge could be divided into three developmental stages: the theological, the metaphysical, and the positive. In his *Cours de philosophie positive*, Comte stated that the physical sciences had reached the final stage during the seventeenth century, when "positive conceptions were effectively and with precision set free from the superstitious and scholastic alloy that more or less disguised the veritable character of all previous efforts."[13] In other words, the history of science was interpreted as the story of the accumulation of empirical knowledge about the world and would be framed as a story of the increasing separation of science from external religious influences. Moreover, this was presented as a story of progress.

Positivism influenced the writing of history in general, as historians in the early twentieth century strove to establish their discipline as a scientific one and distance it from its earlier associations with literature and rhetoric.[14] As well, it became the predominant approach to the history of science. In many ways, it is not surprising that those who developed the academic discipline of the history of science took a positivistic approach. They were, for the most part, either scientists or philosophers, not professional historians. Their contemporaries in the historical profession were primarily interested in political, diplomatic, and military history, and were generally quite happy to leave the history of science to scientists. Therefore, it is not unreasonable to expect that scientists looking at history would focus on those aspects that elucidated their current problems and would bring their assumptions of the workings of science to their study of its history. This phenomenon has been succinctly explained by Floris Cohen: "What has made positivism so appealing to scientists with an interest in the past of science is that this doctrine fits in beautifully with working scientists' virtually inborn prejudices regarding the achievement of their predecessors."[15] In other words, the history of science was first written by scientists and philosophers as a history of progress toward the knowledge that they possessed and the methods upon which they based their own work. It reflected their own assumptions and concerns, laying the groundwork for seeing the history of science as the progress of knowledge over ignorance and superstition for subsequent generations.

One of the clearest examples of this approach is George Sarton, who worked, more than did anyone else, to develop the history of science as a professional discipline. He founded the journal *Isis* in 1913 as the first journal dedicated to the history of science and worked to establish a history of science institute at Harvard.[16] His own work was systematic and comprehensive. His goal was to chronicle the entire history of scientific achievement, a goal he never completely attained—his *Introduction to the History of Science* ultimately ran into five volumes and reached only the year 1400. Sarton's work was rather humanist oriented. He emphasized science as a human activity and compared it in this sense to art or religion.[17] Nonetheless, he was influenced by Comte and wrote his history based on what he called his "theorem on the history of science," which stated that "the acquisition and systematization of positive knowledge are the only human activities which are truly cumulative and progressive" and concluded that "the history of science is the only history which can illustrate the progress of mankind."[18] Moreover, he felt that by studying the history of science, one could learn tolerance.[19] He considered intolerance to be one of the evils of the world and believed that the Church had hindered scientific inquiry by its reluctance to accept new ideas. Sarton stated: "The history of science is not simply the history of discoveries and new ideas that are closer to reality; it is also the history of the defense of these ideas against recurrent errors, illusions, and lies. We must replace darkness with light; that is the main function of science."[20]

So as the history of science became defined as an academic discipline early in the twentieth century, it was characterized by an approach that emphasized the separation of science from theology and interpreted the history of science as the history of progress. These still-apparent assumptions were popularized in the writings of Herbert Butterfield, who was one of the first general historians to write the history of science. In his *Origins of Modern Science*, it was clear that Butterfield still based the value of the history of science on the role of science in modern society: "Considering the part played by the sciences in the story of our Western Civilization, it is hardly possible to doubt the importance which the history of science will sooner or later acquire."[21] As we have suggested, he inherited the assumptions of those who were already working in the field. What makes this somewhat surprising is that it was Butterfield who, as early as 1931, pointed out the "Whig" fallacy in the writing of political history, that is, the error of evaluating the past by the extent to which it contributes to the present.[22]

Such an approach led to a focus on the developments of the late sixteenth and early seventeenth centuries as the period when science became modern, that is, recognizable to us. It reinforced the notion of the Middle Ages as a period dominated by a church that hampered intellectual development. From this perspective, one of the greatest leaps forward in the history of science was its separation from Christian theology. Modern science was born when the medieval synthesis between Christian theology and Aristotelian science was shattered, through the concepts of Copernicus, the calculations of Kepler, the observations of Galileo, and the insights of Newton. The underlying assumption was that Christianity had been a hindrance to the development of science, a view that Sarton declared quite explicitly.[23] The textbook interpretation had been formulated, and it continues to predominate today. One of the most important popularizers of this interpretation is James Burke, whose books and films tend to imply that both the symbolic worldview of the Christian Middle Ages and the power of the Church hindered the development of anything like real scientific discovery. What is significant is that the attitudes toward the relationship between religion and science were a major factor in understanding the chronological development of science.

Revisionist Interpretations

The traditional narrative was based on an assumption that religion and science were more or less in conflict. However, other historians would problematize the relationship of Christianity and science and question the chronology that saw the Scientific Revolution as the liberation of reason and knowledge from superstition. We will now examine some of the most significant challenges, with a view to examining how attitudes toward religion and science affected these other interpretations. One of the most obvious examples is found in the work of the French physicist and philosopher of science Pierre Duhem. Duhem was a Catholic priest who began his research into the history of science by looking at Leonardo da Vinci, and who spent years of research working back through time to find the earliest traces of scientific thought. When this was accomplished, he concluded that the origins of modern science actually lay, not in the seventeenth century, but in the Middle Ages. In the end, he rejected the notion that the Scientific Revolution occurred in the seventeenth century, and in fact, that there had been a revolution at all. He claimed that science proceeded by a series of small steps rather than by abrupt changes. So not only did he reject the traditional chronology, but he used a different assumption about the way science changes over time. For Duhem, Christianity was not a handicap to scientific development, but the context in which it evolved. His work has been influential, although many of his ideas have been superseded by subsequent research.

What is significant for our purposes is how Duhem's findings confirmed his own religious convictions and in his mind served to vindicate the Church. He is described in the *Dictionary of Scientific Biography* as "Right-wing, royalist, anti-semitic, anti-Dreyfus, anti-Republican, and a religious extremist."[24] He was famous for an essay published in 1954, "Physics of a Believer." This religious and political agenda has been continued by Duhem's most fervent promoter, Stanley Jaki, a physicist, theologian, and Catholic priest, who has written many works on the history of science, as well as a biography of Duhem.[25] Jaki called Duhem "the most universal French genius around the turn of the century."[26] Jaki's work is often viewed as primarily polemical or at least apologetic in tone and is thus controversial.[27] The approach taken by Duhem and pursued by Jaki is an example of how histories of science are shaped by religious assumptions, but as well, of how they have served as a vehicle for reevaluating the relationship between religion and science.

Another revision of the traditional thesis came from a very different quarter, that of sociology. In 1938, Robert Merton published his doctoral thesis, entitled *Science, Technology, and Society in Seventeenth Century England.* In this work he argued that the early scientists had not divorced themselves from Christian faith. On the contrary, he argued, this faith had actually furnished some of the impetus for scientific research. Merton identified a correlation between Protestantism, most notably English Puritanism, and the rise of science. He argued that because Puritans valued work and study, they were led to an interest in science. He cited individuals like Robert Boyle as examples. In effect, he was expanding the thesis put forward by Max Weber that Puritanism had been a factor in the rise of capitalism. Almost every aspect of the so-called Merton thesis has generated discussion, but it continues to persuade many. What is significant is that Merton argued that, in this case, Christianity was a more positive factor in the development of science than had been previously considered. It was, however, a reformed Christianity, one that had been purged of its magical elements.

Other historians would question this relationship as well, and it is worth looking at those scholars who began to examine the issue of magic and science. With the exception of Lynn Thorndike early in the twentieth century, the topic of the occult had been avoided by historians as a legitimate field of inquiry.[28] It had been deliberately excluded by George

Sarton because, for him, scientific progress was assumed to involve a separation from superstition, both magical and religious.[29] Butterfield had considered the relationship of magic to science and concluded that the two phenomena were at opposite ends of the spectrum.[30] Other examples of this dismissive attitude toward the history of magic are Charles Singer's history of medicine and H. W. Picton's history of chemistry, the final section of which was entitled "The Triumph of Truth."[31] The reexamination of the relationship between magic and science was largely the result of the work of three individuals: Alexander Koyré, Walter Pagel, and Frances Yates. They would reshape scholarship for the next several generations.

Koyré approached the history of science from the perspective of a religious scholar; he had initially done graduate work on the theology of St. Anselm in Paris and published research on sixteenth-century German mystics. Although he retained a progressivist view of the history of science, Koyré expressed sympathy with pre-seventeenth-century mystics and alchemists and considered them worthy of study.[32] He emphasized the Platonic and mathematical nature of early modern science rather than its empirical side.[33] Koyré's study of Galileo was first published in 1939. When the English translation appeared in 1978, the stage was set for a reassessment of the relationship between religion and science.[34] By this time, a new generation was ready to broaden the scope of traditional histories of science. Rather than viewing magic and the occult with distaste or disinterest, this generation more often regarded them with curiosity.[35] Moreover, the discipline of history had been profoundly reconfigured by the *Annales* historians in France, who deemphasized the idea of change and progress in history and tended to view continuities instead. They reconfigured the history of ideas into the history of *mentalité*, by which they meant the mental apparatus shared by a culture in a particular period. This led to increased interest in understanding the participants in the Scientific Revolution within the cultural context of their own time rather than as forerunners of our own.

A related development was the redefinition of the Scientific Revolution in conceptual terms. In the first part of the century, the Scientific Revolution had been defined largely as the history of physics, with an emphasis on the work of Galileo and Newton. The Scientific Revolution was a revolution in physics. However, other sciences had a different historical evolution. This had been recognized early on by Herbert Butterfield, who had extended the chronological limits of the revolution to 1800 in order to take into account the history of chemistry, which had its most significant breakthroughs after the Newtonian revolution in physics. However, the real pioneer in the history of chemistry was Walter Pagel, who attacked the positivist framework as anachronistic.

One of Pagel's students, Allen Debus, has argued that it is historically inaccurate to judge the past from the perspective of the present. For example, he pointed out that the sixteenth-century physician Paracelsus had a greater immediate impact in his day than did his contemporary, Nicholas Copernicus.[36]

One of the most significant and controversial developments is found in the work of Dame Frances Yates. Going even further than Koyré and Pagel, she argued that the magical worldview as it existed in the sixteenth century was not a hindrance to the development of science, but was, in fact, a stage in its development. She based her argument on the notion that natural magic and alchemy as developed in the Renaissance involved an examination and manipulation of the world in a way that was new for that time. Even though the alchemists' assumptions were wrong, she argued, their impulses were correct, and in this they can be considered precursors to scientists. Yates's purpose was not to refute the notion of the Scientific Revolution—she continued, like others, to see the seventeenth century as a watershed—but she believed that examining Renaissance magic was crucial to understanding how science evolved. Yates had her critics. One of the most vehement is Brian Vickers, who dismisses an interest in Renaissance occult as a sort of nostalgia on the part of modern historians and argues for a rigid distinction between occult and scientific thought.[37] Vickers in turn is criticized for being anachronistic in his portrayal of seventeenth-century scientists as modern empiricists.[38] The debate is largely between those who view the history of science as a process of the elimination of irrelevant or incorrect ideas and those who suggest that we must look at the byways in order to understand the path that was taken.

A notable legacy of this attempt to understand the early modern worldview on its own terms is that it has helped to shed light on the participants in the Scientific Revolution. Recent biographies of seventeenth-century scientists no longer neglect the fact that many of them were either deeply religious, involved in magical or occult practices, or both. It is useful to examine the development of historical scholarship around Isaac Newton as an example. Earlier generations of historians of Newton tended to shy away from his work on alchemy and biblical studies and focused on his physics. However, this approach was increasingly perceived as inadequate and anachronistic. Historian Margaret Jacob described the frustration historians felt after an international symposium on Isaac Newton revealed the complexities of his mind and range of his interests.[39] In her own work on Isaac Newton, Betty Dobbs began to see that there must be some way to understand both his alchemy and his science. In Dobbs's writings, Newton is no longer a prefiguration of the Enlightenment, but the last of the magi.[40] This trend to reevaluate the role of religion and magic has extended to other historical figures as well. For example, a recent biography of Robert Boyle highlights his alchemical activities, a topic previously disregarded.[41]

The State of the Art

It is difficult to summarize the state of the art at this point. The history of science has exploded in the last few decades, in all directions. Debates continue to revolve around the questions raised at the beginning of this chapter. One of the most important developments has arisen from postmodern quarters, or what is often referred to as the "linguistic turn." In the history of science, the reluctant herald of this development was Thomas Kuhn, whose book *The Structure of Scientific Revolutions* has become a reference that is tossed in cavalierly by anyone who wants to suggest that the practice of science is entirely relative, merely the result of shifting paradigms. Kuhn tried to distance himself from the charge that he promoted any such view of science. With or without Kuhn, some historians are now accustomed to bracketing the entire issue of whether science is correct or not, and to examining the external factors that shape it.[42]

To those outside the historical profession, many of these debates may seem pedantic or irrelevant. Even within the profession, there are those who are rather dismayed by the broad spectrum of voices. In the preface to *Reappraisals of the Scientific Revolution*, written in 1990, Lindberg and Westman express dismay that there is no longer any standard view of the Scientific Revolution.[43] However, others see this as a more positive sign of renewal and lively debate and an expansion of the boundaries of the historical profession. More importantly, the current rewriting of the history of the Scientific Revolution is indicative of the wider social debate regarding the role of science in society. William Shea has aptly identified a key reason behind the current furor in the field of the history of science: "When a society is perfectly satisfied with its method of knowing, it is not greatly exercised about the way it was first acquired. As long as science was considered to be the embodiment of rationality, its history was less an examination of actual events than a celebration of heroes and a quest for anticipations."[44] We might add that the current interest in examining the relationship between religion and science in the past is a reflection of our own society's attempt to deal with the question in our own time. In a recent study entitled *Rethinking the Scientific Revolution*, a significant number of chapters deal with issues of the interaction of religion and science in the early modern period.[45] This suggests that the complexities at the center of the debate as identified by Ronald Cole-Turner, which we outline in the introduction, are genuine and are important for the historians of our generation.

Moreover, the story of the history of science reveals a shift in our assurance that science will save and protect us. Earlier generations of historians looked confidently at the history of science as the history of progress and victory over superstition. Current generations tend to have a different emphasis. The writing of the history of science from the early twentieth to the early twenty-first century is a story of increasing skepticism about the salvific powers of science and of the desire to develop a more integrated understanding of the relationship of religion and science. Perhaps the wide range of interpretations that now exists among historians reflects the fact that our generation, rather than relying on science to look after us, is, in Saint Paul's words, working out its own salvation "with fear and trembling."[46]

PART II | *Saintliness*

3 The Iconography of Science

Many of our pictures are incarnations of concepts masquerading as neutral descriptions of nature. These are the most potent sources of conformity, since ideas passing as descriptions lead us to equate the tentative with the unambiguously factual.
—Stephen Jay Gould, *Wonderful Life*

Close your eyes for a moment and visualize a scientist. The odds are very high you imagined either a white male in a lab coat surrounded by scientific apparatus or Albert Einstein. The odds are very low that you imagined a woman or person of color. Why should these images come to mind? Linguists call them *default assumptions*, that is, what we assume to be the case unless we are given information to the contrary. In North America the default assumption of a scientist is a white male. Much of what and how we think about science and scientists is shaped by the images and pictures we hold, which unfortunately all too often have only a passing resemblance to how science is actually done. Because most of us in the science-religion dialogue are not practicing scientists, this iconography has the potential to distort the debate itself.

Following soteriology as the first characteristic of religion, Max Weber identifies the second characteristic as saintliness. This refers to the idea that there are always special individuals who stand out because of their dedication or genius and who demonstrate that religion (or science), when taken seriously, is a vocation or, in theological language, a calling. Saints provide exemplars for the community. They serve as guides in times of trouble, as sources of inspiration, and as models to be emulated. The saint is a potent image. But here ambiguity enters in. First, the image is always different from the reality. Images of science create a gap between how science is portrayed and how it is practiced. Second, images have power, and we often accept them unconsciously. The unintended consequence of images of scientific saints is to establish science as authority. The social sciences can make important contributions to the science-religion dialogue by analyzing science as the active practice of discovery and debate engaged in by a community. As a practice, science becomes a process of knowing rather than a corpus of truths about the natural world, divorced from any context, which the nonexpert must accept on faith.

What these images mean for the science-religion dialogue is the subject of this part of the book. This chapter examines the images of science, scientists, and the scientific method presented in textbooks. The next chapter analyzes the greatest of scientific saints, Isaac Newton. Both alert us to the difficulties these images can create for the science-religion dialogue.

Ambiguous Images

Images dominate discussion of science, in both the media and the academy. Recent controversies, such as the so-called science wars, reveal a great deal of ambiguity in people's attitudes toward science. Expressions of fear and distrust are regular occurrences, yet science retains enormous authority. Saintly Albert Einstein can be named "man-of-the-century" one week, and geneticists can be accused of "playing God" the next. Even a short perusal of contemporary discourse reveals deep ambiguity about basic questions. Is science a worldview, a method, a body of knowledge, or the practice of a community? Are the people who do science saintly geniuses, dispassionate experts, self-interested ideologues, or arrogant seekers after godhood? Such images do not spring up overnight. Perhaps they can best be understood as the sedimentation of tradition.

For example, where do the default assumptions we mentioned earlier come from? Until very recently, the vast majority of scientists (like most others in the learned professions) were indeed white and male, and to the extent that people had any personal experience with scientists it would reinforce the stereotype. On the other hand, relatively few people have much personal experience with science or scientists. What most of us know about science comes either from the media or from the classes we took in high school or at university. Of these, the media is by far the more important. As sociologist Dorothy Nelkin reports: "For most people the reality of science is what they read in the press. They understand science less through direct experience or past education than through the filter of journalistic language and imagery."[1] And people learn about science, unlike most other areas, primarily from print, rather than electronic, media. While we will return to media images in chapter 7, in this chapter we want to look first at education in order to examine some of the images from which people's basic understanding of science arises.

As a basis for this study we randomly chose five recent (1991 to 1999) university-level introductory biology textbooks.[2] We chose them all from the same discipline for continuity and ease of comparison. One of the tasks of any introductory textbook is to portray the discipline to neophytes, and in these days of competitive enrollments, this is not a task to take for granted. All of these texts rise to the challenge. They are all large (more than one thousand pages), colorful, well-organized books loaded with graphics and illustrations. It is this last element, together with their metaphors and "word pictures," that particularly interests us. We should not underestimate the potency of such images. As one of the textbooks says of itself: "Vivid illustrations help fix otherwise abstract ideas in our minds in the same way a mordant fixes a dye."[3] A striking image or vigorous metaphor may display enormous longevity, persistence, and power to shape discourse.

The textbooks are, of course, primarily concerned with teaching the content of the discipline. But they also try to communicate who scientists are and what they do. What are the images of scientists and science presented to people who have little or no prior experience with science? What are the assumptions, symbols, and myths that underlie these images? And what are some of the implications of these images for the science-religion dialogue? In this chapter we look first at the portrayal of scientists and then at how they do science, that is, the scientific method. We will next make a few remarks about how the content of biology is depicted and conclude with some reflections on the significance of all this for the science-religion dialogue.

The Scientist as Saint

One of the things an introductory textbook usually does is present the novice with exemplars of the discipline. Four of the five texts did this by presenting vignettes of biologists at work.[4] Most of these depicted science as an interesting, fulfilling, and rewarding career, much as would texts in any field. (Who, in any discipline, wants to tell youngsters considering their life choices about months on end of tedious academic grunt work?) But at least some of the vignettes in all four books portrayed scientists in a particular way. We can call this the myth of the heroic scientist.

The heroic scientist is the individual who, convinced of the truth, stands alone against the crowd, often at personal risk. A particularly good example is in Allan Tobin and Jennie Dusheck's *Asking About Life*. They begin their text by telling the story of Barry Marshall, the Australian doctor who discovered that ulcers are caused by bacteria. In the 1970s,

Marshall and a colleague noticed that tissues removed from their patients with ulcers were infected with bacteria. Marshall began ordering biopsies of all his patients and discovered they all were infected.

> Marshall, however, had insignificant credentials as a doctor and none as a researcher. In 1980, he seemed to have no more chance of selling his idea to the bio-medical community than his bacteria had of flourishing in the corrosive environment of the stomach. Nevertheless, in 1983 Marshall presented his hypothesis at a scientific conference in Brussels. His presentation was a disaster. He was unknown; he was young, inexperienced, and overexcited; and he had a seemingly screwball idea. . . . When Marshall's presentation was over, his audience of eminent medical researchers shifted uneasily in their seats, embarrassed. A few laughed. They couldn't believe he was serious.[5]

Marshall was undeterred by this humiliation. He returned to his lab and tried experiment after experiment, but he was unsuccessful in duplicating the phenomenon in an animal. "Desperate to prove that he was no nut," Marshall decided to take the risk of experimenting on himself. "He told no one ahead of time—not the medical ethics board at the hospital, not his wife. They wouldn't have approved, he knew." Marshall survived the bacterial cocktail he drank and "in time, other, more-established researchers began to take an interest. Mainly they were interested in proving Marshall wrong. But by the end of the 1980s, the evidence that the bacterium could infect the stomach was unassailable." Because he knew the truth and had the courage to keep going, Marshall had triumphed.

This is an inspiring tale, and other vignettes are just as uplifting—Darwin facing down the prejudices of his day to establish the truth of evolution; Edward Jenner risking lynching by a mob to conduct experiments that would lead to vaccination for smallpox; Barbara McClintock overcoming the sexism of the scientific establishment to win the Nobel Prize. What gives these stories their potency, however, is that they are all symbolic narratives. They all resonate with a fundamental myth in Western culture. There are many versions of the heroic scientist myth—it is not restricted to textbooks. The archetypes are the trial of Galileo and the martyrdom of Socrates.

If we look beneath the surface details, we find that all these stories (in textbooks and elsewhere) share a common structure. There are five elements to the myth. First, the hero is a lone individual, an outsider. Often he or she is of obscure origins. Barry Marshall was a humble Australian doctor. Galileo came from a poor family and, refusing a scholarship, had to leave university. Einstein was a patent clerk who had trouble with arithmetic. Even in the case of Charles Darwin, who came from a distinguished, wealthy family, the textbook retelling emphasizes his failures as a youth before he signed on to *HMS Beagle*.[6] In no version of the myth is the hero a project manager in a large, well-funded research lab.

Second, in the myth, the hero has to struggle against adversity. There is, of course, a lack of resources. Darwin sets sail equipped only with his notebooks and his keen powers of observation. Some, like Galileo or Pasteur, have to invent the equipment with which to make their discoveries. Mythic heroes do not arise out of the Lawrence Livermore Lab or the Mayo Clinic. Furthermore, nature does not want to give up its secrets. As with Marshall, there are long hours of struggle and dozens of failed experiments before the eureka moment, not infrequently achieved by breaking the rules or risking the self.

Third, the hero faces opposition. This may take two forms. The first is the individual against those in authority, be they the church, the state, or the learned establishment of the day (or occasionally, as in the cases of Socrates and Galileo, all of them at once). It is a conflict of knowledge against power, which makes the myth a story of liberation. The other form of opposition is the ignorant mob. Socrates, Galileo, Darwin, and Pasteur, for instance, all challenged the commonsense notions of their day. Ridicule is the universal fate of the heroic scientist, and sometimes the dangers are much worse.

Fourth, heroes triumph because they know the truth. The objective knowledge of the heroes is in contrast to the mere beliefs of their opponents. Pasteur knows microbes cause decay, while Pouchet believes decay spontaneously generates microbes. Galileo knows the Earth orbits the sun, while the Church only has faith in the opposite. Marshall is able to prove bacteria cause ulcers, demonstrating stress as their cause was "just a theory."

Fifth, heroes can do all this because of their exemplary character (what Weber would call charisma). The heroic scientists are geniuses. They are exemplars, models to be followed, to be pointed to when asking "how it should be done." In theological language, we call such persons saints.

Genius has several aspects. One is its incomprehensibility. The media come up with all sorts of fanciful theories to explain genius. Some say it is IQ, others say it is nurture, still others that it is in our chromosomes. Someone has even claimed that Einstein's brain was structurally different from normal. And like the relic of a medieval saint, Einstein's brain has been preserved in a jar. Charisma is mysterious, and whatever theory is au courant, the prevailing attitude toward genius is awe: "Yet though we can't define genius, we know it exists. Genius has made our world: From electricity to theology, we both enjoy and suffer from its effects."[7]

A second characteristic is that, while genius is portrayed as the reason for the hero's triumph over all the obstacles discussed earlier, genius appears to be conditional upon those obstacles. As Steve Fuller explains: "The genius typically confounds all expectations by making an extraordinary discovery while under adverse intellectual and financial circumstances. Indeed, humans appear hard-pressed to identify any genius who did not suffer hardship, be it prior neglect or scanty material resources, although that biographical fact is officially irrelevant to what makes someone a genius."[8]

A third characteristic is that, like medieval saints, geniuses are miracle workers. They see and do things that others cannot. Not only are heroic scientists masters of those arcane rituals we call the scientific method, allowing them to pierce the veils of subjectivity to find "the thing in itself," they exhibit a creativity beyond that of ordinary scientists. As we have seen, in doing this they frequently extend, or even break, the rules.

Fourth and finally, geniuses are nearly always portrayed as male. One can think of a few women recognized as geniuses—Barbara McClintock and Marie Curie come to mind—but not very many more. With the notable exceptions of physics and computer science, women have made significant advances in the natural sciences over the past twenty years. Women have done particularly well in biology. The textbooks under study here are more or less encouraging to women. McClintock and Mary Leaky are mentioned, and most texts are careful to include pictures of female researchers. Yet the people held by our culture to be exemplars of science are nearly all male. At the level of our myths, science is still a male activity. This, in part at least, explains why default assumptions have been so slow to change.

The myth of the heroic scientist is one of the central myths of modern society and, in the form of the martyrdom of Socrates, goes back to the very beginnings of the Western intellectual tradition. Textbooks incorporate the myth to inspire the young and introduce them to a noble calling. It functions to inculcate values and models of behavior. This is reflected in the attitude expressed in Robert Wallace, Gerald Sanders, and Robert Ferl's *Biology: The Science of Life* as "doing the damnedest with one's mind, no matter what," or in the dedication of a scientist in Ticki Lewis's *Life* who, seriously scalded in a hot spring while collecting, cries out "save that thirteenth sample."[9] But there is also a dark side to the myth. We have already seen how it helps perpetuate gender stereotypes. There are other consequences as well.

For one thing, the myth sets science apart from normal activity. If those who engage in science are geniuses, it follows that science is beyond the grasp of ordinary people. If heroic scientists are saints, lesser scientists are made into priests. Science slides from being a system for knowing the world into a system of authority. As Steve Fuller notes: "It would seem that because the average difference in the knowledge of the experts and the public in the case of science is much greater than in that of any organized religion, . . . faith in science marks a degree of deference to authority that is unprecedented in human history."[10] This creates a contradiction. On the one hand, by elevating scientific knowledge above the beliefs of both those in power and the crowd, the myth proclaims science to be liberating. On the other hand, in that scientific knowledge has itself become authoritative and cannot be challenged by the ordinary citizen, it is profoundly anti-democratic.[11] We have yet to resolve that contradiction in our society.

If the bright side of the myth is the scientist as saint, its shadow is the mad scientist or evil genius. From Victor Frankenstein to Dr. Jekyll to Professor Moriarty to Dr. Strangelove, romantic art has imbued scientists with hubris. Arrogantly believing they are above conventional rules, these characters quickly lose self-control, becoming embodiments of immorality and evil. Over the last fifty years, the growth of big science in both power and authority has been matched by a growing suspicion of science among the public. Confronted with everything from atom bombs to genetic engineering, increasing numbers of people are coming to see scientists as "playing God."

A final consequence of the myth is, ironically, the legitimation of what Robert Park calls "voodoo science."[12] A key element of the myth is the heroic individual standing alone against the learned authority of the day. Take a trip to the local bookstore or spend an evening watching cable TV. Is there a crackpot anywhere not wrapped in the mantle of Galileo, proclaiming self-righteously, "I will not be silenced"? If certain books and TV shows are to be believed, the accumulated wisdom of practicing scientists, on anything from the age of the pyramids to UFOs, should count for no more than the opinion of the Curia. But how is a layperson to decide if someone peddling, say, an alternative medical treatment today will be regarded as a quack tomorrow, or as the next Barry Marshall?

The Infallible Method

Textbooks have to do more than motivate undergraduates with inspiring vignettes of great scientists. They also have to introduce them to how science is done. In the first or second chapter of each of the five textbooks under study is a section on what it is that makes someone a scientist—the scientific method.

Science education in North America is almost universally done using an apprenticeship model. In addition to lectures and textbooks, students take labs where demonstrations (euphemistically called experiments) give them hands-on experience. By the time they reach the graduate level, they have acquired a good deal of craft knowledge in the practice of their discipline. It is a system that works, although critics charge that it produces scientists who have little knowledge of the history or philosophy of science. However, we are not concerned here with the totality of science education but with the images in introductory textbooks. For most undergraduates (in colleges and universities that require a science class at all), an introductory class is all the experience of science they will have.

A student reading any one of these books acquires an image of how science is done. Those reading more than one of these books, however, might come away quite confused. All of the books describe the "scientific method," but in no two is it the same. In all the books, the scientific method is presented as a series of steps scientists must go through (Sylvia Mader's *Biology* and Lewis even have tidy diagrams), but only one step—formulating a hypothesis—is the same in all five books. Four of the books (all except Burton Guttman's *Biology*) have a controlled experiment as one of the steps. Only one book mentions prediction or scientific laws, only one other mentions models or statistics, and only two mention publication or reports of findings. For two books, hypotheses may be confirmed. For the others they may only be falsified. Two books are strongly hypothetical-deductive in their logic, while the others emphasize inductive reasoning as well. Now, none of this may matter very much. The differences between the books may represent no more than a healthy variety in their philosophy of science or pedagogical technique. Still, we think these presentations of the scientific method raise a few important issues.

First, all the books represent the scientific method in terms of what philosophers of science call the context of justification rather than the context of discovery. The one point they all have in common is that the method begins with the formulation of a hypothesis to be tested, and they go on at some length talking about the procedures for testing it. They deal with how a scientist justifies confidence in her or his hypothesis. The origin of the hypothesis in the first place remains rather mysterious, however. For those texts that even try to answer that question, hypotheses emerge—somehow—from curiosity, puzzle solving, or "mulling, dreaming or inspiration."[13] What happens at the end of the procedure is equally mysterious. Several of the books mention publication, and Lewis and Mader emphasize the cyclical nature of science, but none talk about how reports are received by the scientific community or how disputes among scientists are resolved. The image the novice is left with is of an incredibly detailed method that rises out of the fog and disappears back into it. Is it any wonder that discovery is pictured as the work of genius?

The presentation of scientific method in these texts thus bears only a passing resemblance to the way science is actually practiced. As depicted, the scientific method is unitary, abstract, and individual. First, these texts present science as a unity—*the* scientific method (even if they cannot agree on what all the steps are). Only Guttman devotes more than a sentence to the differences between sciences. Yet as philosopher Henry Bauer establishes, methods and instruments that are taken as paradigmatic in one discipline are irrelevant in another.[14] Even subdisciplines may have little by way of common practice. Molecular biology, for instance, approaches the world very differently than does either ecology or paleontology.

Second, the textbooks' presentations of method are abstract, if not arcane. The deductive-predictive methods of physics are taken as a model for all of science. Most of the books simply equate field observation and controlled experiment. As sociologists Harry Collins and Trevor Pinch state: "The picture of a quasi-logical deduction of a prediction, followed by a straightforward observational test is simply wrong." Rarely is the real world so neat, unambiguous, and free from "noise" as the textbook picture. Nor are the demonstrations in an introductory lab likely to provide much of a correction. If the outcomes are fully known in advance, all the demonstration does is confirm the hypothesis-prediction-observation abstraction. But in the actual practice of science, where the result of an experiment is not known beforehand, this may lead to what Collins and Pinch call the "experimenter's regress," in which the scientist is caught in a circle (whether or not the experiment "worked" is dependent on the outcome, but the outcome cannot be verified unless the experiment worked). [15] The scientific community has, as a community, of course worked out ways of going beyond the experimenter's regress, but students will not read about them in the textbooks.

Finally, in the textbook version the scientific method is practiced by the lone scientist. The scientific community, let alone the broader social context of science, more or less disappears (with the exception of a brief mention of technological benefits that flow from science). In none of the texts is there anything of what Karen Knorr Cetina calls "epistemic culture" or Diane Vaughan calls "workgroup culture," that is, nothing of the institutionalization of science and how that affects the way scientists do their work. Certain values, such as curiosity, are discussed in terms of the motivation of individual scientists, but the norms of the scientific community are absent. Indeed, even scientific ethics are mentioned in only two texts (Guttman and Lewis—and in Guttman only in terms of human genetics). This asocial view of science fosters what sociologist Sal Restivo calls the myth of pure science, in which science is portrayed as, and only as, the production of knowledge for its own sake.[16]

This leads to the third issue: How does one distinguish between what is science and what is not? Wallace, Sanders, and Ferl are straightforward: "In its broadest sense science might be defined as the way one gets at the truth, or at least as close to the truth as possible." Guttman tries to answer the question with a lengthy list of characteristics, none of which is unique to science, but which together distinguish between science, pseudoscience, and nonscience. For Mader, "anything less than a completely objective observation or conclusion is not considered scientific."[17] In all of these texts, science is defined by its content. Its boundary is objective reality. Only Lewis talks, briefly, about the limitations of the scientific method and the importance of interpretation. All the texts depict science, to use philosopher Ian Hacking's words, as a product rather than as a process, that is, as a corpus of truths rather than as a practice.[18] Science is presented as the authoritative statement of "the way things are."

In sum, the textbook discussion of scientific method pictures science as individualistic, asocial, and authoritative. Now, for science majors, who are slowly inducted into the practice of science over the course of their studies, what introductory books say about method is probably not all that important in their formation as scientists. But for the bulk of students, this is their only exposure to how science is done. For those whose inclusion in science will go no further than an introductory class, science has to be taken on authority.

Images of Content

At more than one thousand pages each, these textbooks focus massively on content. As we have just seen, relatively little attention is paid to science as a process. This is significant. Many people, nonscientist and scientist alike, have the image of science as a corpus of truths about the material world. This has important consequences for the science-religion debate, as we shall see shortly. But first we need to look at how the content of science is depicted. To keep our discussion manageable, we will concentrate on a single issue. Stephen Jay Gould begins *Wonderful Life: The Burgess Shale and the Nature of History* with a discussion of the iconography of evolution. Since evolution remains a central issue in the science-religion dialogue, and since many readers will be familiar with Gould's work, we will continue his discussion by examining the pictures the textbooks use to illustrate the theory of evolution.

These pictures are important because they are more than just illustrations. Each represents a model of a process, in this case of evolution. "A model," Ian Barbour says, "can be grasped as a whole, giving a vivid summary of complex relationships, which is useful in extending and applying the theory as well as in teaching it."[19] Models may be as simple as a picture or as complex as a computer simulation, but the level of complexity affects neither the accuracy nor the utility of the model. Every model is a selection and compression based upon what the model builder wants to emphasize—it is not reality in miniature (see chapter 10). Models are indispensable, but they also contain risks. Reification is inherent in the process of model building, and what makes a model useful in simplifying and illustrating a complex process may also give unwarranted facticity to those elements selected. We have a bias toward the visual and, as the old saying goes, "seeing is believing." The danger is that, as Gould points out: "Many of our pictures are incarnations of concepts masquerading as neutral descriptions of nature. These are the most potent sources of conformity, since ideas passing as descriptions lead us to equate the tentative with the unambiguously factual."[20]

Charles Darwin used a potent metaphor to describe the process of evolution. The history of life, he said, was like a great tree: "The limbs divided into great branches, and these into lesser and lesser branches, were themselves once, when the tree was young, budding twigs, and this connection to the former and present buds by ramifying branches may well represent the classification of all extinct and living species in groups subordinate to groups."[21] The tree of life has been a standard depiction of evolution ever since.[22] Built into that model, however, was the idea of progress. Those organisms at the top of the tree were higher or more advanced than those lower down. Human beings were always placed among the topmost branches, of course. Evolution became a story of linear development climaxing in the present order of things. It was Whig history on a grand scale. This is the point Gould challenges in his book.

The tree of life has a number of variations—the ladder of life, the cone of increasing diversity (see fig. 3.1), and the famous "March of Progress from Ape to Man" (in which the figures are always male). But in whichever format, Gould argues, these icons all depict evolution as linear and progressive.

In its conventional interpretation, the cone of increasing diversity propagates an interesting conflation of meanings. The horizontal dimension shows diversity—fishes plus insects plus snails plus starfish at the top take up much more lateral room than just flatworms at the bottom. But what does the vertical dimension represent? In a literal reading, up and down should record only younger and older in geological time: organisms at the neck

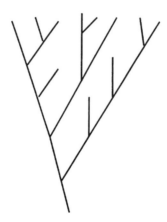

Figure 3.1 Cone of Increasing Diversity

of the funnel are ancient; those at the lip, recent. But we also read upward movement as simple to complex, or primitive to advanced. *Placement in time is conflated with judgment of worth.*

However much biologists today may want to deny such preconceptions, these biases are inherent in the iconography. Gould continues: "The fatuous idea of a single order amidst the multifarious diversity of modern life flows from our conventional iconographies and the prejudices that nurture them—the ladder of life and the cone of increasing diversity."[23] He goes on to argue that the fossils of the Burgess shale (unusually well-preserved fossils from the mid-Cambrian period found near Field, British Columbia) show a wider diversity of basic body plans (as opposed to number of species) than are found among animals today. Instead of linear progress, Gould argues for a model of evolution characterized by decimation and diversification (see fig. 3.2). For him, evolution is less like a tree than a badly pruned bush. Evolution is driven not by progress but by chance.

Gould's theories remain controversial, and it is not our place to judge between him and his critics.[24] The point he does establish is that, however we depict it, a model will bear within it assumptions (including extrascientific ones) that are both inherent and concealed by the reification of model building. Well-grounded theory, debatable assumptions, or baseless speculation can all be given equal facticity by the icons we use.

Returning to the textbooks, we find that all of them have read Gould, and the majority has taken at least some of his admonitions to heart.[25] All the books mention his theory of punctuated equilibrium as an ongoing controversy, although none use his model of decimation and di-

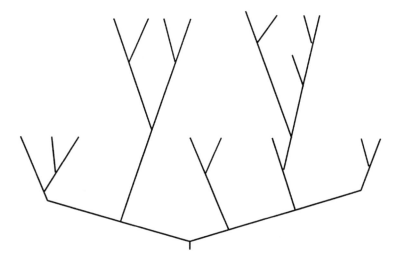

Figure 3.2 Decimation and Diversification

versification. Only Lewis (human ancestry) and Wallace, Sanders, and Ferl (horses) have illustrations that portray evolution as linear, while Guttman makes the strongest representation of the alternative view, using pictures of two different reconstructions of horse ancestry to emphasize that linear models are incorrect.[26]

The point, however, is not that these textbooks have kept up with current theorizing. Whether a model shows evolution as linear progress or random chance is less significant than the certainty that whichever theory it illustrates will have facticity bestowed upon it. A nonlinear model of evolution may very well be more "accurate" in that it encompasses a broader range of empirical data, but it is no less imbued with assumptions or philosophy than its predecessors. But for the reader of the textbook, the illustrations present a picture of "the way things are." Models are indispensable to the practice of science, but we have to see them as part of a process of knowing rather than as a picture of the natural world itself, divorced from any context, which the nonexpert must accept on faith.

Implications for the Science-Religion Dialogue

No one who has been teaching for very long has many illusions about what students come away with from an introductory class. A year or two after the class, most students will be left with a smattering of vocabulary and, we all hope, a bit of inspiration. But what sticks in people's memory are the images, both pictures and metaphors. While the media are more important in shaping most people's everyday knowledge of science, their educational experiences give them a framework that filters and shapes later information. Those whose science education ends after the introductory class will, quite obviously, have a very different experience of science than those who become professional scientists.

Throughout this chapter we have seen that there is frequently a gap between how science is portrayed and how it is practiced. Images have power, and we often accept them unconsciously. The unintended consequence of the textbook presentations is to establish science as authority. What are some of the implications of all this for the science-religion dialogue?

The textbooks, as we have seen, portray science as content, as a body of truths about the material world. So do many people in the science-religion dialogue. Both the Barbour and Gould models, discussed in the introduction, picture science as an entity, a body of discoveries to which religion must respond. So we have any number of articles along the lines of "the theological implications of X" (fill in the blank with your favorite scientific finding). But is this a very useful way of thinking about, and debating with, science?

It has become common in science studies to speak of two aspects of science. We mentioned Ian Hacking's distinction between science as product and science as process. Others have spoken of frontier science versus textbook science (Bauer), ready-made science versus science in action (Latour), controversial versus noncontroversial science (Collins and Pinch), and, most recently, Science (with a capital *S*) versus research (Latour again). What all these have in common is the distinction, on the one hand, between science as an active practice of discovery and debate and, on the other, science as the substance of what is discovered after the debates have closed. We think this is a useful distinction.

There is a qualitative difference between the kind of science found in, say, *Nature* or *Science*, and that found in the textbooks. The journals are full of frontier science, science in action, where scientists engage in lively debate. What is at issue is nature itself. For example, was the Earth hit by an asteroid sixty-five million years ago or not? Did an asteroid kill the dinosaurs, or were they killed by volcanoes, or did they die off slowly from disease and climate change? Until scientists come to a conclusion, we do not know the answer. So long as the arguments continue, nature is in dispute. Textbook science is what is left at the end of the process. What in the journals is a hotly disputed hypothesis becomes a mundane fact by the time it reaches the textbooks.

This is what makes textbook science authoritative. No one disputes the periodic table or the laws of thermodynamics, because generations of scientists have used them and confirmed that this is indeed the way nature works. No one has the same level of confidence in, say, superstring theory or sociobiology. The problem in scientific controversies is a tendency for authority to move "upstream," for frontier science to claim the same authority as long-established knowledge. This is very clear in the science wars and can be found in the science-religion dialogue as well. Nobody would be much interested in an article on "the theological implications of the periodic table," but there are risks in discussing the latest cosmological theory or research in neuropsychology as if it were the same kind of science.

The first risk is exemplified by the Galileo affair. In spite of the mythology, the trial of Galileo did not simply pit science against religion. At the time of Galileo, far from being in conflict with science, the Church was using what Barbour would call an integrative approach. The Church developed its theology by integrating it with the science of its day, that is, Aristotle's. Unfortunately for the Church, Copernicus and Galileo changed the science out from under it. This risk is inherent in any integrationist approach. The aim of theology has always been to guide the community of the faithful in its moral reflection and help it find meaning in the world. Science, on the other hand, changes continuously, and even the textbooks get rewritten.

A second risk is that, other than a few extraordinary individuals, such as Ian Barbour or John Polkinghorne, who are cross-trained in science and theology, most people in the dialogue are nonspecialists trying to deal with very specialized knowledge. (This applies to scientists looking at any specialty outside their own as much as it does to others.) Apart from the difficulty in simply understanding another discipline, since we tend to identify science with its content, how is the nonspecialist to decide what is "good" science and what is not? Science on the frontier is by its nature unresolved. How can a nonspecialist find the assumptions built into a model or decide an issue if the experts have not? No one wants to confine the dialogue to the periodic table, but who wants to publish "the theological implications of cold fusion"?

Of course, we could limit the dialogue to "safe" subjects, scientific findings upon which nearly everyone agrees (but as the anti-evolution movement demonstrates, even that may be hard to find). The risk of doing so is irrelevance. Science and technology regularly pose moral and policy dilemmas which as a society we must face. The greatest contribution the science-religion dialogue can make is to provide insight and ethical guidance, but to do so we have to engage the issues precisely before they are resolved. It is futile to allow science or technology to develop without comment and then decide after the fact that it would have been better had it been done differently. The time to debate whether or not human cloning should be allowed, for instance, is before someone has cloned a human being.

These dilemmas are inherent and unavoidable so long as we identify science as a corpus of truths about the natural world. The alternative is to see science as an active practice of discovery and debate a community engages in. As a practice, science becomes a process of knowing rather than a body of objective truths divorced from any context, which the nonexpert must accept on faith. And it is precisely because of their ability to analyze science as the practice of a community that the social sciences can make important contributions to the science-religion dialogue.

Viewing science this way has advantages for the dialogue. First, it puts scientists back into science. Science becomes what the scientific community does. As a community, scientists have norms and values, standards of evaluation and criteria for judgment, even if different subgroups employ distinct standards and criteria. As in any community, scientists have disputes and their own means of resolving them, ways of determining what is most important and allocating resources, and means for deciding who is a member of the community and who is not. Viewed this way, science becomes less of an abstraction, and scientists cease being mythic heroes. Instead, when science becomes the practice of real people, we have a much more solid basis for partnership and dialogue.

Second, if we see science as its content, religion can never be more than added on, and its legitimacy will always be suspect. Science will always be the active partner in the dialogue, and religion can do little more than listen. If we understand science as a practice, however, theological insight and ethical reflection can become part of the process from the beginning. By engaging scientists and engineers in their day-to-day activities, the science-religion dialogue can make a difference in the way science and technology are practiced. Making reflection on values and ethics part of everyday scientific practice could be one of the most important reforms generated from the science-religion dialogue.

4 | The Newtonian Revolution

Nature and Nature's laws lay hid in night:
God said: Let Newton be! and all was light.
— Alexander Pope, epitaph for Sir Isaac Newton

Newton was not the first of the age of reason. He
was the last of the magicians.
— John Maynard Keynes, "Newton, the Man"

Scientific revolutions have been a major focus in our attempt to understand the nature of science and the nature of the scientific enterprise. How a system of knowledge comes into being must reflect both the nature of that knowledge and the environment or culture in which it is created and later operates. The Newtonian revolution, often referred to as the Scientific Revolution, stands out as both the foremost scientific revolution and its archetype. A special feature of this revolution is its perceived birth from the mind of one man, who eventually became the prototype for the rational mind of the modern scientist. This association of modern science with Isaac Newton as the ideal model of the modern scientist was promoted by generations of scientists and historians partly in order to create the self-serving myth of the Scientific Revolution as a clean, discontinuous triumph of rationalism and inquiry over ignorance, tradition, and the occult.

The traditional story is of a Newton standing on the shoulders of Bacon, Galileo, Kepler, and Descartes and seeing the promised land, where the external, real world was conquered by the methods of experimentation, rational analysis, and deductive reasoning. This view of the Newtonian revolution is self-serving in that it supports the idea of inevitable progress in the scientific enterprise. It also justifies the belief in an objective, real world and the superiority and triumph of the philosophical approaches and systems of rationalism, objectivity, materialism, and naturalism. In addition to these fundamental philosophical beliefs, the structure, nature, and successes of Newtonian mechanics imply the auxiliary doctrines of mechanism, determinism, reductionism, and realism. In essence, Newtonian mechanics became the basis for the Newtonian worldview, a radical change from the earlier holistic and organic Aristotelian worldview.

As we saw in the previous chapter, major movements tend to be associated and identified with single individuals who then become the symbolic human icons for those movements. For Newtonian mechanics and its accompanying worldview, the human icon was of course Isaac Newton, who was born on Christmas Day in 1642 (in the Julian calendar), the same year in which Galileo had earlier died.[1] How strange and puzzling it must be, then, for physics students today to read from John Maynard Keynes's famous essay: "Newton was not the first of the age of reason. He was the last of the magicians, the last of the Babylonians and Sumerians, the last great mind which looked out on the visible and intellectual world with the same eyes as those who began to build our intellectual inheritance rather less than 10,000 years ago."[2] What could Keynes possibly have meant by these cryptic remarks? Has history presented a false image of our icon, or was it, in fact, only a partial image?

In this chapter we argue that Newton was not the model modern scientist but was instead a living Faust who in his own life combined science, religion, and magic. Newton's ambitious life goal was to understand God's universe and purpose. His raison d'être was to understand everything, and Newton's everything was greater than our everything.[3] Those who elevated him to the status of a scientific saint did so by suppressing the memory of both his religion and his magic. It is therefore ironic that Newton's authority as a scientific saint is used to bolster a metaphysical naturalism that aims to replace religion.

Newton, the Genius

What did Newton accomplish? *Annus mirabilis,* sometimes whimsically paraphrased *annus physicalis*, is a favorite term of physicists, especially in association with the years 1905 and 1932. Ironically, the term originated with the British poet John Dryden in reference to the year 1666, which saw the confluence of the plague, the Great Fire of London, and the war with the Dutch.[4] If Dryden had been blessed with a gift of prescience, he would have also included the unprecedented intellectual achievements of Newton, when as a young, undistinguished scholar he was forced to leave Cambridge University and return to the family farm in Woolsthorpe to avoid the plague.[5] Denied the usual academic resources and stimulation, his initiative, brilliance, and tenacity facilitated an unparalleled explosion of achievement that included the discovery of the law of universal gravitation, the formulation of calculus, and the crucial experiments that elucidated the nature of light.[6] If genius is the capacity to transcend limitations and expectations to achieve the unachievable, then Newton was undoubtedly a genius.

Even after three hundred years, the breadth, depth, and style of Newton's remarkable lifework continue to amaze us. "Nature to him was an open book," reflected Albert Einstein, "whose letters he could read without effort. In one person he combined the experimenter, the theorist, the mechanic and, not least, the artist in expression."[7] With a slight touch of ironic poetic license, the historian I. Bernard Cohen describes the sweep of Newton's accomplishments and reputation:

> Newton, thrice great like the magical patron of alchemy Hermes Trismegistus, dominated the rise of three major sciences in modern times: rational mechanics, experimental optics and pure mathematics. Known in his day for achievements unsurpassed by any predecessor or contemporary, he had penetrated the mysteries of light and color (and had invented a new type of telescope), had found the law of universal gravitation (thus to explain at once why the planets move around the sun in accord with Kepler's three laws and why stones fall to earth as Galileo had found they do) and was an inventor of the "fluxional calculus," the new language of the exact sciences. With the kind of admiration usually granted to superheroes in war or athletics, Newton's contemporaries asked whether he was at all like ordinary men: did he eat and sleep like other mortals?[8]

In 1687, Newton's work on gravity was transformed, with the assistance of Edmund Halley's midwifery, into the greatest and single most influential scientific work ever written, *Philosophiae Naturalis Principia Mathematica*—more familiarly, *Mathematical Principles of Natural Philosophy*—usually referred to today as simply the *Principia*. In this book Newton was able to establish the subjects of classical kinematics and dynamics as the first comprehensive physical theory, as well as to develop a novel approach to the creation of scientific theory that became the standard for all later physical theories. Newton's modus operandi for his mechanics included all known relevant observations and measurements, accounted for observations and measurements with minimal complexity (or maximum economy), and led to new and different experiments that produced results consistent with the predictions of the theory. The extraordinary success of Newton's theory and approach convinced the scientific community that the primary criteria for the acceptance of any theory should be its utility, that is, its usefulness as a tool for further scientific inquiry and publications. The publication of the

Principia caused an immediate furor in the English scientific community that later spread to continental Europe, eventually crystallizing into the icon of Newton and the myth of his work.[9]

What was the basis of this myth? How did Newton revolutionize science?[10] Newton's mechanics, which included his law of universal gravitation, was the fulfillment of Galileo's dream of overturning the Aristotelian worldview. By unifying terrestrial and celestial physics, Newton destroyed the foundations of Aristotelian physics forever. One important byproduct of this overthrow of tradition was the effective separation of physics and chemistry, so that each could develop into an independent science.[11] How an object moved became a question independent from what substance the object was made of. Another important consequence of Newton's system was the decoupling of physics from the authority of traditional Aristotelian philosophy and the replacement of philosophical argumentation and syllogisms by a system of axiomatic mathematical modeling. This foundational and functional change was poignantly reflected by a shift in the training background of physicists from philosophy to mathematics.

The importance of the problem Newton solved was assessed by the British historian Herbert Butterfield in his *Origins of Modern Science*: "Of all the intellectual hurdles which the human mind has been faced with and has overcome in the last fifteen hundred years, the one which seems to me to have been the most amazing in character, and the most stupendous in the scope of its consequences, is the one relating to the problem of motion."[12] Newton's system of mechanics initiated an unprecedented paradigm shift involving several aspects of science, which resulted in the transformation of science into modern science. The efficacy, utility, and successes of Newton's mechanics made it the archetype for all subsequent modern science, and it became the practical foundation and inspiration for the Enlightenment and the Enlightenment ideal.[13]

It has been said that the journey to truth is usually more holy than the arrival. And in the journey of scientific development, as with life in general, timing is everything. "The most important thing for a genius," noted Lev Andreevich Artsimovich, "is to be born at the right time."[14] And it was fortunate for science that Newton was born at the right time. He was able to use and incorporate several seminal innovations developed by Kepler and Galileo in his own system of mechanics. Newton was one of the great synthesizers of knowledge in the tradition of Euclid and Ptolemy, but his principal synthesis—unlike those of his predecessors—was not of results but of ideas. In common with the later great syntheses of James Clerk Maxwell (involving electricity and magnetism) and Albert Einstein (involving space, time, mass, and energy), Newton's creation was much greater than the sum of its parts.

Newton was obsessed with learning and knowing everything in God's universe. His system of mechanics was the Holy Grail that he and others successfully used to assault numerous previously unsolvable problems. The Newtonian worldview was the realization of the classical Greek belief in an ordered, regular universe that is rational and understandable. Newton and his followers eventually believed that all aspects of our rational universe could be analyzed and understood by a combination of carefully obtained data, reason, talent, and, last but not least, persistence. When asked how he made his discoveries, Newton gave his famous response: "By always thinking unto them. I keep the subject constantly before me and wait till the first dawnings open slowly, by little and little, into a full and clear light."[15] As a result of its utility and success, Newtonian mechanics became the archetype for all modern science and the standard against which other scientific, especially physical, theories were to be measured.

Newton's Science

What are the features of modern science that were derived from Newtonian mechanics? It is useful to separate these features into four categories: content, approach, methodology, and epistemology.

Content

It is truly amazing that the first semester of almost any calculus-based physics course taken anywhere in the world will be Newtonian mechanics, unchanged in spirit from Newton's groundbreaking work.[16] For as E. N. da C. Andrade noted: "From being the preoccupation of a few curious spirits science has grown to be a universal study, on the fruits of which peace among people and the prosperity of nations depend, but the great principles enunciated by Newton and their orderly development by him remain as the foundations of the discipline and as a shining example of the exalted power of the human mind."[17] The new concepts, realizations, and theories needed to create the complete structure and approach of today's physics were primarily additions to the foundations laid by Newton in the *Principia* published in 1687.

Approach

The Newtonian revolution presented a gestalt shift in the way scientists viewed nature and how they thought about it. To understand this shift, it is useful to summarize pre-Newtonian physics. Before the Scientific Revolution, the accepted view of nature was based on the Aristotelian approach in which the motions of objects were considered phenomena that were directly related to qualities possessed by the substances that made up those objects.[18] To Aristotle, physics was the study of phenomena that were changeable and a source or cause of motion.[19] In the heavens, phenomena were circular and repeated themselves without deviation as a result of the celestial objects being made of the perfect heavenly substance called quintessence (ether). Since celestial objects never left their natural place, celestial motion was perpetual circular motion having neither beginning nor end. This perfect motion was due to the celestial objects being in direct communication with the Prime Mover (First Cause or Aristotle's God). There was no need for other forces, since celestial objects were doing what they naturally should do, and, in fact, they could not do otherwise.

Terrestrial motion, that is, motion on the Earth, was divided by Aristotle into two different classes of phenomena: natural motion that proceeded from the nature of the object, and violent motion that derived from external forces acting on the object. According to Aristotle, all objects of the Earth were made of combinations of the four elements of Empedocles: earth, water, air, and fire. Each of the four elements had a natural place of existence within the Earth that reflected its position in a natural hierarchy, for example, the natural place of earth material is at the center of the Earth. All objects naturally wanted to travel in straight lines toward their natural place, where they would eventually come to rest. In essence, this natural motion represented a transition or change from a potentiality to an actuality of an object. For example, a stone that is dropped will fall straight downward toward the center of the Earth. Another example of Aristotelian analysis of nature is the process of burning paper, which causes a separation of the earth, air, and fire elements that made up the paper. The ash, being made of earth, will fall straight down, while the fire will move upward, striving to be above the air.

Violent motion, on the other hand, was understood in terms of external agents or forces, which implied that these forces caused movement. If an object was moving as a result of a violent motion, then there had to be a specific force responsible for this motion. Conversely, if there is no applied force, there can be no violent motion. Though equating forces with any motion seemed to make perfect sense to Aristotelian philosophers, it turned out to be completely wrong and created a large barrier that prevented future progress in mechanics.

Galileo and Newton, in stark contrast to Aristotle, believed that objects did not possess any innate qualities that dictated their motion. In particular, since inanimate objects are not alive, they do not want or strive to do anything. Things happen in the physical world because other things previously had happened to them. Phenomena occur because of processes involving forces that act on the object from the outside world (its environment). Objects interact with each other only through forces; in other words, forces are how objects "communicate" with each other.

Galileo and Newton replaced Aristotle's concept of a natural place, which they did not believe existed, with the concept of a natural state of an object that was either at rest or in uniform motion having constant velocity. This altered viewpoint required forces in order to explain the celestial circular motions, as well as any accelerated motions on Earth. An object's state of motion is defined as its velocity (speed and direction), and its acceleration is the rate of change of its velocity. An object couples with its environment through forces that connect the object and the environment, and these forces act on the object causing its velocity (state of motion) to change. Newton's famous second law, $F = ma$, or net force = mass times acceleration, emphasizes this difference in perspective from Aristotelian thought. If there are no forces acting on an object, or alternatively, if there is no net force, then there are no changes in the object's state of motion, and the object continues to move with the same velocity. Thus it is possible in the Newtonian framework to have motion without the presence of any net force. Forces connect an object to its environment, and their net action produces a corresponding acceleration, which is the response by the object to this influence. This is the origin of causality, that is, cause and effect, in the Newtonian world of mechanics. It answers the question of why objects move the way they do through observing how they move.

As part of the philosophical foundation of his system, Newton rejected occult, mystical, teleological, or religious explanations for natural phenomena in the physical world. Certainly this reflected his total rejection of Aristotelian thought and methodology, which were replaced by his focus on the study of repeatable phenomena. In Aristotle's world, objects were the primary entities of study in the attempt to understand the order and purpose of the world. Objects had innate qualities that manifested themselves in both the nature of the objects and in the phenomena associated with these objects. It was the goal of Aristotelian science to understand objects in terms of their nature, potentiality, and actuality. Celestial phenomena were cyclical and repeatable, while terrestrial phenomena were directed, linear, and nonrepeatable. For Newton, on the other hand, objects were just the vehicles through which natural processes were carried out, and it is these processes that are repeatable and universally applicable to all objects in the universe. The outcome of any phenomenon in the Newtonian worldview was independent of either its location or its time of occurrence (a result that later was to be generalized as the principle of universality). Instead of attempting to understand why the phenomenon was occurring in terms of some purpose or some grand design, it was the phenomenon itself that was important in understanding nature. A corollary to this new attitude in science was the gradual decoupling of religious dogma and precepts from the knowledge and study of science.

Methodology

Newton began the *Principia* with a set of rules—"Rules of Reasoning in Philosophy"—the first two rules being articulations of what are now referred to as Occam's razor and the principle of universality:

> We are to admit no more causes of natural things than such as are both true and sufficient to explain their appearances. To this purpose the philosophers say that Nature does nothing in vain, and more is in vain when less will serve; for Nature is pleased with simplicity, and affects not the pomp of superfluous causes. . . . Therefore to the same natural effects we must, as far as possible, assign the same causes. As to respiration in a man and in a beast; the descent of stones in Europe and in America; the light of our culinary fire and of the sun; the reflection of light in the earth, and in the planets.[20]

Interestingly, Newton's "Nature does nothing in vain" was taken directly from Aristotle, but obviously with a different intent.[21] "Natural philosophy [science] consists in discovering the frame and operations of Nature," remarked Newton, "and reducing them, as far as may be, to general rules or laws—establishing these rules by observations and experiments, and thence deducing the cause and effects of things."[22]

Newton's approach to studying nature was completely revolutionary in scope and method. The structuring of the principles, problems, and results in a completely mathematical form allowed for a diminishing focus on the causal aspect while allowing model building to emerge. Eventually, it became encapsulated in the view that physics is the art of problem solving of systems of nature by successive approximation of mathematical models using calculus and differential equations. Newton and the physicists who followed him studied specific problems that are mathematically solvable instead of general philosophical problems that were typical of the earlier Aristotelian philosophers.

Epistemology

Newton's methodology had its genesis in the work of Galileo and later became formalized in the epistemology of modern science: hypothesis testing by controlled experiments. In Newton's hands, this marriage between the ideals of Bacon and Descartes became a ménage à trois in which Galileo's Platonism became the framework that held empiricism and rationalism together. Generally speaking, most scientists would agree on what constitutes good and valid scientific methodology. It is reductionistic in nature and involves the careful analysis of observations and experiments in terms of orthodox theory. The problem is that there is little agreement on the specific details of this methodology, and certainly it is not possible to reduce it to a concise formula to be followed, as was pointed out in the previous chapter. The so-called scientific method, which is a variation of Baconian empiricism, is generally acknowledged to be a myth.[23] Imagination, intuition, and lucky guessing play as large a role as any rational process in constructing good ideas. A more realistic view of scientific methodology, which also reflects the method used by Newton, is the hypothetico-deductive method that constructs hypothetical models based on and inspired by observations and then tests them by deducing the various consequences generated by the models.[24] It is the consequences that are important and that require detailed checking against controlled experiments. The epistemology that this methodology naturally supports is reductionism and a tempered realism, referred to as either critical realism or scientific realism.

Newton's system was materialistic, mechanistic, deterministic, reductionistic, and progressive. The effect of the success of Newtonian mechanics immediately influenced social institutions and intellectual thinking throughout European society, especially in England. It became the intellectual genesis of the Enlightenment ideal, a belief that all aspects of the world, including human behavior and institutions, can be understood through the use of scientific methodology and reasoning.[25] A corollary to this belief is the view that the only reliable knowledge is knowledge obtained through science. For those who supported the Newtonian worldview and the Enlightenment ideal, it was essential to use Newton as a symbol and epitome of this worldview and ideal. In his lifetime, Newton was often regarded as a demigod of rationalism. It was this image that was self-serving to his followers to the point that it had to be preserved and sanitized in order to promote Newtonianism.

Newton the Magician

But what about Newton's interest in alchemy, the occult, and biblical prophesy? These activities were well known to his inner circle of friends and yet are nearly absent from the earlier biographies of Newton.[26] Since their existence became widely known in the 1930s, they have posed a set of difficult questions for historians. Why were these activities omitted from the portrait of Newton handed down to us? What else about Newton has been hidden from us? Were Newton's alchemy, occult activities, and studies of biblical prophecy connected with his scientific activities? And more importantly, did these disparate activities influence each other?

In a remarkable coincidence of history, the renowned British economist and scholar John Maynard Keynes bought a huge collection of Newton's papers in 1936 at a Sotheby auction fifty years after they had been offered to Cambridge University.[27] These papers brought to light many facets of Newton that had been hidden from the public at large by a conspiracy of scientists and historians who either could not deal with the truth or had agendas to be served. When these papers were originally examined shortly after Newton's death, they shocked his contemporaries who generally viewed modern science as the antithesis of alchemy and superstition. It became convenient to consider these activities as amateur dabblings that had nothing to do with Newton's scientific work. This view was reinforced by the belief that modern science is evolutionary and progressive in nature. Science is assumed to be self-correcting over time, and many of its ideas and methods naturally become extinct through the conscious act of rejection by the scientific community.

How do we reconcile these contradictions in Newton's intellectual life? How could the first and greatest modern scientist, who became the godfather of the Enlightenment, have a secret life that was deeply involved in the seemingly irrational? First of all, we must acknowledge that it was fortunate that the Keynes papers, known as the Portsmouth Collection, became available during a period that could accept them as part of a larger and more human Newton.[28] At the same time that the extent of Newton's involvement with alchemy, the occult, and biblical prophecy was being recognized, the dark side of Newton was surfacing to public scrutiny. In addition to being a very private man, Newton was seen to be obsessive, egotistical, jealous, insecure, and spiteful.[29] His ambition to understand everything drove him to physical lapses, a major nervous breakdown, and the alienation of colleagues and former friends. Newton, the man, was as unsuccessful as Newton, the physicist, was successful. These aspects of Newton are complementary and present completely different impressions of the same man when viewed separately. In fact, Newton's abused and tortured soul plays a role in bridging the worlds of natural science and the occult. Keynes concluded his famous Newton Tercentenary Celebrations essay with a description of Newton as "this strange spirit, who was tempted by the Devil to believe . . . he could reach *all* the secrets of God and Nature by the pure power of mind—Copernicus and Faustus in one."[30]

These revelations can lead us to view Newton not as the greatest modern scientist, but instead as a real Faust with one foot in the magical tradition of the past and the other in the modern science of the future.[31] Newton became obsessed with the goal of understanding all of God's universe and purpose. He believed that a universal synthesis had been achieved in the fabled ancient wisdom, or *prisca theologia*, a divinely inspired knowledge thought to date back to the time of Moses, which needed to be rediscovered (see chapter 5). Newton's goal of synthesizing all knowledge led him to believe that all of his enterprises in mathematics, mechanics, optics, the occult, alchemy, and biblical criticism and prophecy were part of a single enterprise.[32] His eclecticism expressed itself in his use of different methods of inquiry for different domains of activities involving this search. Newton, unlike modern scientists, did not see his alchemical studies as conflicting with his scientific studies, for they were complementary in scope.

And most importantly for our purposes, behind all of Newton's activities and studies was the belief in a real God who is in direct control of everything in the universe.[33] Newton believed that a complete understanding of God's universe and purpose involved questions that required methods different from those used by physicists in answering mechanical questions. This motivation to go wherever truth led him was reminiscent of Robert Boyle's struggle to balance science, alchemy, and God. Both men wanted to use reason to serve their spiritual beliefs, an approach that creates a tension that is at the heart of all science-religion interactions and disputes. Modern historical research and analysis has shown that the rationalist Newton is a myth created by the Enlightenment and its followers, who attempted to deny religious motivations and connections in the development of science.

There is a revealing parallel between the internal tensions that existed within Newton and those created by his revolution. Usually one thinks of the Scientific Revolution as a series of events or a period of scientific history, but it is more useful to think of the Scientific Revolution as a process that affected the different sciences at different periods of time and that ended with the synthesis and crystallization of the many features that are usually associated with modern science. Newton was the catalyst for both the revolution in mechanics and its aftermath, while at the same time a transitional figure who strangely reflected the changes and tensions occurring during the process of the Scientific Revolution itself.

Newton, Science, and Religion

One of the major results of the Scientific Revolution is a radical change in the view of reality and of the various domains within it.[34] Before the Scientific Revolution, reality included the natural world and the spirit world, and magic was the realm in which they intersected and interacted. At the end of the Newtonian revolution, intellectuals were increasingly associating the natural world with reality and at the same time exiling magic to the irrational and putting the spirit world and miracles into limbo. This redefining of reality and the boundaries of its domain was a process that occurred parallel to the Scientific Revolution and has its own evolutionary history. The process of redefining reality occurred concurrently with the development of the philosophical concepts of naturalism and metaphysical naturalism as the basis of modern science.

Naturalism is the epistemological imperative that requires modern science to consider and include only natural phenomena, natural processes, and natural principles. In other words, only natural mechanisms need apply as explanations for events in nature. Supernatural explanations are not permitted to play any role within the domain of scientific explanations or understandings. Metaphysical naturalism, on the other hand, is the ontological precept that the universe consists only of matter, natural processes, and forces. Supernatural forces, spirits, and events do not exist nor can they be entertained in scientific speculations. Since the seventeenth century, the scientific world has increasingly accepted the concept that reality is synonymous with the domain of the natural world. An important corollary to the concept of metaphysical naturalism is this limiting process of identifying reality with the natural world. The associated belief that reality is the physical universe composed only of matter and energy is referred to as scientific materialism (or monistic materialism). The only phenomena that are considered real within the scope of scientific materialism are things that are physical, measurable, or deducible from scientific observations.

When Newton was struggling with his attempt to balance his rational head and his spiritual heart, the process of redefining reality was in an early stage, and reality often was viewed as nature plus, where the plus could contain spiritual and occult components. God was generally viewed as the real Creator and power in the universe. One of the goals of Newton's science was to understand how the universe operated in order to gain insight into God's mind and purpose. Purpose in the Newtonian worldview could be derived from its meaning, which in turn could be inferred from the order and design that the natural world revealed to the scientist as a result of his or her attempt to understand the knowledge obtained from observation and experimentation of natural phenomena. Newton made many references to this motivation for his work, and in this regard he was similar to Bacon and Boyle before him. A rational God should be reflected and revealed in an ordered and rational universe—a universe that could be deciphered using rational means and methods.

The Newtonian world was so immediately successful at unlocking the secrets of nature that it became associated with the metaphor of a clockwork universe. Nowhere was this viewpoint more eloquently expressed, and at the same time coupled with the idea of a divinely governed unity, than by Alexander Pope in his *Essay on Man*, epistle 1:

> All are but parts of one stupendous whole,
> Whose body Nature is, and God the soul;
> That, chang'd thro' all, and yet in all the same,
> Great in the earth as in th' aethereal frame,
> Warms in the sun, refreshes in the breeze,
> Glows in the stars, and blossoms in the trees,
> Lives thro' all life, extends thro' all extent,
> Spreads undivided, operates unspent,
> Breathes in our soul, informs our mortal part,
> As full, as perfect, in a hair as heart;
> As full, as perfect, in vile Man that mourns,
> As the rapt Seraph that adores and burns;
> To him no high, no low, no great, no small;
> He fills, he bounds, connects, and equals all.[35]

Over time, Newton's clockwork metaphor for creation eventually developed a life of its own that naturally created a shift from the glorification of the Creator to the glorification of the creation. As the Newtonian worldview grew out of its adolescence, the concept of naturalism also grew to the point of being able to stand on its own feet.

In the apocryphal, though often reported and historically influential, conversation between the French mathematician Pierre Simon de Laplace and Napoleon Bonaparte, Laplace came to symbolize the idea that modern science no longer needed God. "You have written this huge book on the system of the world," Napoleon supposedly noted when Laplace presented him with a copy of his celebrated *Mécanique céleste*, "without once mentioning the author of the universe." "Sire," courteously responded Laplace, "I had no need of that hypothesis."[36] It almost seemed that the universe had outgrown its parent and did not need God any longer.

Today a further evolution can be seen in the interaction and conflict between the concept of naturalism that starts with the assumption of a universe that allows for the existence and operation of only natural processes and the intellectual understanding of God's role in the universe. From its inception, the concept of naturalism has continuously gained acceptance and influence in the academic world. Most scientists today (if they think about it at all) would subscribe, in relation to their work "I the lab," either to a strong version of naturalism or to metaphysical naturalism.[37] Ironically, if God created the universe, it was done so efficiently many contemporary scientists regarded God as either obsolete or superfluous.

This historic change in our understanding of the world and corresponding beliefs is often seen in contemporary science-religion interactions. In the not-too-distant past, one usually heard theologians, and some scientists, starting with the assumption of a real (Christian) God who literally created the universe and who is forever in control of this creation. Today, that viewpoint has been increasingly replaced with the perspective of naturalism.

When discussing their view of what constitutes valid religion and its appropriate domain, some modern scientists, such as Albert Einstein and Stephen Jay Gould, are often concerned only with the ethical aspects of religion and not with any issues of God, especially a personal God, nor with the role of divine action in the universe.[38] Three hundred years after the publication of Newton's *Principia*, many modern scientists no longer see their science as a celebration of the Creator of a rational, ordered universe. Under these conditions, the issue then becomes: What role do we allow God to have in our universe? For God is no longer the starting point of our relationship to the universe but appears instead to be an appendage to it, if God appears at all.

So naturalism seems to have triumphed, at least in academia, over the domain of religion. But is the situation really that simple? There are other clues pointing to other possibilities for our predicament at the beginning of the twenty-first century. In spite of the tendency of an increasing number of intellectuals during the three centuries since the creation of Newton's clockwork metaphor to view reality in strictly naturalistic terms, religion has never disappeared. Interestingly, the prominent science philosopher Michael Ruse chose *Can a Darwinian Be a Christian?* as his title for a recent book on contemporary science-religion issues and engagements.[39] Maybe this is a sign that the pendulum of naturalism is starting to swing back to a more balanced position.

So, while Isaac Newton may be a saint of modern science, this image is a distorted one that ignores his religious nature. By looking at Newton in the context of his time, we see the irony that the father of naturalism was not a proponent of it. If Newton had not been convinced of the existence and origin of the order in God's created universe, he would not have looked for it. One lesson to be learned from this episode in the history of science might be that we need to continually reassess whom we sanctify and the reasons for doing so. In the case of Newton, this reassessment may allow the real Newton to emerge from his distorted image and again serve as an exemplar, this time as a reconciliation between science and religion that opens up rich possibilities for further research and debate.

PART
III

Magic

5

Magicians, Reformers, and Scientists

Scientists of today can read and recognize works done after 1687. It takes a historian to comprehend those written before 1543.

—Richard Westfall, "The Scientific Revolution Reasserted"

Now we go right to the heart of the "fuzzy stuff in the middle" of Ronald Cole-Turner's model, that is, of what we have called the seamless web of relationships between religion, science, technology, and ethics. Specifically, we look at the issue of instrumentality, that is, how religious and scientific ideas are used in a practical sense. This brings us into the realm of magic, which historically was a natural outgrowth of belief in the supernatural. It is helpful to consider magic as an instrumental component of religion, in the same way that technology is the instrumental counterpart to theoretical science. This relationship may be surprising, because most of us would consider our age a scientific one in which magic has no role. However, at one time science, religion, magic, and technology were all intimately linked. We begin by examining the history of those relationships. We will see that there was an important historical moment, the Reformation, during which attempts were made to draw boundaries between magical and religious beliefs. It was followed by another attempt, which we call the Scientific Revolution, to separate magical practices from scientific ones. After this historical analysis, we will be better positioned to understand the boundaries that we have inherited. However, in chapters 6 and 7, we problematize those boundaries. Has magic really disappeared from our worldview, or is our thinking still magical in some ways? In chapter 6 we take a functional approach, that is, we look at how magic works and examine two contemporary instances where it implicitly operates. In chapter 7 we focus on the symbols of magic and look at how these symbols still have power to move us, no longer in the service of religious belief, but in the service of science and technology.

Explaining Causation—Then and Now

Our sense of identify is reflected in our understanding of our own history. It is commonly assumed that we now live in a scientific age, a legacy of the Scientific Revolution of the seventeenth century. Our modern scientific worldview is contrasted to that which preceded it, which is labeled medieval and characterized as magical. As Richard Westfall suggests, we feel that there is something qualitatively different about this earlier period, about the way people thought and, specifically, how they thought about the natural world. One way to explore the history of this human tendency is by examining some of the underlying assumptions that informed prescientific thinking about nature.

There are two important differences between the assumptions of the late Middle Ages and those of our own day. In order to highlight these differences, it is worth reflecting briefly on our own assumptions. First, we might look at the example of how a physics teacher explains magnetism to her or his class. Students learn about electrons, which they cannot see, but they assume that they exist as something that belongs to the material world. In the Middle Ages, magnets were considered magical, and the forces that made them work were thought to be supernatural. Sailors used magnets for compasses but needed to keep them hidden, lest they be charged with using an instrument of the devil. What has changed is our attitude toward the invisible world. We can accept the idea that something can be physical, yet invisible to the human eye. In the medieval period, which lacked the tools to extend people's visual perceptions, the invisible was not part of the material world.

Second, we need to reflect on our attitudes toward that which we do not know. For example, physicists are not really able to explain what gravity is, although they are able to study its effects. However, they assume that they will one day find out more than they know today and that the answer will belong to the material world. This confidence in our own ability to understand causation is our legacy from the Scientific Revolution. In the Middle Ages, what was unknown was considered to operate on magical principles. What has also changed, then, is our attitude toward the things we do not understand. In short, what has characterized the modern worldview for the last several centuries is a spirit of optimism. Before the seventeenth century, the manner in which causation was approached differed from our own hopeful assumptions about our future abilities.

On the other hand, it is worth reminding ourselves that even though we live in a scientific age, most people are still motivated by a desire to find ultimate explanations. For example, we may understand the physics involved in why a car crash occurred but on a different level we seek to understand why a loved one was injured in it. Certainly, if one is a metaphysical naturalist (see chapter 4), that is, if one believes that there are no forces beyond those of the physical world, explanations become more straightforward. However, the revival of interest in all things occult within the last few decades suggests that many people still turn to ideas like fate, or God's will, or even the stars, when scientific explanations are psychologically unsatisfactory. It is this impulse that allows us to view our medieval and early modern forerunners with a more sympathetic eye than we might otherwise have.

In this chapter, we examine how causation was understood in the past. Our approach is necessarily broad, in both time and scope. We will begin by discussing medieval attitudes (specifically, those of the scholastic theologians), and then focus on the early modern period (that is, the sixteenth and seventeenth centuries). Moreover, we are working beyond the traditional divisions into which history is generally compartmentalized—the Renaissance, Reformation, and Scientific Revolution—fields that historians often treat in isolation from one another. Instead, we argue that underlying each of these processes is a common desire to find a satisfactory epistemology, that is, to figure out a way to understand how the world works. At every stage, there is a renewed attempt to understand, explain, and even control the forces that are immaterial or invisible.

Magicians

In a medical book written by the court physician to King Edward II of England in the early fourteenth century, one can find this remedy suggested to stop a nosebleed: "Go to a place where the *sanguinaria* (i.e., shepherd's purse) grows and kneeling say Our Father and Hail Mary, etc. Then [say] this versicle: 'You, who have redeemed us by your Precious Blood, we ask you to come to the aid of your servants.' And then collect one or two plants. . . . And then hang this plant about the neck of the patient from whom the blood flows, and instantly it will stop and surely constrict."[1] It is difficult for us to know what to make of such a remedy: Is this medicine, religion, magic, or a combination of all three? To the medieval mind, the material and the spiritual worlds were closely integrated and interacted with one another. Such a cure (one of many examples that could be cited) made perfect sense.

One reason for the difficulty in discerning where religion ended and magic began was that magic made logical sense in a universe that was thought to contain not only plants, animals, and humans, but angels and demons. Medieval Christianity had been profoundly influenced by Neoplatonism, a philosophy that emphasizes the continuum between the physical and spiritual realms. Reality was thought to be organized into a great chain of being, proceeding upward from inanimate matter to plants, animals, humans, and into the realm of angels, with God at the pinnacle. It was the sixth-century Neoplatonist Dionysius, the pseudo-Areopagite, who perfected this system by outlining in detail nine levels of angels who mediated between God and humans. It was also thought that there existed a variety of spirits that held an intermediary position between the purely spiritual nature of the angels and the physical bodies of humans.[2] This made possible a world containing everything from angels to demons. It is important to note that, as spiritual beings, both angels and demons were thought to possess knowledge unknown to humans. As fallen angels, demons were still superior to humans in their knowledge of the natural world, due to their immaterial nature.

This worldview created theological problems, however. It raised issues not only of how things worked, but also of the proper Christian response. The Church's attitude throughout the Middle Ages was that magic was done with the help of demons and therefore was evil. It was Saint Augustine (354–430) who laid the foundations for this attitude. He posited a distinction between miracles wrought by God and magic performed with demonic aid. His distinction was to undergird the Church's view for centuries: "People attempt to make some sort of a distinction between practitioners of illicit arts, who are to be condemned, classing these as 'sorcerers' (the popular name for this kind of thing is 'black magic') and others whom they are prepared to regard as praiseworthy, attributing to them the practice of 'theurgy.' In fact, both types are engaged in the fraudulent rites of demons, wrongly called angels."[3] In other words, according to Augustinian doctrine, there is no such thing as good magic.

Medieval philosophers articulated three categories of causation: natural, supernatural, and preternatural. Events with obvious material causes were natural. Events that God caused, such as miracles, were supernatural. In between natural and supernatural events were events caused by forces superior to humans, that is, by angels and demons. In this mindset, then, it was possible to distinguish between miracles caused by God and magic caused by lesser spiritual forces. So magic could be natural in the sense that it used natural means, but it was demonic because it required the help of the demons.[4] If we understand these three categories of causation—natural, preternatural, and supernatural—we can understand the scholastic attitude toward magic and superstition. It was not seen as qualitatively different from religious belief. Magic used the same mechanisms that religion used, but they were directed toward an incorrect end, that is, a being other than God. For example, Thomas

Aquinas (c.1225–1274) looked at the issue of the healing powers of Christian relics and concluded that the powers were supernatural, since the relics healed some patients and not others.[5] In this case, he attributed the healing to angelic intervention not to demons. So we may summarize the scholastic position as one in which belief in the invisible realms was assumed, demons were considered part of those realms, and the occult, or hidden, aspect of natural phenomena was explained through recourse to either supernatural causes (that is, a miracle of God) or preternatural ones (caused by demons).

However, by the late Middle Ages, challenges to these distinctions came from the direction of technology, which had begun to surpass the philosophers' ability to explain how things worked. If occult, hidden forces in nature resulted from spirits, how did one understand, for example, a clock? William Eamon has argued that by the late Middle Ages, magic consisted of explanations for technologies that had been developed but for which there was no scientific explanation:

> The medieval mind was equipped with few scientific concepts with which to explain the phenomenal amounts of power that could be produced by such familiar machines as water wheels, windmills, and cannons. Nor was scholastic science able to explain the manifold conversions of power and motion that were, by the fifteenth century, commonly accomplished by means of complex gears, crank-shafts, connecting rods, belts and chains. The only analogy available to explain such marvels was the idea that the universe was a vast reservoir of occult forces and energies which could be tapped at will by various means: talismans to draw down the virtues of the celestial bodies, mixtures of herbs designed to exploit sympathies and antipathies, and above all, machines.[6]

The outgrowth of this development were attempts by the end of the Middle Ages to make magic into a science, as a branch of knowledge involving the study of occult qualities, whose effects could be seen, but which could themselves not be perceived. One twelfth-century work considered necromancy and alchemy branches of natural philosophy, along with medicine, agriculture, navigation, and optics.[7] By this time, European scholars had been introduced to Arabic scientific writings, such as the *Secreta secretorum*, which was attributed to Aristotle and thought to contain secret knowledge available only to the adept. The boundaries where legitimate natural philosophy ended and demonic magic began became increasingly blurry from this point on.

About the middle of the fifteenth century, natural magic experienced an intellectual revival. The Italian philosopher Marsilio Ficino (1433–

1499), working under the patronage of the Medicis in Florence, began translating previously inaccessible texts into Latin. His primary interest were the writings of Plato and of the Neoplatonists. While working on a Latin translation of Plato, another text fell into his hands—the writings of Hermes Trismegistes, which contained magical and mystical ideas. One of the most infamous passages in the Hermetic texts refers to the process of creating life itself, specifically, how to make a homunculus, or a living statue that could predict the future and both cause and cure diseases.[8] Ficino was requested to prepare a Latin translation of the Hermetic texts. Shortly thereafter, another body of purportedly ancient literature was introduced to the West through Ficino's student Giovanni Pico della Mirandola (1463–1494).[9] This was the Kabbalah, the Jewish mystical writings. The kabbalistic texts describe the magical power contained in the letters of the Hebrew alphabet and their numerical equivalents.[10] What Ficino and Pico were doing was, of course, entirely in line with the great interest in ancient texts that had impassioned Italians for several generations, but it introduced into Italian society new sources of magical "wisdom."

Ficino and his followers believed that God's wisdom was communicated not only in the Scriptures but also to Hermes, Pythagoras, and Plato. They were thus merging pagan and Christian knowledge into what came to be called the ancient theology, or *prisca theologia*. The thread that united them was a Neoplatonic emphasis on the relationship between the spiritual and natural realms, the correspondence between these realms, and the possibility of attaining real scientific knowledge about the nature from these correspondences. Magic became, in some circles at least, a respectable intellectual pursuit in late-fifteenth-century Italy. Renaissance magicians claimed what they were doing was not a demonic exercise, but an intellectually valid and even moral pursuit. What excited the Renaissance Neoplatonists was the belief that they had discovered the textbooks that held the keys to unlocking the secrets of the universe. Neoplatonic magic worked on the assumption that if one knew the correct formulae, incantations, and symbols, one could draw down the spiritual energies of the universe and utilize them for human purposes.

The elements of Renaissance magic were compiled and categorized in a book that would become the textbook of Renaissance magic, *The Occult Philosophy* of Henry Cornelius Agrippa (1486–1535), first published in 1531. Agrippa distinguished three types of magic. First was natural magic, involving the manipulation of natural objects, that is, alchemy. Celestial magic or astrology was second. Third was religious magic, which involved the conjuring of angels and spirits, or necromancy. These forms of magic corresponded, respectively, to the physical, celestial, and supercelestial spheres.[11] Alchemy was based on the belief that the natural world is composed of four elements—earth, air, fire, and water—that are combined in different ways. It seemed reasonable to conclude that one might be able to learn how to recombine them, for example, to produce gold. Astrology was based on the belief that God had written wisdom into the stars and that one could predict events through understanding the stars. And necromancy, as we have seen, was based on the assumption that spirits—including here angels, demons, and departed human souls—have superior knowledge that humans can discover and manipulate.

If knowledge is power, we have no better illustration than that of the attitude of the Renaissance magi toward their crafts. Neoplatonists believed that people could control their own destiny and environment, and this was a selling point for their activities. Magic was intellectually seductive. It is a beguiling thought that the cosmos is ordered and meaningful, and it is thrilling to imagine that one can find all of the ways in which its components are connected. We get a taste of this excitement by listening to the words of the sixteenth-century Italian astrologer Girolamo Cardano (1501–1576):

> Nothing comes closer to human happiness than knowing and understanding those things that nature has enclosed within her secrets. Nothing is more noble and excellent than understanding and pondering God's supreme works. Of all doctrines, astrology, which embraces both of these—the apotheosis of God's creation in the shape of the machinery of the heavens and the mysterious knowledge of future events—has been unanimously accorded first place by the wise.[12]

Moreover, this worldview was psychologically appealing or, as we might say today, empowering. The Neoplatonists had an essentially optimistic view of human nature based on the notion that humanity, having a soul, was linked to God and could in some measure perform the work of God on Earth. They went so far as to describe their learning as a process of "divinization."[13] For the Renaissance Neoplatonist philosophers, the purpose of life was defined as the perfection of the soul through the attainment of wisdom.[14] Pico della Mirandola articulated this view in his treatise *On the Dignity of Man*, in which he argued that God had created humans with the ability to either descend to the beasts or rise up to the divine realms. In either case, they were free to determine their own fate. Paul Ricci, an Italian Kabbalist, defined this as one of the basic premises of the Kabbalah: "Whoever is constructed in the likeness of God and as a microcosm, and resembles the Most High and Macrocosm in manner of activity, seeks his own perfection."[15] For the Kabbalists in particular, the notion of salvation as the attainment of wisdom was central. It was based on the notion that the soul had existed before it entered the body and resided in heaven; when it descended to earth, its goal was to learn how to perfect itself through living a human life. Salvation was, in their minds, an intellectual exercise.

By the early sixteenth century a new figure had emerged in European culture: the magus. He was perhaps an astrologer, prophet, alchemist, or all three. One of the most notorious was Nostradamus (1503–1566), whose predictions still grace the covers of supermarket tabloids (the only sixteenth-century personage of whom this can be said). Nostradamus was the court astrologer to the Valois kings of France. In fact, it was not uncommon for sixteenth-century monarchs to have astrologers on hand to give them counsel on issues such as the best time to go into battle. In the same way universities today compete in hiring the top research scientists, Renaissance monarchs tried to have the best alchemists on their payrolls. The potential benefits to be gained from someone who might be able to transform lead into gold were obvious.

Agrippa's *Occult Philosophy* contains a clear articulation of magic as a higher calling, one that required study and wisdom but also morality and pureness of heart. Those who attained this and performed their religious duties faithfully would be rewarded with divine power. What is noteworthy here is that religion and magic have become almost completely integrated. Agrippa illustrates how this works: "If therefore now thou shalt be a man perfect in the sacred understanding of Religion, and piously and most constantly meditatest on it . . . and art such an one on whom the authority of holy rites and nature hath conferred dignity above others . . . thou shalt be able by praying, consecrating, sacrificing, invocating, to attract spiritual and Celestial powers, and to imprint them on those things thou pleasest, and by it to vivifie every magicall work."[16] For Agrippa, magical activity was entirely consistent with—and a natural extension of—Christianity. Some Catholic alchemists explicitly compared their activities to the eucharistic transformation.[17] So we find with the rise of Renaissance magic an almost complete unification of magical activity, religious devotion, and scientific inquiry. The basic ideas were formulated, as we have seen, in Italy in the last half of the fifteenth century and were disseminated throughout Western Europe in the first half of the sixteenth. However, no sooner had the Renaissance synthesis of magic, religion, and science been formulated, than the boundaries came to be challenged.

Reformers

The Reformation of the Christian Church was many things. But most historians would agree that one of these things was an attempt to redraw the boundaries between religion and magic. With the Protestant Reformation and, to a lesser extent, the Catholic or Counter-Reformation, attempts were made to purify Christianity of superstitious and magical elements. Protestants reformulated the Christian faith by attacking the Renaissance synthesis. The basis of much criticism of the Church was the "magic" in its rituals. For Protestants, the process of boundary formation was thus relatively straightforward. They rejected anything they thought smacked of superstition, and so they discarded the doctrine of transubstantiation, the use of images and relics, and the veneration of the saints and the Virgin Mary. Protestants argued that transubstantiation was magic, because the Church believed that the words "this is my body" brought about the transformation of the elements.[18] Since, as we have seen, the alchemists were themselves making this comparison, the Protestants may have had a legitimate claim. Other rituals were called into question as well. For example, the French Protestant Pierre Viret ridiculed the way the Catholic clergy performed the Mass, for which there were rules concerning the number of prayers based on their correspondence to three (the Trinity), five (the wounds of Christ), or seven (the sevenfold grace of the Godhead). He argued that this approach made the priests into "pythagoreans" using a magical art.[19]

It was not only the notion that rituals were magic but also the claim that pagan texts had been inspired by God that created some unease. Protestants were appalled at the concept of the *prisca theologia* and turned back to the Bible in their varied attempts to restore the primitive church. They saw Catholicism as imbued with pagan concepts. For example, we might look at a sarcastic attack on the Catholic Church, entitled *The Bee-Hive of the Romish Church,* by Philip van Marnix van Saint Aldegonde. He explicitly ridiculed the Church for incorporating pagan and Jewish or kabbalistic traditions. He stated, "the Church of Rome hath gathered all these before named pieces together, and taken out of them, what shee hath thought good, which are called . . . the traditions of the church of Rome, and the foundation of our beliefe."[20] He argued that because the Church had taken this direction, its authority ought no longer to be respected.

Another relevant feature of most Protestant theologians was a desire to return to an Augustinian view of human nature, that is, an emphasis on human inability to avoid sin and on the necessity for God's grace and forgiveness. As we have seen, the Neoplatonists had envisioned the world as one in which human souls could fly upward through their own diligent study and pure morals. However, both Luther and Calvin stressed the absolute impossibility of the human soul saving itself. Calvin argued that to believe such a thing took sovereignty away from God, who had the authority to condemn to heaven or hell. For their part, Christian

Kabbalists, like Guillaume Postel (1510–1581), opposed Calvinist doc-trines of grace. Postel produced a treatise explicitly attacking Calvin's notion of predestination. He argued that Calvin's pessimistic view of human nature and emphasis on sin was extremely harmful to a person's health and well-being.[21] Postel believed that since humans were made in God's image, they were capable of distinguishing and of choosing be-tween right and wrong.

It should be clear from this discussion that Protestant theologians tackled the issue of boundary clarification head on. The Catholic Church also made some attempts to redefine the boundaries. Its task was rather more difficult, however, as it had to try to distinguish legitimate prac-tices, such as that which effected the transformation of bread and wine into flesh and blood, or made prayers to the saints efficacious, from de-monic magic. This process did not occur immediately, however. While the Renaissance philosophers were developing their theories, the popes were relatively unconcerned about theological issues and governing the Church and were more inclined to focus their energies on directing mili-tary campaigns and enhancing their own prestige through art and pag-eantry. Initially, then, there was little opposition from the Church to the developments of the Renaissance Neoplatonists. In fact, Cardinal Egidio da Viterbo possessed one of the largest collections of kabbalistic texts in Italy and was commissioned by Pope Clement VII to publish his own writings on the Kabbalah.[22] This attitude would change only with the pontificate of Paul IV (1555–1559), who opposed the syncretism of pa-gan, Christian, and Jewish thought that had been more or less tacitly accepted by his predecessors. The Council of Trent (1545–1563) tried to establish some boundaries; for example, it decreed that there ought to be some attempt to avoid popular superstitions involving the use of images, the saints, and the Virgin Mary.[23] Around this time, books of magic were included in the *Index of Prohibited Books*.

By the late sixteenth century, the Catholic Church was even more clearly evaluating its position on magic. The Jesuit theologian Martin Del Rio (1551–1608) tried to distinguish good from bad magic in his trea-tise *Six Books of Inquiries into Magic*, published in 1599. He differenti-ated legitimate Catholic practices from superstitious ones. For example, he examined the practice of wearing relics of the saints as amulets. He permitted the wearing of amulets but was careful to point out that if they had any effect, it was due to God's supernatural power rather than to any magic inherent in the object itself.[24] He denied that words could hold any magical power in themselves, yet he maintained that prayers were still efficacious and that the words "this is my body" possessed a supernatural force because God had decreed it.[25]

In spite of such attempts to clarify the issues, Catholicism would still be linked to magic for decades. The tradition established in the fifteenth century continued to receive some support. Jacques Gaffarel (1601–1681) prefaced his book *Unheard-of Curiosities*, which is a catalogue of magic, with this comment: "If thou thinke it strange, that a man of the Church, as I am, should adventure on so bold, and daring a Subject, as this seems to be, consider, I pray thee, that many of my Profession have put forth things much more bold than these; and even such as have been esteemed Dangerous too."[26] He then lists two full pages of individuals who preceded him in the study of magic, to justify his work. Nevertheless, by the seventeenth century, the tide had turned and individuals such as Gaffarel were swimming against it.

It may appear at this point that the story is relatively clear: magic and religion were separated during the Reformation. However, the story is not this straightforward, because of an issue raised earlier. How does one retain a belief in God's power to act in the world, yet remove the temptation to appeal to the spiritual world and try to manipulate it? An even greater risk in the sixteenth century than magic was atheism. "Atheist" became a catchword tossed at one's enemies, much as "communist" was in the 1950s. Nevertheless, there were a few materialist philosophers in the sixteenth century who argued that the immortality of the soul was illusory and that the soul died with the body. In particular one might think of the Italian philosopher Pietro Pomponazzi (1462–1525), who denied God's role in the world and attributed causation solely to natural forces rather than supernatural ones.[27] Taken to its extreme, this position would invalidate the miracles of the Bible and erode the Christian faith itself. To deny the existence of supernatural forces in the world was thus to risk atheism. To reject magic completely could be seen in some way as a rejection of the spiritual world and of the existence of God.

So it is premature to conclude that the separation of magic, religion, and science was an easy process, and it would be a mistake to think that during the Reformation anyone rejected notions of correspondence between the spiritual and natural realms. We find that even Protestants had to think through how they understood the distinctions. Those who condemned magic usually still acknowledged the existence of some conformity between the stars and planets and human bodies.[28] John Calvin (1509–1564) wrote a treatise on astrology in which he pointed out that doctors use astrology to help them in their treatment of patients, for example, to know when to perform a bloodletting, which shows that "there is a certain convenience [between] the starres or planets and the disposition of mans body."[29] However, Calvin rejected the idea of judicial astrology, that is, that the time of birth and the alignment of stars at that time affect nature and temperament. His reasoning was that if this were the case, it would interfere with God's will.

The notion of correspondences was similarly fuzzy. The Lutheran theologian Philip Melanchthon (1497–1560) argued that there were "predictions" that were not magical, such as when a doctor checks a patient's pulse or when a sailor predicts the weather from the direction of the wind. He defended this correlation as part of God's creation: "There is no doubt that such divinations have been permitted because they are simply a consideration of the natural order, and should anyone maintain that this is not natural or that it is illusory, he would be offending God with a manifest untruth."[30] Beyond this, he believed, there were auguries based on demonic spirits that have no connection to the natural world. Such discussions were common in the sixteenth century. The French philosopher Jean Bodin (1530–1596) objected to the use of the Kabbalah not because it did not work but because he considered its magical effects to be of demonic origin.[31] Even the German Protestant physician Johannes Weyer (1515/16–1588), one of the few who opposed the belief in witchcraft, continued to believe in magical cures. What we find in the sixteenth century, then, are continuing attempts to distinguish good from demonic magic.[32]

So rather than finding people rejecting magic because it is not true, we find that during the sixteenth century the argument was more likely to be made that magic is dangerous because it is true. The solution to determining the place of magic did not entail a rejection of the supernatural but a more thorough demonizing of it. It is therefore not surprising that throughout the sixteenth century we find a new genre of literature, the demonologies, which were academic discussions of the role of demons in the world.[33] These works set out to demonstrate that to believe in the power of the devil was central to the Christian faith. The most infamous of these is one of the earliest, the *Malleus Maleficarum* (Witches' Hammer) written by Heinrich Kramer and Jakob Sprenger, two Dominican friars, in 1486 as an inquisitorial manual useful for detecting witches. They provide a "scientific" explanation for the way in which devils can assume a human form: "The air which forms the devil's assumed body should be in some way inspissated [thickened], and approach the property of the earth, while still retaining its true property as air. And devils and disembodied spirits can affect this condensation by means of gross vapours raised from the earth, and by collecting them together into shapes in which they abide."[34] Demonologies were produced throughout the sixteenth and early seventeenth centuries, such as those written by Jean Bodin and King James I of England. Here too, we find the demonologists working toward cataloguing and categorizing events and distinguishing between those caused by demonic forces and those not so caused, much as their medieval predecessors had done.[35]

These works still assume that the spirits possess knowledge supe-

rior to that of humans. This belief informs the investigations into demon possession, of which there were many in early modern Europe, especially in France (for example, Laons in 1566, Aix-en-Provence in 1611,
Lille in 1613, and Loudun in 1633).[36] Tests were devised to determine
whether someone was actually possessed by a demon or whether they
were suffering from a natural illness like epilepsy. If they demonstrated
knowledge they would normally not possess, for example, if they could
speak Greek or Hebrew, it was an indication that the devil was speaking through them. The European witch trials, which reached their peak
around 1600, were a complex phenomenon with many causes. The presence of an extensive demonological literature was, however, an important contributing factor.

This process of demonizing magic that occurred through the early
modern period meant that the Renaissance magicians would come to be
portrayed as black magicians. Bodin considered Agrippa to be the worst
sorcerer of his age.[37] An obscure German scholar, George (or Johann)
Faust, would be immortalized by Christopher Marlowe in 1604 as Dr.
Faustus, a black magician who sold his soul to the devil in return for
knowledge and ended up in hell for his efforts.

Even though they were not subject to the Inquisition as vigorously
as women accused of witchcraft, magicians became increasingly notorious. And certainly those who continued to hold magical opinions were
in danger. We might cite Tommaso Campanella (1568–1639), who was
imprisoned by the Inquisition, and Giordano Bruno (1548–1600), who
was burned at the stake in 1600. The English magus John Dee (1527–
1608), although favored by Queen Elizabeth, had his library vandalized
by a mob that perceived him to be a wizard.[38] Earlier in the century,
the use of the Kabbalah in magic was considered a guarantee against demonic influence, but by the 1580s there are strong denunciations of the
Kabbalah on Catholic as well as Protestant sides.[39] So the Renaissance
notion of the magus doing his work as a moral individual had, by the
seventeenth century, given way to the view of the magician who sells
his soul to the devil for the sake of power. It was a way of retaining belief
in the supernatural, but warning people away from interacting with it.

Scientists

Thus far, then, we have suggested that demonizing
magic was a way of guarding the Christian faith against the danger of
atheism and yet to redefine the boundaries between religion and magic.
There is, from this point on, another story to be told, the separation of
science from magic. This is a complex issue, and we will simply note a
few important developments that signal the eventual abandonment of a
belief in supernatural forces.

One nail in the coffin of Renaissance magic came from the area of critical textual analysis, resulting in the discrediting of the *prisca theologia* early in the seventeenth century. Critical analysis revealed that the texts beloved by the Renaissance Neoplatonists were in fact not as ancient as they had thought. In 1614, Isaac Casaubon dated the Hermetic texts as originating after the Christian era.[40] One of his contemporaries, the Jewish scholar Leon Modena, suspected that the *Zohar,* the most important kabbalistic text, had been written in the twelfth century. He argued, the reason for parallels with ancient texts was that it was written later and was influenced by them.[41] The similarities that had seemed so remarkable to Ficino, Pico, and others were explained in the seventeenth century by the common origins and historic settings of the texts, not by God's divine revelation that had communicated eternal wisdom at the time of Moses, as originally thought.

There were other, even more significant, developments. One of the most important factors was the increasing reliance on empirical data. As an example we might look at the person of Johannes Kepler (1571–1630), whom physics students will remember as the author of the three laws of planetary motion. Kepler was heavily influenced by Neoplatonic ideas, and his astronomical studies reflected a desire to discern the harmonies between planetary orbits, which he initially thought would reflect Plato's five solid figures. His abandonment of circular orbits for elliptical ones represents not only a rejection of the idea of the Aristotelian spheres, but also an indication that the search for harmony and correspondence had to be mitigated by an examination of the available evidence. In Kepler's case, this was provided by the vast amounts of empirical data available to him after the death of Tycho Brahe.

Moreover, by the middle of the seventeenth century, we start to see a critical analysis of the correspondences that the Renaissance magicians assumed to exist. A key figure in this context is the French scholar, priest, and mathematician Marin Mersenne (1588–1648), known as a lifelong friend of Descartes. His major work, the *Quaestiones in Genesim,* was published in 1623 and has been described as one of the key works marking the transition out of Renaissance modes of magical thinking.[42] Mersenne attacked both the "atheists" on one hand and the magicians on the other. Mersenne's desire to clarify the boundaries moved mathematics away from numerology.[43] He suggested that one could always find correspondences but that they had no basis in reality and were merely products of one's imagination.[44] We see him beginning to articulate a view that suggests that harmonies and forces do exist but not in the way that had been conceived. For example, he questioned one of Ficino's ideas, that music could draw down stellar influences and thus affect the emotions. Mersenne's response was "that any influences whatever have been brought down from the stars by singing has been entirely repudiated, for this or that song does not provoke us to sadness or happiness because it is performed under this or that star, as is indicated by the fact that the same song has the same power when heard under various stars, as experience will confirm."[45] What we see here is that Mersenne is testing Ficino's hypotheses and rejecting them. He similarly discredited the connections between planets and metals by showing that the comparisons do not bear up to critical analysis.

Of even more profound significance, however, is the redefinition of "occult" forces as hidden forces, but not necessarily supernatural ones. Descartes (1596–1650) followed a discussion of the magnet with this statement: "There are no qualities that are so occult, no effects of sympathy or antipathy so marvelous or so strange, . . . that its reason cannot be given by [the principles of the mechanical philosophy]."[46] In other words, just because something is hidden does not mean that it is inaccessible through study. This point is made explicitly by one of Descartes's contemporaries, Walter Charleton (1619–1707), who pointed out that to say a quality is occult is not to explain it. He believed it was the hidden forces in nature that must be the object of science.[47] In other words, hidden forces are not necessarily supernatural simply because they are not apparent.[48] It is not accidental, of course, that this intellectual shift paralleled the technological development of exactly those kinds of instruments that would extend human capabilities beyond the level of normal sense perception: the telescope and the microscope. As we will see in the next chapter, scientists are now using new equipment to try to measure phenomena like the effects of prayer.

Finally, what was beginning to change by the seventeenth century was not so much the knowledge base, but the attitude toward knowledge. Francis Bacon (1561–1626) outlined the goals of science thus: "The end of our foundation is the knowledge of causes and the secret motion of things, and the enlarging of the bounds of human empire, to the effecting of all things possible."[49] Implied here is that the causes of things can be discovered. The implications of this belief are powerful. It means that if a physician does not know what causes an illness, it need not be relegated to the presence of demons. It may simply mean that the cause has not yet been discovered. Such an insight was profound and was a contributing factor to halting the persecution of individuals for the crime of witchcraft.

The Dilemma Continues

The purpose of this chapter has been to illustrate the transformation of the view of reality from a magical to a naturalistic one. The journey from scholastic thought to the Scientific Revolution uncovered some of the dilemmas scholars faced at various points along the way. Specifically, we saw the necessarily thin boundaries between a theistic worldview and one where magic is possible. We would like to conclude with a quotation from the Internet version of the *Catholic Encyclopedia*. The article on necromancy contains the following comment: "The Church does not deny that, with a special permission of God, the souls of the departed may appear to the living, and even manifest things unknown to the latter. But, understood as the art or science of evoking the dead, necromancy is held by theologians to be due to the agency of evil spirits, for the means taken are inadequate to produce the expected results."[50] Of course it is not surprising that the Church would consider necromancy to be demonic. What is surprising is that even today we see a dilemma caused by belief in the spiritual realm that results in a cautionary approach to dealing with it. Unless one is a pure materialist, there are difficulties that must be dealt with during any age.

For the most part, people today acknowledge that the world operates on the basis of physical principles. But we still call on religion to fill in the explanations when no others are adequate. What is worth thinking about are our own categories of causation. Since the Scientific Revolution, scientists have looked at causation in physical terms, and occult forces lost their supernatural element. However, the popular revival of interest in areas like astrology, the Kabbalah, and spiritualism suggests that the scientific explanations still fail us periodically. And, as we will see in the following chapter, we are still often puzzled by issues of causation and resort to magical ways of thinking when no others satisfy us.

6 As If by Magic

Physician, heal thyself.

—Luke 4:23

We have seen that prior to the Scientific Revolution, magic, religion, technology, and science were closely intertwined and separating them was the work of many decades of intellectual effort and debate. However, this process was never complete nor was it systematic. As suggested at the end of chapter 5, for individuals who believe in some form of spiritual realm, important issues are raised regarding causation. In this chapter we will explore further some of the relationships between religion, science, and medicine by examining two phenomena that have been receiving a great deal of attention over the past decade or so, namely, AIDS and the healing power of prayer. The AIDS epidemic is an important social phenomenon for many reasons. Not only is it threatening the lives of millions of people around the world, it appears to have come out of nowhere, as if by magic. As we will see, among the several theories that have been proposed to explain the origin of this epidemic, some are based on the notion that AIDS is the result of divine retribution or even the arrival on Earth of alien organisms. Similarly, evidence is mounting in support of the healing power of prayer, as public faith in traditional medicine declines and the members of the medical establishment, both researchers and caregivers, are becoming more open to studying and using prayer as a treatment.

Our current understanding of both AIDS and the healing power of prayer rely far more on aspects of magical causation than we perhaps realize or are willing to admit. Consequently, before looking more directly at these phenomena, we have to first explain causation in general terms and then discuss specifically what we mean by magical causation.

Magical Causation

The word *magic*, like the words *religion* and *science*, is used extensively in popular and scholarly literature, and yet it defies precise definition. One (though not the only) important element of the various conceptions of magic, however, appears to be the assertion of a causal relationship between phenomena where evidence for that relationship does not exist.[1] In other words, the existence of a causal mechanism is taken for granted rather than being based on any kind of empirical verification. To take an anthropological example, there are tribes that dance in order to bring rain. If after the dancing the rain comes, then the dancing is said to have caused the rain. If, on the other hand, after the dancing it does not rain, the members of the tribe are unlikely to abandon their explanation. Rather, they might suggest they made a mistake in the dance or one of the dancers did not properly prepare for the dance. So, even though there is no evidence that dancing brings rain, people are more likely to look to their own inadequacies than they are to suggest that the explanation is wrong. Anthropological and historical data from many cultures suggest that in most instances an explanation based on magic (lack of evidence) is better than no explanation at all and that explanatory mechanisms, and the systems of meaning they are based on, are essential to the maintenance of social order.[2] To the extent that religion and science rely upon causal explanations in the absence of empirical evidence, we suggest that they are employing *magical causation*.

Our interest in magic in this chapter is functional rather than substantive or symbolic. In other words, we are concerned with what magic can do for us, what role it plays in society. In particular, we will look at how magic functions to provide causal explanations. While the practices associated with magic differ among cultural groups, magic performs three functions that are fairly similar. First, as Rodney Coe indicates, "magic serves to allay anxieties about the unknown." Whenever you whistle while walking alone down a dark street or sit at your favorite desk when writing an examination, you are using magic. Second, "magic is extensively used in combating disease and illness." Coe explains that in many instances magic is used to explain why someone gets sick, and so it makes sense that magic would be used to explain how someone was cured. For example, there are untold numbers of cases of so-called miracle cures that leave physicians scratching their heads. Third, "magico-religious beliefs and practices act as agents of social control."[3] In other words, they provide an orderly system within which people come to understand their roles and responsibilities as members of society and through which they come to define the objects they encounter in their daily lives. Within the context of medicine, not only is the relationship between the patient and the caregiver subject to this ordering process, the whole idea of what it means to have a cold or have cancer is determined within these systems of meaning. The term *magico-scientific* would also be relevant here. Both religion and science contain elements of magic and yet, as we will see, society tends to view scientific beliefs and practices as more legitimate than religious ones.

This raises the question of what constitutes legitimate authority. In the case of religion, legitimacy is likely to stem from belief in a supreme being, while in the case of science it is the objectivity and rigor of the so-called scientific method that provides the authority. Max Weber hypothesized that authority has its basis in one of three possible sources: charisma, tradition, or legal-rational structures. With charismatic individuals, it is their personal presence, their ability to draw people to them that forms the basis for their authority. Political figures like Adolf Hitler or John F. Kennedy, religious leaders like Billy Graham or Jimmy Swaggart, and outstanding scientists like Carl Sagan or Stephen Hawking are able to exert tremendous influence over their audiences. In many ways the exact content of their messages is secondary to their ability to convince people to accept what they say. Alternatively, the social aversion to almost any kind of change forms the basis for the authority vested in tradition. When presented with a challenge, too often groups revert to tried-and-true ways of doing things, not because those ways are necessarily the most effective but because they are the ways things have always been done. The reluctance of many church members to change any aspect of their Sunday morning ritual is a familiar example. Legal and rational bases for authority share the characteristic in that they appear to be objective and codified, and therefore immune from the subjective whims of a potentially dangerous individual or the folly of mob rule. Religion presents us with rules for behavior and lists of acceptable beliefs and practices, and so does science. It is often argued, however, that religious ideals must be accepted on faith, while scientific ideals are empirically testable. As we saw in chapter 1, this distinction is open to question.

When their authority is threatened, scientists frequently pose two sorts of questions to their challengers. They will often ask why humans trust airplanes to deliver them unharmed to their destinations, implying that we have faith in scientific principles. In response, Steve Fuller suggests that people are more likely to put their faith in a complex social network of engineers, mechanics, schedulers, pilots, and so on, who work together to ensure safe air travel, than they are to rely on the science of aerodynamics.[4] In fact, the history of flight is much more a testament to the ingenuity and creativity of skilled and daring tinkerers than to the power of scientific knowledge. A second sort of question scientists often ask is why humans would recoil from the prospect of walking out of the windows in skyscrapers if they didn't believe in gravity. Simply put, you do not need to know anything about gravity to understand from practical experience that you will fall to your death. For millennia before Isaac Newton's observation of the proverbial apple falling from a tree, people were just as subject to the force of gravity as we are today. No amount (or lack) of scientific understanding of Newton's laws of motion alters the ability of individuals to get on with their daily lives.

In attempting to determine what it is that scientists are trying to say with these two questions, we can interpret the first line of reasoning as an example of how science claims to have helped us exceed our natural limitations. Science produces technology. By this argument the scientific establishment justifies the extremely large amounts of public and private money spent on research, on the basis that the resultant increases in scientific knowledge will provide tangible benefits for people everywhere. It is also an example of what Fuller calls "methodological ventriloquism," whereby scientists project their explanations onto various phenomena and onto the public.[5] In other words, as part of the legitimating process, scientists recast everything into the language and meaning systems of science. Similarly, the second question demonstrates the scientific claim of being able to explain our natural limitations by rational means. Fuller points out that scientists are hostile to what they call "intellectual recidivism," whereby commonsense explanations are substituted for more sophisticated scientific explanations. We might interpret this to mean that where there is more than one possible explanation of a phenomenon, the most scientific explanation is to be preferred. From this standpoint, while a small child may learn by painful experience that stepping off a raised surface can result in an assortment of nasty bumps and bruises, scientists seem to suggest the incident will take on real significance only when the child learns that bodies fall to earth at 9.8 meters per second squared.

Accepting for a moment the purported rationality and objectivity of the scientific enterprise, let us take a closer look at the notion of causality. Generally, causation is predicated on three criteria. The first is the idea of temporal order, whereby the cause must precede the effect. Second, the cause and effect must be correlated, or statistically associated, such that a change in the cause will lead to a proportional change in the effect. Finally, the relationship between the cause and effect must be nonspurious, that is, the relationship must be actual and not just apparent. For example, when the number of births shows a sudden increase nine months after a power blackout, it is spurious to suggest that it was the lack of electricity itself that resulted in a large number of pregnancies. Take the example of a bacterial infection. In order to establish with certainty that bacterium X causes disease Y, it is necessary to show that the sufferer was exposed to the bacteria prior to becoming sick, that signs of disease, such as fever, are related to the concentration of the organism in the blood, and that the signs being displayed by the sufferer were not caused by something else. This final criterion is often verified by testing whether the isolated bacteria will cause the same disease in others. In most cases a laboratory model of the disease is used for verification rather than a human "guinea pig," but not always. In 1995, renowned virologist Peter Duesberg volunteered to inject himself with HIV to support his contention that the human immunodeficiency virus does not cause AIDS.[6] Similarly, as we saw in chapter 3, Barry Marshall ingested bacteria to prove they cause stomach ulcers.

Beyond these three criteria for establishing a causal relationship, we must also recognize the difference between necessary and sufficient causes and the difference between proximate and distal causes. A necessary cause is one that must exist in order for a certain effect to take place. So, for example, oxygen is necessary for a fire to burn. Similarly, male and female gametes are both necessary for sexual reproduction to take place. However, neither of these alone is sufficient. A sufficient cause is one that acts on its own, requiring no assistance to produce an effect. Many religious belief systems hold that God is a necessary and sufficient cause of the universe. A proximate cause is one that is closer in time to the effect than a distal cause that may have existed, say, since birth. Thus, particular individuals may be genetically predisposed to certain diseases, and yet these may only manifest themselves at some point later in life as the result of exposure to certain environmental factors. Similarly, a patient may be admitted to the hospital for some ailment and while staying in the hospital may develop a fatal case of pneumonia. While pneumonia would be considered the proximate cause of death, the original ailment for which the person was admitted would be the distal cause.

In the case of AIDS, infection with HIV may be necessary but not sufficient to cause the appearance of this syndrome. In fact there may be a more distal cause, something that leads to the suppression of the human immune system that provides fertile ground for HIV to thrive. Precedent for this idea can be found in tuberculosis, for instance. Poor nutrition and overcrowding due to poverty proved as important to the development of TB as was the tubercle bacillus.[7] Similarly, prayer may be neither necessary nor sufficient to cause a cure of some disease or other. In this sense, prayer would be a spurious variable in the treatment regimen. The fact that people who are prayed for get well, just like the fact that people who have AIDS prove positive on tests for HIV antibodies, demonstrates the principle that correlation is not causation.

By way of summary, then, we are using the notion of magical causation to characterize those instances where a causal relationship is assumed to exist even in the absence of valid and reliable empirical evidence to support the various criteria set out to demonstrate causality. However, there are bound to be instances where one or more of the criteria appear to be satisfied and, based on the propensity of evidence, people jump to the conclusion that the "cause" has been found. In our view, the decision in such cases would still constitute an invocation of magic.

HIV and AIDS

In his opening speech to the twelve thousand delegates at the Thirteenth International AIDS Conference in Durban, South Africa, Thabo Mbecki, the president of the host country, indicated that he found it difficult to believe that the problems millions of Africans have with their immune systems could be blamed on one single virus, namely, HIV. Mbecki pointed to the poverty of Africa as the single most significant determinant of the health of the people of that continent. It is important to emphasize that Mbecki was not saying that HIV does not cause AIDS but that a considerable level of uncertainty exists in the scientific community about whether HIV alone is a necessary and sufficient cause of AIDS. At the same time, he drew attention to the fact that, at least in Africa, the socioeconomic status of the people may be a critical element in the causal chain, no matter how remote (distal) from the epidemic, or spurious, it may be.

It is difficult to deny the power of AIDS (acquired immune deficiency syndrome) to incite panic, cause governments to spend billions of dollars on research and care, and cause moralists to rail against everything from drug abuse to indiscriminant sex to homosexuality. It is not very difficult to see why this is the case. In her book *Illness as Metaphor*, Susan Sontag writes, "nothing is more punitive than to give a disease a meaning—that meaning being invariably a moralistic one. Any important disease whose causality is murky, and for which treatment is ineffectual, tends to be awash in significance."[8] Before the term *AIDS* came into use, this seemingly new medical phenomenon was referred to as GRID (gay-related immune disease), in recognition that its first sufferers in the United States were homosexual males. Soon afterward, it was recognized that a certain set of social groups was at high risk of contracting the disease, namely, hemophiliacs, homosexuals, Haitians, and heroin-users (the four *H*s). Membership in one of these groups was viewed as a distal cause of AIDS, predisposing certain individuals to HIV infection. Curiously, a few years later, when health officials and researchers became aware of the staggering number of people suffering from AIDS in Africa, the search for the cause and a cure still tended to focus on the American experience. In a very real sense, the level of attention focused on AIDS reflected a broader concern with being able to differentiate between social groups. AIDS was something they had and we did not want. The sociopolitical activity around the epidemic masked the fact that we actually know very little about AIDS from a medical point of view, and this is perhaps most obvious when we look at explanations for the source of AIDS.

In his encyclopedic examination of the origin of the AIDS epidemic, Edward Hooper describes the five major categories of theories that have been put forward to explain the source of this new disease.[9] While a series of papers in 1995 finally contained a convincing demonstration of the link between HIV and AIDS, no adequate theory yet exists to explain how AIDS originated and erupted into an epidemic in Africa and elsewhere in the early 1980s. Three of the theory categories characterize AIDS as a recent phenomenon, and Hooper refers to these as "the heavenly, the malevolent human, and the unwitting human" models. The fourth category, which we will call the archaeological, contains theories that assume that AIDS-related disease has existed for centuries or longer and has merely been unrecognized as such. The fifth category of theories, which we will call the socially constructed, posits AIDS as a "creation of semantics," a sort of neologism for a cluster of existing conditions lumped together to serve some sociopolitical end. Of course, as Sontag might suggest, AIDS is more than a name, it is a moral judgment and a social force of immense magnitude.

In the "heavenly" category, two major theories exist. The first is the "scourge of God" theory in which AIDS is seen as divine retribution for a licentious lifestyle associated with homosexuality, sexual promiscuity, and drug addiction. Not only does this theory have strong moralistic overtones (not to mention little if any scientific merit), it is extremely difficult to sustain when applied to newborns with congenital AIDS, recipients of blood transfusions, and the unsuspecting monogamous female partners of men who engage in indiscriminate recreational sex. Of all the theories of origin, this one is the most literally religious in nature, and consequently it is the most difficult to disprove. The second theory is the celestial origin theory, which suggests that a number of extraterrestrial viruses, including HIV, might have come to earth as debris from the tail of a passing comet. This theory gives the impression of scientific merit, but the fact that something sounds scientific and is in the realm of possibility is a far cry from demonstrating correlation, let alone causation. Notwithstanding this cautionary note, some world-renowned scientists, including astronomer Fred Hoyle, think that this theory is plausible.

The "malevolent human" category might be thought of as the "conspiracy theory" category. Theories in this group include accusations that the CIA has on several occasions developed and tested biological weapons on an unsuspecting public, at home and abroad. On a more global level, the Russians and the Americans have been taking turns accusing each other of coming up with something devastating during the cold war years that is now out of control. The basis for these theories is the Hobbesian view that conflict and war reflect the natural state of the human species and that in the ever-escalating effort to destroy others, we often end up destroying ourselves. These theories also tend to demonize science, in that they support the allegation that groups of exceptional scientists are secretly employed by governments to work on leading-edge (and seemingly diabolical) research projects.

The "unwitting human" category might also be called the "unintended consequences" category, because AIDS may in fact be the unintended consequence of another otherwise benign or even beneficial development. Specifically, HIV could have been carried along with a variety of vaccines that were administered in large numbers in the 1950s in Africa and elsewhere in an effort to eradicate malaria, polio, smallpox, and other epidemic diseases. This is in fact the theory that Hooper supports in his book.[10] These theories are based on a conception of human ignorance rather than malevolence, as if to say that what you don't know may hurt you. In this sense, they constitute a warning against the uncontrolled proliferation of scientific, and especially medical, experimentation. Not only does such a position pose a threat to the further funding of medical research, but also it gives rise to a number of ethical issues around what limits should be placed on human intervention in the natural world. Recent controversies over experiments in cloning and the genetic modification of foodstuffs come to mind.

The theories in all three of these categories are based on recent events, and so, even if they had some validity, they may be reflecting only the proximate and not the more distal cause of the epidemic. They also reflect the notion of magical causation inasmuch as they provide an explanation in the absence of supporting empirical evidence. However, rather than acknowledging and accepting the fact that we do not know, various interest groups construct theories that fit their view of the world. So, for example, from the viewpoint of science, it may be suggested that we just do not know yet. Alternatively, from a religious perspective, it might be suggested that we might never know. Either way, for the present at least, with many of these theories, there is no adequate way to put them to the test.

Theories in the fourth category view AIDS as an older condition that has just recently been recognized. In support of these ideas is the discovery that HIV–1 and HIV–2 are closely related to two simian immunodeficiency viruses (SIVs) that are found in certain nonhuman primates, namely SIVcpz and SIVsm, which infect chimpanzees and sooty mangabeys, respectively. So, at some point, it is argued, these viruses jumped across the species barrier and entered humans. Viruses have the ability to mutate very rapidly, and we now recognize several different strains of HIV that display a broad spectrum of virulence and ease of transmission. While theories in this category may explain the evolution of HIV, they do not tell us very much, if anything, about AIDS as a disease and as an epidemic. For many years, the media and the medical establishment have talked about the search for a cure for cancer. Critics are quick to point out that the use of the word *cancer* disguises the fact that there are several varieties of cancers with vastly different characteristics. As more research is carried out on HIV and AIDS, we are coming to realize that there are many HIVs and that AIDS, like cancer, is a collective term for a complex and ever-changing phenomenon.

The final category of theories contains those that call into question the very notion that HIV causes AIDS. Peter Duesberg has been the leading proponent of this line of reasoning. This formerly well-respected member of the National Academy of Sciences, who once held a $350,000 per year grant and who is credited with the discovery of oncogenes (genes that cause cancer), has argued that there is no scientific basis for the claim that HIV causes AIDS. Duesberg argues instead that HIV is just one of a number of opportunistic organisms that take advantage of a suppressed immune system brought on by long-term recreational drug use and exacerbated by having indiscriminate sex with multiple partners.[11]

Kary Mullis, who won the Nobel Prize in chemistry in 1993 for his invention of PCR (polymerase chain reaction), also argues that there is insufficient evidence to support the HIV theory of AIDS. Mullis suggests that the decision to put the HIV hypothesis forward was to provide a legitimate framework for government spending on AIDS research, even in the absence of concrete scientific justification for such a hypothesis. As he says: "Years from now, people looking back at us will find our acceptance of the HIV theory of AIDS as silly as we find the leaders who excommunicated Galileo." As Mullis goes on to observe, the important question we are left with is, "If HIV isn't the cause of AIDS, then what is?"[12] In the face of uncertainty, combined perhaps with the fear of undermining their own livelihood, scientists appear more willing to take the position that an inadequate explanation is better than no explanation at all.

As we have observed, one major problem with these categories of theories of origin is that none of them provides an explanation for how AIDS burst onto the scene in about 1980. Starting with a few isolated cases as early as 1959, the exponential growth of the epidemic over the last twenty years has been astounding. It is estimated that by early 2001, thirty-six million people worldwide were living with AIDS, two-thirds of which in sub-Saharan Africa, and more than twenty million have already died.[13] It seems ludicrous that at this point in our history, in the presence of such a global phenomenon, we are still left floundering for an explanation of a crisis of such proportions. As ludicrous as it may sound, in response to questions regarding how AIDS came about, we are still left shrugging our shoulders and observing that it is as if by magic.

For centuries, the leadership of church and state worked together to protect their own interests, partly by creating and enforcing moral codes and authority structures designed to circumscribe the thoughts and activities of the majority of the population. We are often schooled to believe that the Enlightenment and the industrial revolution brought an end to this sort of arrangement. For at least the last one hundred years, however, democratic governments have worked with leaders of high-technology and science-based industry to provide their own codes of behavior and systems of meaning for the citizens of the world. The conspicuous consumption of durable goods has replaced tithing as the mechanism to ensure that the power structure is maintained. The HIV theory of AIDS provides not only the theoretical grounding for a massive scientific research network, particularly in Western capitalist countries, but also a mechanism through which the systematic discrimination and exploitation of underdeveloped, and racially different, nations can take place. We believe that this is one of the points that Thabo Mbecki was trying to make.

The Healing Power of Prayer

In 1988, Randolph Byrd published the results of a randomized, controlled, double-blind experiment in which certain patients recovering from heart attacks were prayed for while another group was not.[14] Those in the prayed-for group required fewer antibiotics, were less likely to develop pneumonia, and had fewer cases of congestive heart failure. This highly publicized study marks the point at which the healing power of prayer leaped into the public consciousness. Of course, prayer has been used in healing for millennia, but now science was getting in on the game, and somehow that made prayer a more legitimate subject of discussion. Over the last decade, a large number of articles and books on the subject have appeared. For example, a quick search at amazon.com yields a list of seventy-four titles that contain the words "healing" and "prayer." However, like AIDS, the healing power of prayer is a highly controversial issue.

The source of the controversy is that relating prayer to healing transgresses the boundary between religion and science, which poses a particular threat to established medical science. In this regard, we could recast Sontag's comment on disease to read that any treatment whose mechanism of action is unknown, and for which specific diseases are unspecified, will tend to be awash in significance. Religion, because of its link to the supernatural, is by its nature inexact and mysterious. Science, on the other hand, is held up as the very epitome of exactness and clarity. For people to retain their faith in medical practice, medicine must be based in science not religion. As Cohen and colleagues state: "From the standpoint of modern scientific medicine, no treatment should be employed without evidence of its effectiveness and safety."[15] Prayer does not lend itself readily to this kind of evaluation.

Many scientists reject prayer-based healing. Larry Dossey, following the work of Daniel J. Benor, discusses potential reasons why.[16] For present purposes, we can group the objections into three categories that roughly correspond to religion, science, and magic. Let us examine each of these in some depth. First, in the religion category, scientists argue that the healing prayer is often specific to one religion or another. So, for example, in his study of patients in a coronary care unit, Byrd concludes that prayer to the Judeo-Christian God had positive effects. What if certain patients, or those praying, had been Muslims or Buddhists? Is it the act of praying or the specific religious context within which the praying takes place that does the healing? One implication here is that the faith of the person praying or of the person being prayed for might have some part to play in the healing process. However, we must be careful not to confuse the issue. If prayer heals, it does not prove the supremacy of one religion over another or of religion over science. For example, Cohen and colleagues cite a passage from C. S. Lewis wherein he comments that the successful use of prayer in healing does nothing to demonstrate the truth of Christianity. Rather it proves "something more like magic—a power in certain human beings to control, or compel, the course of nature."[17]

Similarly, some scientists view healing through prayer as associated with mysticism. The reason they find this association objectionable is that the mystical realm is often viewed as irrational (or at least nonrational), and therefore antithetical to the logical and objective workings of science. Also, mysticism implies mystery and thus provides an opening for appeals to the unknown, and perhaps unknowable, that may include appeals to the supernatural. It may also point to the limits of scientific exploration as opposed to the limits of scientific knowledge. These things are very different indeed. In many situations, scientists argue that given enough time and money they will be able to understand some particular phenomenon. We must recognize that when we accept that something is truly mysterious, we are acknowledging that it is literally beyond our grasp.

Second, in the science category, four objections to healing through prayer are commonly raised. The first, and strongest, objection is that healing phenomena cannot be replicated. In other words, there is no way to demonstrate in the laboratory through experiments that prayer heals. There are several aspects to this. Part of the problem is that prayer as a form of therapy is nonspecific. It can be used to treat any disease condition. As a consequence, it is difficult to demonstrate that prayer is either necessary or sufficient to bring about a cure. At the same time, however, prayer may be viewed as the proximate cause of healing, on a personal or a social level. Even when someone has been receiving treatment or medication for an extended period, if that person thinks that the prayers recently offered on their behalf precipitated a cure then on a personal level prayer is part of the causal chain. Similarly, if a particular group of people have faith in the healing power of prayer, then no amount of scientific evidence for or against their position is likely to alter their view.

In an effort to bring studies of healing prayer more closely in line with the demands of science, Herbert Benson has argued that prayer, like meditation and some other so-called alternative therapies, works through a mechanism he calls the "relaxation response."[18] Lowering the blood pressure, slowing the heart rate, and lowering the metabolic rate strengthens the immune system. The details of the physiology behind this response are complex and poorly understood, but it does lend itself to scientific examination. As a case in point, the emerging field of psychoneuroimmunology is devoted to studying the interactions between thought processes, the brain, the central nervous system, and the immune system.[19] While this new field represents a more holistic and interdisciplinary approach to medicine, it appears to be firmly rooted in the scientific paradigm. Others might argue that a term like *psychoneuroimmunology* is just another word for magic.

Alternatively, the healing power of prayer can be viewed as an example of the placebo effect, whereby healing takes place based on the belief that some treatment that can otherwise be shown to have no medicinal value has worked. Coe indicates that "placebos are magic in modern dress."[20] In many ways the placebo effect merely demonstrates that we just do not know how healing takes place, and that we can often trick ourselves into letting nature, or perhaps the supernatural, take its course. Coe goes on to explain, for example, that there are a large number of common illnesses from which a person would recover even in the absence of treatment altogether. Furthermore, treatments that match cultural expectations can be very effective. If a patient expects to be given pills, even when none are warranted, the physician can prescribe sugar pills, and the very act of following the medical model seems to facilitate the healing process. From this perspective it could be argued that if the patient feels that prayer is helpful, then why should physicians object to its use? As Christina Hughes suggests, it is irrelevant whether it is a placebo or something else.[21] From a holistic perspective, as long as it helps the patient, medical caregivers should be supportive.

A second scientific objection to the use of prayer is that modern medicine is materialistic, relying on such techniques as surgery, radiation therapy, and drug treatment to cure patients. Many of these techniques are invasive and often do collateral damage to the patient, but they are tangible. In a recent book that purports to take a scientific approach to explaining how prayer heals, Walter Weston reports that people have the ability to emit an eight-hertz electromagnetic signal that is the physical correlate of the healing power of prayer.[22] Anyone familiar with basic brain function will recognize this frequency (eight cycles per second) as that of alpha waves, which are typical of people in a deeply relaxed or passive state. Elsewhere, however, Weston indicates that the frequency given off by spiritual healers is eight megahertz, or eight million cycles per second. Even those with a rudimentary knowledge of physics will know that such frequencies are in the microwave realm and are thus quite capable of disrupting cell integrity and cooking popcorn. While Weston's book is full of scientific language and contains summaries of several studies, no citations are provided. Unfortunately, the sort of sloppy scholarship, not to mention sloppy manuscript editing, that this book represents is more likely to hinder rather than to help establish the acceptance by members of the scientific community of the healing power of prayer.

The third objection in the science category makes two quite similar arguments, in that they concern the beliefs and thought system of modern science, rather than its practices and methods. First, there is the issue of cognitive dissonance that comes about when the things that we see or experience do not match our beliefs. The easiest and most comforting response to such situations is to reject them out of hand. In other words, to accept that prayer heals would require a new way of viewing the world, one that is inconsistent with the scientific method, and so scientists choose not to believe. Second, the laws of healing appear to be different from those of other sciences. This objection can be interpreted as an example of the reductionism that characterizes the natural sciences. According to this view, at a fundamental level, all natural phenomena follow the same set of rules. If prayer heals, we should be able to write an equation that not only explains the mechanism of healing but also allows us to predict what will happen in any particular application of prayer. Another way to think of this issue is to try to imagine what a standard dose of prayer might be. What unit of measurement would be appropriate, and what kind of apparatus could be used to measure it? Both of these objections easily lead to the conclusion that, from a scientific perspective, prayer is unnatural and therefore outside the purview of science. People can believe what they will about the healing process, but scientists will continue on their quest for explanations consistent with their own beliefs.

The fourth objection in the science category has to do with the fact that careers and financial security are at stake. Billions of dollars are regularly pumped into medical research and into equipping hospitals with the latest technologies for diagnosis and treatment. Even if there is substantial merit in the healing power of prayer, there is a great deal of inertia in the medical establishment to overcome before significant resources will be allocated to studying it or to using it in a clinical setting. The instinct for self-preservation is very strong among professional groups, and compelling reasons must exist in order to induce change in the existing social order. Similarly, the multinational pharmaceutical conglomerates that control the entire process from lab research and clinical trials to the production and distribution of drugs are unlikely to give credence, let alone actual support, to something that would place healing resources in the hands of independent individuals.

In the third category, magic, we have put together those objections that appear to us to be, in some ways, the least rational. First among these is the truism that we are all resistant to change. Unfortunately this is very much a throwaway argument that has little explanatory power and serves only to reinforce the perception that scientists' faith in their enterprise is far more tenuous than they might perhaps care to admit. A second objection is that prayer-based healing may be beyond conscious control. If that is the case, then it has the potential to disrupt social order by introducing random and unpredictable elements into medical practice. Magic is used to preserve order and the status quo.

The next three objections in the magic category are similar in that they involve aspects of stigma and witchcraft. The arguments go something like this. If some people have the power to heal through prayer, then we may come to fear those people, lest they somehow turn their power against us. If someone can cure disease, does that person perhaps have the power to cause it? Similarly, if we have the power ourselves, we may come to fear our own ability to restrict the application of those powers to beneficial ends. Could we lose control? Finally, people who possess the power to heal may be seen as odd or unacceptable. As a result they may be shunned by society and subjected to all manner of ridicule, suspicion, and derision.

Notwithstanding all these objections, studies of prayer are breaking boundaries between religion and science and raising questions crucial to our understanding of causation. Dossey reports that several studies have found that prayer can impact nonhuman organisms.[23] Groups of randomly selected individuals have been able to retard or increase the growth of various molds and bacteria. In one instance separate colonies of *E. coli* were influenced to mutate in specific ways. In all of these cases, it is impossible to invoke the placebo effect or to expect that the emerging research program in psychoneuroimmunology will help. There must be something more to prayer than can be explained simply in terms of human physiology.

In spite of several studies that clearly demonstrate the healing power of prayer, the fact that the mechanism through which prayer works to heal is still unknown means, as a therapy, it is relegated by the medical establishment to the realm of magic. In the preface to *Healing Words*, Dossey states: "A body of knowledge that does not fit with prevailing ideas can be ignored as if it does not exist, no matter how scientifically valid it may be."[24] Curiously, even though magical causation is employed positively in trying to explain AIDS, when it comes to prayer, magical causation is used negatively. In other words, it would appear that when magic is used to support science it is okay, but when it is used to support religion it is not. Part of the reason for this contradiction might have to do with the perceived benefits of science and technology. In the absence of thorough explanations, we are willing to accept a certain amount of rhetoric and sleight-of-hand from the scientific establishment because we observe multiple benefits from what it has accomplished to date. However, it appears that we are much less willing than we might have been in the past to extend this same consideration to religion.

Religion and Science

To suggest that HIV does not cause AIDS and that prayer does cause healing threatens the medical establishment and, by extension, the scientific model that is at the core of contemporary society. Opponents would argue that there is no scientific basis to demonstrate that HIV is not the cause of AIDS. Similarly, this same group might argue that there is no scientific basis to support the idea that prayer has therapeutic properties. Both arguments point to a lack of evidence and therefore a lack of knowledge.

In either case, the vast financial support for medical research and what seem like the ever-escalating expenditures on drugs around the world would be threatened. Consequently, we might suggest that to some extent the religion and science debate is about the control of limited resources to support the activities and belief systems of a specific group of people. In the absence of sufficient rational justification for their position, however, group members invoke magic in an effort to discredit the positions of others. In the case of AIDS they argue that alternative hypotheses to the HIV hypothesis are irrational and unscientific. In the case of prayer they argue that no experiment yet devised is capable of demonstrating that the efficacy of prayer is nonspurious.

Even though a recent textbook in medical sociology contains an entire chapter to alternative therapies, nowhere in the entire work does the author mention prayer even once.[25] However, the same text devotes nearly three full pages to AIDS. How is it that AIDS is identified as a socially relevant issue, but the healing power of prayer is not? As already stated, part of the explanation is to be found in the fact that, at present, science has a much higher profile and level of general acceptability than religion. Beyond this, though, religion is often considered to be something personal and private, while science is seen as objective, comprehensive, and universal. People might generally agree that prayer is individual, a matter of personal choice, while AIDS is indiscriminate, infecting people of all races and creeds around the world. It is unfortunate that this line of reasoning is extended to justify the social significance of AIDS, and simultaneously to deny the social context and relevance of prayer. Perhaps one task for the science-religion dialogue would be to establish some balance to such questions.

7 Technology as Magic

As information has been disseminated, the demand for the miraculous, which has been one of the great contributions of science, has increased. To supply this demand for the miraculous has always been a highly remunerative task.

—Harold Innis, *The Bias of Communication*

Human beings are technology from the skin out. Lacking fur and claws and fangs, slow of foot and with dull senses, humans are unimpressive animals. In place of our natural deficiencies we have substituted technology. Since technology is essential to our very survival, it is not too surprising that we spend a lot of time trying to make sense of it.

Throughout history, most human cultures have surrounded technology with myth and ritual. To engage in creation was to participate in (or to encroach upon) the preserve of the gods. Weavers and potters, and especially smiths, were commonly perceived as immersed in the sacred. There was often a strong element of magic associated with the creation of technology. Many crafts included elaborate initiation rites and an occult tradition. Before the modern era, most peoples saw the material world as alive, and they often personified nature as female. Those who would penetrate the mysteries of nature thus had to engage in propitiatory rites, particularly miners and metalworkers, who were often perceived as violating Mother Earth and who had to go through elaborate rituals of purification and sexual cleansing.[1]

As we saw in chapter 5, during the Renaissance, magic was widely accepted and boundaries were not clearly established. To the extent that magic was distinguished from religion and science, it was so by its instrumental character. "Because its aim was some useful accomplishment, not mere knowledge," says historian Bert Hansen, "magic was a practical technology rather than a science."[2] Indeed, what today we would think of as ordinary technology was commonly perceived to be magical. Early clocks, in particular, were often thought to be magical.

Today, boundaries are apparently more clearly defined. The modern world tries to claim that technology is separate from religion and magic. We live in a secularized society. We are realists. Nature for us is dead matter, shaped by the impersonal forces described by science. Myth and ritual, to the extent they have any meaning at all, are matters of individual preference. We leave symbols to the poets and guide policy with fact and reason. Or so we claim.

In October 1999, IBM distributed an eight-page advertising supplement in Canada's two national newspapers—the *Globe and Mail* and the *National Post*—to introduce its new line of Internet servers. The first two pages are pictures showing children gathered around a large black monolith. The text reads: "What if there was a <u>box</u> . . . <u>A magic</u> box." If the modern world is so secular and scientific, why would IBM want to violate accepted boundaries and portray its new machines as magic? No one talks about power saws as magical, yet magic is a persistent trope in our discourse about computers.

This ad provides a useful case study through which we can uncover broader themes in our discourse and explore the place of technology in the science-religion dialogue. As we will see, magic language is spiritually and morally ambiguous. It is an expression of a mythic narrative that is in turn a manifestation both of people's hopes and fears and of their powerlessness. We repeatedly look to technology to save us, or we fear it will destroy us. This is symptomatic of a malaise at the roots of our political order. As a symptom of deeper trends in our society, magic language thus reflects both the breaking down of the boundaries drawn centuries ago and a legitimation crisis in advanced industrial society. The spiritual and practical dilemmas thus created require ethical insight on the part of the science-religion dialogue.

Advertising Magic

The IBM ad has very strong visual images. Four and three-quarters pages out of eight are photographs, all with a multicultural and international theme. Four of seven photos portray children. Should anyone miss the implication of the pictures, the captions emphasize "the magic box brings people together" in the global village. Most portray the box as a large black monolith suggestive of the film *2001*, an image not likely to be lost on boomer-age decision makers. The picture on the final page is a little different. It shows an "African" girl pulling a small black box in her red wagon down a dusty road through desert scrub (although the Joshua trees in the background betray the locale as southern

California). The parting image seems to say, "you too can take a magic box home." In addition to the photos, there are two childlike cartoon drawings reiterating the globalization theme and five line drawings of IBM equipment.

The text is just as striking. The font on the third page (the first full page of text) and in the picture captions and transitions imitates a child's printing. The taglines on pages 3, 7, and 8 are in an "adult" cursive. The rest of the text is in normal fonts, but much of it uses very short, simple declarative sentences. The cursive text is especially interesting. On page 7 is the reassuringly parental "The magic box is always there for you," while at the very bottom of pages 3 and 8 is the adult declarative, "The magic box is an IBM [trademark] business server."

Of most interest for this study, however, are the frequent and repeated references to magic. The word *magic* is used forty-two times in eight pages. The sociologist of religion Joachim Wach defined magic as a "means to force the numen to grant what is desired."[3] Its power is ours to use but not to understand. IBM agrees on page 4. Servers are "so complex that only a handful of wizards understand their inner workings. Yet so effortless to use that hundreds of millions of people use them everyday."[4] The company engages in divination: "Servers are the most important tools of the next century. Servers will hold virtually all of our intellectual capital." Even more, what the box itself does is magical. It is described (in childish print) as:

> A box that contained all the answers to all the questions you've ever had. A box that contained every invention and every idea you've ever wondered about. A box that could help doctors figure out how to cure diseases. A box that could help leaders of industry deliver products faster. Help professors produce better books. Astronomers find new galaxies. Well there is such a box. A magic box.

The new machines are the philosopher's stone.[5]

This childish, fairy tale–like text clashes oddly with the technobabble and what propagandists call scientific slant in the fine-print portions of the ad. For example, one inset paragraph declares: "An IBM RS/6000 SP UNIX server is capable of 3.88 TRILLION calculations per second." That certainly sounds impressive, but without any basis for comparison with rival machines, how is the reader to know if that speed is good, bad, or indifferent? There is also an element of science fiction when IBM boasts that its processors were on the Mars Pathfinder mission: "Only an IBM server has reliability proven on two planets." At one point, IBM even intimates that its machines are alive: "That's why reliability, scalability, accessibility, and security aren't just selling points—they're part of the DNA of every server IBM makes." This is language used for effect, rather than communication.

A lot of themes are packed into this one ad. Globalization is presented as an incontrovertible reality. The world is shown as a place for children and for happy cooperation between nations, races, and cultures. The future is determined, and IBM is able to foretell what it is. Technology is magic, and engineers are wizards. IBM's new machines are magic boxes that, like the philosopher's stone, have enormous transformative power and, like the black monoliths of *2001*, can raise consciousness. And the readers (and potential users of the technology) are spoken to as if they were children, as the corporation appropriates to itself the role of wise and reassuring parent.

Explaining Magic

The question remains, why would IBM want to portray its new machines as magic? The ad is obviously hype and hyperbole, but we should not let that obscure the question. The corporation is spending a great deal of money on the ad campaign, and undoubtedly hiring the best talent available. We can be sure that nothing is there by accident. Any words and images used would be deemed plausible and effective. So why would IBM think that magic language would work? Why would it want to transgress well-established and usually strongly defended boundaries? Since anyone in a position to buy a server is likely to have postsecondary education, one would reasonably expect that magic language would alienate rather than entice potential buyers to buy— although the "let's pretend" air of the ad's beginning ("What if there was a box") and the scientific slant of the fine print may take the edge off for some scientifically oriented readers. Now, obviously, an ad designed for mass circulation is aimed at the general public and therefore has a larger agenda than just selling machines, but even so, why do the hype and hyperbole not just appear ridiculous?

There are several possible explanations. First, magic language has long been associated with new technology. As Arthur C. Clarke said in his famous third law: "Any sufficiently advanced technology is indistinguishable from magic."[6] Clarke was not making a new observation. At the beginning of the seventeenth century, Tommaso Campanella recorded:

> Everything done by skilled men in imitating nature or helping it by unknown art is called magical work, not only by the vulgar crowds but by all men in general. . . . Since the art was not understood, all this was called magic. Later, all this became ordinary knowledge. The invention of gunpowder . . . and of print-

ing and the use of the lodestone were magical. But today they are common knowledge. The reverence for making clocks and for other mechanical arts is lost, for their methods have become obvious to everybody.[7]

The introduction of new technology, like any other form of social change, is potentially threatening to many people.[8] Many ask themselves, what do these changes mean and how will they affect me? However, conventional machines with which people are familiar and comfortable are not discussed in magical terms. Computers may be magical; toasters are not. However, while there has been an enormous increase in the size of the Internet in the past few years, we are not dealing with a particularly new technology here. Personal computers have been on the market since 1977, the Internet was begun in 1985 (and its predecessor, ARPANET, goes back to 1969), and Web browsers have been available since 1993, so why use magic language now (especially since servers are rather mundane pieces of equipment that few users will ever see)? Thus technological change may be a factor in this case, but it is not a sufficient explanation.

A second possible explanation may lie in the economic context of the ad. In part it can be seen as an attempt to tap the speculative frenzy on the stock markets in 1999 for "dot.com" companies. In a delirium that can be compared only to the Dutch tulip mania of the seventeenth century, IPOs (initial public offerings) and corporations that had never earned a nickel of profit saw their stock prices rise by hundreds of percent.[9] IBM obviously stood to benefit if the bubble continued. As the ad claims on page 4: "Servers are where virtually all transactions will take place. E-business is transforming the worlds of commerce, manufacturing, finance, education, aerospace, retailing—the whole world. And without servers there can be no e-business." The aura of magic is here combined with a bandwagon appeal—you do not want to be left behind. This is magic language as mystification. Asserting that all these claims about the future and e-business are magical means that they do not therefore require empirical justification. Proof is not needed. Actual performance, or even some black ink on the bottom line, is unnecessary. In effect, IBM is saying that the future is determined, IBM has divined it, and you should accept it on blind faith. Yet while this is certainly part of the explanation, it still is not sufficient. The ad does not appeal directly to the stock market frenzy, and, even if it did, that would just push the question back one level. Market bubbles can be exploited without recourse to magic language. Even taking this ideological use of magic into account, there is a surplus of meaning. If the ad did not tap into a deeper, mythic understanding of computers, the hype and magic language would lack plausibility and would just appear ridiculous.

A third explanation may be that the ad retains its plausibility because it is grounded in ancient myths. If we read the ad closely, we find a mythic narrative hidden between the lines that is surprisingly similar to the quests of the Renaissance magi. It goes something like this. The magic box will give you omniscience, a godlike knowledge, and with it prescience, the ability to know the future. With this unlimited knowledge will come unlimited power. This is progress.

Let us analyze each part of the myth. The magic box will give you omniscience, says the ad on page 3. It contains "all the answers to all the questions you've ever had" and "every invention and every idea you've ever wondered about." It will help doctors heal, professors produce better books, and astronomers find new galaxies. This is godlike knowledge. The ad recalls some of the deepest myths of Western civilization which, like that of Prometheus, express the yearning of humans to be like gods. Recall, in particular, the myth of the Fall. As recounted in the third chapter of Genesis, the serpent tempts the woman to eat forbidden fruit, promising that "your eyes will be opened and you will be like gods." She and the man eat, gain the knowledge of good and evil, and as a consequence are cursed and expelled from Eden. The longing to return to Eden, to regain the lost earthly paradise and be like gods, has been one of our civilization's most persistent wishes and lies behind countless messianic and apocalyptic hopes.[10] This ad implies that, as magic, technology can reverse the Fall and recover Eden.

With omniscience comes prescience, the ability to know the future. The future tense is prominent in the text of the ad and, as we have already seen, IBM believes that the future is determined and that IBM has divined it. Again, this resonates with long traditions in Western culture. For thousands of years people have paid astrologers, soothsayers, psychics, and futurologists to predict what will happen. This quest to know the future goes beyond mere curiosity. To know the future is to be able to change it, and prediction has always been intimately linked with control.

One hundred seventy years ago, Auguste Comte founded the discipline of sociology upon the slogan "Knowledge for prediction, prediction for power." But Comte was merely echoing the ideas of Francis Bacon from two hundred years before. Bacon's slogan, "Knowledge is power," set the agenda for the new natural sciences, but he in turn was only elaborating a theme from the Renaissance alchemists and magi. That knowledge is power is the great Faustian theme of modern civilization. It is also a central theme of the magic-box ad. "E-Business changes everything. Absolutely everything," says IBM on page 7. The omniscience and prescience delivered by the magic box will allow its users to transform the world.

All of this is progress. While the ad is more oriented to profits than prophecy, progress lies just beneath its surface. The magic box will do all sorts of remarkable things to make life better, says the ad on page 5; it "can help you close a hole in the ozone layer, find a lost friend, or sell 50 shares of stock."[11] This kind of language continues a long tradition. As the Canadian philosopher George Grant observed: "What makes the drive to technology so strong is that it is carried on by men who still identify what they are doing with the liberation of mankind."[12] For the early scientists, and even more for the Enlightenment, science and technology were the means by which humans would be freed from want and suffering and fate. The growth of scientific knowledge was seen as irreversible and cumulative and was equated with the growth of freedom. Technology was the means by which utopia would be achieved.

So it is as mythic narrative that we can begin to see why magic language remains salient at the beginning of the twenty-first century. To understand the magic in this ad, we have to go beyond its appeal to greed and self-interest, although that is there. We have to go beyond its appeal to the fear and excitement of novelty and change, although that is there too. The magic language of this ad, like so much of our discourse about technology, spins the web where technology and religion meet.

Interpreting Magic

To recount this myth is not yet to understand it, however. This myth, like all symbolic narratives, needs to be interpreted. Here we run into a paradox. We do not live in the Renaissance anymore, and we cannot pretend that the past five hundred years have not happened. The symbols of alchemists and magi ring false when spoken by advertisers for the largest computer company in the world. The ad may have expropriated some of the deepest myths of Western civilization, but in doing so it twists them out of their mythic matrix and turns them into a vehicle to sell—sell machines and sell ideas. Magic means something profoundly different at the beginning of the twenty-first century than it did at the conclusion of the fifteenth.

In order to resolve this paradox we will need what Paul Ricoeur calls a double hermeneutic. Interpretation must first be an exercise in suspicion in order to strip away ideology. We have to uncover all the falsehoods, all the deceptions and self-deceptions, that obscure the truth. But removing the masks is only the first step. The second is the recovery of meaning. Once we have removed the idols, we still have to listen to the symbols. As Ricoeur reflects: "Hermeneutics seems to me to be animated by this double motivation: willingness to suspect, willingness to listen; vow of rigor, vow of obedience. In our time we have not finished doing away with *idols* and we have barely begun to listen to symbols." The circle of interpretation never stops. As Ricoeur concludes: "'Symbols give rise to thought,' but they are also the birth of idols. That is why the critique of idols remains the condition of the conquest of symbols." [13]

Magic as Deception

So, as an exercise in suspicion, the first level of interpretation is the narrative as bad faith and mystification. This is myth in its popular meaning of a story that is not true. This is an advertisement, after all. Its aim is to persuade, by any means necessary. We have already mentioned some of the propaganda tricks used in the ad, such as scientific slant and bandwagon appeal. Every part of the mythic narrative illustrates bad faith.

First, the ad promises that the Internet will deliver "all the answers to all the questions you've ever had." The reality, of course, is rather different. The Internet may provide enormous amounts of information, but serious questions have been raised as to how much of it is reliable. Eva Allen, John Burke, Mark Welch, and Loren Rieseberg report in the British science journal *Nature* that the quality of scientific information at the majority of sites studied was poor. In their study they searched the Web and took the first five hundred sites dealing with evolution (EV), genetically modified organisms (GMO), and endangered species (ES). A pair of referees then evaluated the sites for accuracy. They conclude:

> For EV, only 12% (59 of 500) of the web sites examined were considered informative by both referees. For GMO and ES, 46% (64 of 140) and 28% (55 of 200) of sites, respectively, were considered informative. Of informative sites, the proportion that were judged inaccurate ranged from 10% for GMO sites to 34% for EV. . . . Likewise, the proportion of informative sites scored as misleading ranged from 20% for ES to 35% for EV. [14]

So when only 12 percent of sampled Web sites on evolution can be considered informative at all, and 69 percent of those are inaccurate or misleading, the Web as a source of information has to be called into question. The problem is that anyone can put anything on a Web page, and so the Web is crowded with opinion, ideology, and propaganda. Since the Web is not peer reviewed, the individual reader has little way of determining whether the "facts" being presented are reliable or not. The result is that valid science is swamped in a sea of misinformation and distortion. Omniscience, indeed!

If claims to omniscience falter over the question of quality and reliability, those of prescience and power succumb to an internal paradox. The ability to know the future has had an ambiguous history. To the ancient Hebrews, a prophet was one who could read the signs of the times and proclaim the Word of God. Prophets were not fortunetellers. For the Greeks, the ability to see the future was a gift—or curse—from the gods. Recall the story of Cassandra, who was fated never to have her predictions believed. The meaning of prophecy and prediction changed with the coming of the scientific worldview, however. The "clockwork universe" of many Enlightenment philosophers and scientists was a mechanical and completely determined system. In principle, if one had enough knowledge, one could accurately predict what would happen at any time in the future, just as one can predict the motions of a machine. This view lies behind the language of prediction and control used by Comte. The language of the ad is that of technological determinism, the belief that technology is the "motor force" in society. The reason IBM can make such confident predictions of what the Web will do in the future is that the company believes that technology determines what that future will be. But here the paradox enters in. The whole point of knowing the future is to be able to change it. But if the future is determined, there is nothing we can do about it. We are as helpless as Cassandra. The aim of prescience is empowerment; the result is powerlessness.

This paradox is inherent in the nature of prediction. Accurate prediction requires an unvarying mechanical structure, which is why astronomers can predict eclipses hundreds of years in advance. But empowerment is built upon agency, the ability of people to make real decisions and influence the direction of their lives, which makes for an indeterminate future. Natural scientists may indeed be able to make predictions about those aspects of nature that form a mechanical system, but it has been one of the great illusions of the social sciences to try to imitate them. Neither the moon nor molecules have agency; people do. But the only agency left to us by the language of the ad is to buy the technology offered to us and to accept passively whatever the machines determine.

Nor is progress into a utopian future likely. All the loose talk about the so-called new economy proved to be premature. For example, the number of people employed in the computer sector remains tiny. According to economist Jim Stanford, for example, in Canada, less than 2 percent of workers are employed in the production of electrical and electronic products and in the computer services industry combined.[15] Neither are the jobs in this sector much like the hype. As Clifford Stoll says: "Internet employment is cyclical, insecure, and often unrewarding. Today's digital sweatshop is a cubicle, with tight deadlines and often no promise of work beyond the end of the month. Rather than employees, businesses hire consultants and contractors—they do not get benefits and are easier to lay off."[16] While the media touts images of well-to-do programmers, most of the employees of even relatively successful e-businesses are nonunion, low-paid warehouse workers. And after the market crash, many of those much-hyped "dot.com" companies no longer exist.

All this reveals the bad faith of the ad. The magic language is not simply false, it is an attempt to deceive. It is unlikely the ad writers "really believe" in magic, but if enough people can be persuaded to act because of it, their vision will become a self-fulfilling prophecy (and the corporation will grow rich).

This exercise of suspicion, to see the myth and magic of the ad as a con game, is only the first step of a double hermeneutic, however. As cynical as the motives behind it may be, framing computer technology as magic nevertheless speaks to some felt need in many people. As Margaret Wertheim says: "People will only adopt a technology if it resonates with a perceived need. For a technology to be successful, a latent desire must be there to be satisfied. The sheer scale of interest in cyberspace suggests there is not only an intense desire at work here, but also a profound psychosocial vacuum that many people are hoping the Internet might fill."[17] To talk of technology in terms of myth and magic has a persistent appeal for people. Magic is a symptom of deeper trends in society. Magic today is simultaneously an expression of people's hopes and fears and an expression of powerlessness.

Magic as Utopia and Apocalypse

To frame technology as magic is to mine people's latent hopes and fears. A persistent theme in discourse about technology since early modern times is that it will alternately save us or destroy us. From Francis Bacon to the present, science and technology have been seen as key to the perfect society. These utopian expectations express ancient dreams and desires (or fears) that have never been very far away from religion.

The IBM ad is only the latest in a long tradition of visions that prophesy that technology will reverse the Fall and allow us to be as gods. Describing the appearance of utopias such as that envisioned in Bacon's *New Atlantis*, Margaret Wertheim observed: "With these utopian visions we witness the emergence of the idea that man, through his *own efforts*, can create a New Jerusalem here on earth. . . . Technology would thus become a medium for *salvation*. Again and again in the age of science, technology has been viewed as a salvific force, a key to a better, brighter, more just world."[18] Today's cyberutopians continue the tradition. For example, futurologist Frank Ogden believes that by 2035 "there will be new scientific, and harmless, means to deliver physically improved future citizens into a progressive society. We are at the dawn of the age that will find us creating our own successors." Ray Kurzweil, a distinguished computer scientist, goes even further. According to him, the exponential growth in computer capacity means that by 2060 we will be able to download our personalities into computers, extend our abilities a millionfold, give ourselves ready access to all human knowledge, and never die. Others take us even closer to godhood. "The final goal of Computopia is the rebirth of theological synergism of man and the supreme being," said Japanese futurologist Yoneji Masuda. "It aims to build an earthly, not a heavenly, synergistic society of god and man."[19]

The other side of all this optimism is apocalyptic fear. Every hope that technology is leading us to New Jerusalem is matched by the dread that it is building hell on earth, or worse. One of the deepest fears at the beginning of the twenty-first century is that technology is out of control, that our tools will turn against us. A much-discussed essay in *Wired* by Bill Joy, the founder of Sun Microsystems, is a good example. "The 21st-century technologies—genetics, nanotechnology, and robotics (GNR)—are so powerful that they can spawn whole new classes of accidents and abuses. . . . I think it is no exaggeration to say we are on the cusp of extreme evil, an evil whose possibility spreads well beyond that which weapons of mass destruction bequeathed to the nation-states, on to a surprising and terrible empowerment of extreme individuals."[20] Unlike nuclear weapons, which required enormous resources to develop, GNR technology will be widely available to corporations or individuals. Joy fears that terrorists or an accident could unleash a genetically engineered "white plague" or nanotechnology "gray goo" that would annihilate our species. Or perhaps we will be exterminated by our robots. This may have seemed like science fiction when Joy wrote it, but the unhappy events since 11 September 2001 have made the dangers of GNR technology all too real.

It would be easy to be cynical and dismiss all of this. Technology has been imbued with quixotic expectations for a long time. In the 1860s some said the Atlantic cable would put an end to war by putting an end to misunderstanding.[21] In 1890 the telephone was seen as a tool of democracy, allowing Americans to call the president directly. The radio, it was asserted in the 1920s, would enable us to go to work without ever leaving home (a prophecy recycled for personal computers and then again for the Internet). In the 1950s atomic energy would make electricity too cheap to meter, while television was hailed as the redemption of education. Now, when one's operating system crashes every day, one may perhaps be excused for thinking cyberfantasies of godhood are a bit premature. But cynicism would miss something deeper at work.

Utopias are expressions of deep wishes, what Wertheim calls "latent desire" or the German philosopher Ernst Bloch called "anticipatory consciousness."[22] What do people wish for? People want to be warm and well fed. They want to be safe and healthy and happy. They want to be comfortable. And when they have all this, they do not want it to end—they do not want to die. Our ancient myths express these wishes. They are full of striving for more, for fulfillment, for transcendence. As we retell these stories—now in secular form and under the guise of science—we too strive for more, to go beyond the limits. With Prometheus, we will steal fire from the gods. With Adam and Eve, we will eat the forbidden fruit of knowledge. With Faust, we will gain unlimited knowledge and power. Today's cyberutopias are the linear descendents of these myths. But, as in the myths, when we exceed the limits, we fear we will be punished. Prometheus was chained to a rock. Adam and Eve were expelled from Eden. Faust bought knowledge and power at the price of his soul. The other side of the coin of utopian hope is apocalyptic fear. We have transgressed and fear Judgment Day, the wrath to come. Ray Kurzweil speaks to latent desire, Bill Joy to latent fear, but both their visions spring from the same source.

Magic as Powerlessness

Magic is all about power. Through our machines we command the transformative power of the numinous, or at least we appear to. Yet underlying all these hopes and fears is a pervasive sense of powerlessness, what Wertheim calls a "profound psychosocial vacuum." "Magic," says Brazilian theologian Rubem Alves, "is a flower that grows only in impotence."[23]

Perhaps it is ironic that the more technological our society has become, the more "technologically illiterate" the majority of people are. In advanced industrial society our life has become increasingly segmented through the division of labor and the separation of the spheres of work and home. Today we use many complex machines, but most people have very low levels of inclusion in most technologies.[24] Most people are consumers rather than producers of technology. Technology is constructed by others and presented to most of us as an accomplished fact. Today, few see technology built, few know what makes it work, and even repair is often a matter of replacing one "black box" with another. Technology has taken on aspects of nature, an independent force, powerful but mysterious. Technology itself has become more important as display, becoming a commodity, a status symbol, an object of conspicuous consumption.[25] The lower our levels of inclusion, the more technology seems a magical black box and the more wizardlike seem those few who do have high levels of inclusion.

We can see this particularly clearly in the child-adult theme in the ad. As we have seen, the ad speaks to us as if we are children. And in the face of the giant technocratic structures that rule our world, most of us as individuals are indeed as powerless and dependent as children are. Because most of us have low levels of inclusion, as users and consumers of technology we are presented with a take-it-or-leave-it option, and we are constantly told that if we do not "take it" we will be left behind. In an existential situation of powerlessness, the ad appeals to fantasies of knowledge and power. But it does so as fantasy—as magic. At the same time the ad tries to sell us the fantasy of power, it asserts the real power and authority of the corporation. IBM puts itself in the role of parent—wise, powerful, competent, comforting, who assures you on page 7 that it is "always there for you." Magic is thus both an expression of dependence and an ideology for dependence.[26] The most we can do—like the children in one of the pictures in the ad—is dance around the box in a circle.

This is reflective of the declining role of the citizen in postdemocratic society. To those Enlightenment thinkers who made the American and French revolutions, citizenship was the keystone of a free society. Citizens were free individuals who participated in their political institutions and took moral responsibility for the good of society (what was often called republican virtue). For Thomas Jefferson, economic independence was a prerequisite for citizenship. "Dependence," he said, "begets subservience and venality, suffocates the germ of virtue, and prepares fit tools for the designs of ambition."[27] Today, economic independence is a remote dream for the vast majority of people. The ad celebrates globalization as cooperation and multiculturalism, but it omits something. There are no citizens in global society, only consumers. In such a society, the Canadian philosopher John Ralston Saul says, "the citizen is reduced to the status of a subject at the foot of the throne of the marketplace."[28] Freedom has been reduced to the ability to make choices between commodities (be they things, services, or ideas) offered to us by others. Participation in civic institutions, the hallmark of the citizen, has declined sharply across North America over the past thirty years.[29] The widely discussed decline of voter turnout in both the United States and Canada is only the most visible symptom. We may have a high standard of living, our technology is unsurpassed, but most of us are as powerless before the marketplace as our ancestors were before some king.

Magic language is thus a symptom of a legitimation crisis in advanced industrial society. The fact that technology would be advertised as a magical black box already means that most of us are dependent. On the other hand, those with high levels of inclusion are elevated to the status of wizards. As the division of labor, and with it the information explosion, continue to intensify, there is more and more knowledge that we not only cannot master but for which we must trust some "expert."[30] Science slowly comes to be seen (by the general public at least) as based less and less upon reason and more and more upon authority. When scientists and engineers become priests and wizards whose pronouncements cannot be understood by the public and, implicitly, should not be challenged, rational debate is closed off.

Magic, Spirituality, and Ethics

What can all this tell us about the relationship between science and religion? Magic language is both spiritually and morally ambiguous. It seems to us that there are two dimensions to the question, the spiritual and the practical. Ethics, and thus the need for evaluation, infuses both.

Magic language is spiritually ambiguous. On the one hand, magic is an expression of hope. As we have seen, it arises out of our deepest longings as human beings. On the other hand, it is an expression of powerlessness. What makes this discussion so disturbing is that it is some of our most advanced technology that is being discussed as magic. It is one thing to find magic language in Romantic literature or New Age spirituality, and quite another to find it in advertisements for computers. Or maybe it is not.

Margaret Wertheim argues that the monistic naturalism of the scientific worldview closed off any space for the spirit as was found in traditional Western dualistic views of the world. Cyberspace reopens that possibility.

> This projection of essentially religious dreams onto cyberspace is not . . . particularly surprising. As a new immaterial space, cyberspace makes an almost irresistible target for such longings. From both our Greek and our Judeo-Christian heritage Western culture has within it a deep current of dualism that has *always* associated immateriality with spirituality. . . . It was perhaps inevitable that the appearance of a new immaterial space would precipitate a flood of techno-spiritual dreaming. That this site of religious expectation is being realized through the by-products of science—the force that so effectively annihilated the soul-space of the medieval world picture—is surely one of the greater ironies of our times.[31]

What the networking of computers has done is create new possibilities for otherwise secular people to express their spiritual longing. In that this may allow people to find meaning in their lives, it is all to the good. Anything that helps counteract the alienation and anomie of advanced industrial society may be of some benefit. But it raises two additional questions.

First, what kind of spiritual experience are people having? As the elaborate demonologies of our Renaissance forebears testify, to be spiritual is not necessarily to be good. The Renaissance magi, as we saw in chapter 5, envisioned a holistic magic that would unite the material and spiritual and in so doing transcend both. What do today's magi envision? Getting rich. Gaining power over others. Fantasies of sex and violence. In other words, their "spiritual" visions are of more of the same. In cyberspace we find spirituality without transcendence. "The cybersoul," Wertheim says, "has no moral context."[32] It is an expression of the ego without either a vision of the good or a sense of obligation to others. What makes people like Ray Kurzweil frightening is not that they are likely to achieve their dreams of immortality but that their dreams are so shallow.

Second, is cyberspirtuality becoming a new "opium of the people"? Bill Joy writes that, at first comforted by technological visions, "I didn't feel pressed to solve so many problems in the present." If technology was going to bring utopia in the future, "I might as well enjoy life more in the here and now."[33] So when the magic box promises to close the hole in the ozone layer, the rest of us are absolved of responsibility or the need to change our lifestyle. If magic is both an expression of dependence and an ideology for dependence, then one of the effects of cyberspirituality would be passivity. A number of studies have shown that as the amount of time spent on-line increases, interaction with flesh-and-blood people drops dramatically.[34] It seems the more we dream of a magical future, the less likely we are to actively participate in building the real one.

The second dimension is the question of practice. But here is much less ambiguity. There are clear dangers in treating technology as if it were magic. Propaganda like the IBM ad is aimed at shaping public opinion and influencing policy makers, and the combined industry and media hype has had its effect. Policy is habitually made on the basis of the grandiloquent visions of those who have something to gain. As a consequence, we stumble from one expensive boondoggle to the next. There are countless examples of a technical fix gone awry, from claims that atomic energy would make electricity too cheap to meter to computers fixing all the problems in our schools. Or, alternatively, policy is based on apocalyptic fears and resources are wasted on worthless crash programs. The billions of dollars spent on the Y2K hoax is a good example. In neither case is there any realistic assessment of the limits of the technology.

One of the things the science-religion dialogue can contribute to our practice of technology is to restore some perspective and balance to public debate. When we trace the web of reality and find all the interconnections, we are much less likely to become transfixed by any one thread.

All of us are called upon for greater discernment. As Ronald Cole-Turner says: "Informed criticism . . . is only the first step. By itself, such criticism only serves to warn us of technology's pretensions and risks. It does not guide us in the right use of technology, much less offer us a framework of meaning out of which the future course of technology can be anticipated and guided. So a theology of technology must include an assessment of the theological appropriateness of technology."[35] One of the most important tasks the science-religion dialogue can undertake is to criticize the idols and build ethics into our practice.

PART IV

Theodicy

8

The Moral of the Dinosaur

To some people, the idea that extinction is ultimately good is so self-evident that it does not need testing: more fit species can be distinguished from the less fit by the mere fact of their survival. The disturbing reality is that for none of the thousands of well-documented extinctions in the geologic past do we have a solid explanation of why the extinction occurred. . . . Sadly, the only evidence for the inferiority of victims of extinction is the fact of their extinction—a circular argument.

—David Raup, *Extinction*

One of the great blessings of our species is consciousness—we are self-aware. One of the great curses of our species is our awareness of death. The reality every individual on Earth must face is our own death. Consequently death is one of the central issues in every theology of every religion.

Death is the foremost of a class of occurrences the anthropologist Clifford Geertz calls "limit situations."[1] These are events that lack not simply meaning but interpretability, that is, there is not only no answer but also no way of getting an answer. Death, suffering, and intractable moral paradox all have the potential to destroy meaning, not just for an individual but for a society as a whole. As a consequence, every religion has developed means of coping with limit situations, what theologians call *theodicy*. Theodicy is the provisional answer religion offers in a situation that is intrinsically meaningless. Weber saw it as one characteristic of all religions. In the face of death and suffering and evil, religion tells us of sin and punishment, of karma, of resurrection or heaven or reincarnation, of the Fall and of redemption. Theodicy reduces the terror of limit situations, enables individuals to cope, and helps society avoid the potential threats of chaos.

If individual death is a central theological (not to mention existential) problem, what do we do with death on a mass scale? One of the more dubious achievements of the twentieth century is that it raised the issue of mass death. Caught in the carnage of the trenches in 1917, the poet Wilfred Owen wrote: "What passing bells for these who die as cattle?"[2] One of the greatest horrors of the twentieth century is that we coined the word *genocide*—and that we needed to. But even genocide pales (intellectually if not morally) beside the question of extinction. Machine guns and poison gas made mass death a social reality. With the coming of the atom bomb, humanity for the first time became self-aware of extinction.

Extinction has been an intellectual problem for only two hundred years. For the ancient Greeks the doctrine of plenitude, or fullness of the natural world, meant that extinction was not possible.[3] The Bible proclaims that the creation was good and relates how Noah saved a breeding pair of every animal so that none would be wiped out by the flood. The Church consequently believed that God would not take back what had been given, and therefore the idea of extinction was blasphemous. Fossils were not fully understood as the remains of long dead animals and plants until the eighteenth century. It was Georges Cuvier, the founder of paleontology, who in 1796 first proved that many fossils represent organisms that no longer exist anywhere. The discovery of extinction began an intellectual controversy in Europe that was pivotal to the rise of modern geology and the theory of evolution in the nineteenth century. In the past twenty years the discovery that on a number of occasions in Earth history there have been sudden mass extinctions in which most forms of life were wiped out has forced scientists to rethink those nineteenth-century solutions and question some of the central ideas of geology and evolution.

Mass extinction also raises important theological issues, although few in the science-religion dialogue have addressed them. One of the assumptions of many in the debate is that evidence of God's revelation can be found in the "book of nature" as well as the "book of Scripture." It is common in the science-religion dialogue to look to cosmology and evolutionary theory to find evidences of God's design (as in the various forms of the anthropic principle, for instance). A question that is not often debated, however, is what kind of God is revealed through the "book of nature." Many scientists (and others) are motivated by the beauty, awe, and mystery of nature, but nature just as frequently presents another face.

In this chapter, we look at the controversy surrounding the discovery that sixty-five million years ago a comet or asteroid struck the Earth, exterminating the dinosaurs and 70 percent of all other species on the planet. This controversy makes a particularly good case study for several reasons. First, a sociological analysis of the controversy reveals the working of scientific practice. The more we understand about how scientists work, the richer our dialogue can become. Second, the history of the controversy reveals some of the implicitly religious ideas embedded in scientific theory. And third, the content of the discovery itself both challenges many assumptions in the science-religion dialogue and raises in a particularly strong form the question of theodicy.

Extinction and Theodicy

Georges Cuvier had a problem. What was the meaning of the fossil elephants being dug up across northern Europe and Asia, which the Siberians called mammoths? In his first scientific paper in 1796, Cuvier proved that not only were African and Indian elephants distinct species, but that mammoths differed from either.[4] By 1800 he had identified the fossils of twenty-three species that no longer existed anywhere. Over the next few years he determined that the world was "thousands of centuries" old, that there was a time when reptiles dominated the Earth before mammals appeared, and that none of these ancient animals were still alive. But what could have caused all of these extinctions? As he studied the layers of rock (called strata) in the Paris basin, he found that each was characterized by a different assemblage of fossils. Terrestrial and marine environments lay right on top of each other, fresh-water and saltwater deposits alternated. By 1812 he concluded that the only way to explain these dramatic alternations in the rocks was through a series of "revolutions" or catastrophes. The sea had from time to time flooded in, drowning all life in the area. Later the water would retreat, and the land would be repopulated.

A product of the Enlightenment, Cuvier was a careful empirical observer who throughout his career was sharply critical of speculative theories not grounded in the facts (which is why he opposed the evolutionary speculations of Jean-Baptiste Lamarck). Unfortunately, some of his followers were not so careful, particularly in England, where a very bad translation of his *Discours préliminaire* appeared in which the most recent catastrophe was identified with the biblical flood.[5] This did not sit well with one group of English geologists, the followers of James Hutton, who in 1788 had expounded the principle that in geology "the present is the key to the past." The attack on Cuvier was led by an English lawyer named Charles Lyell, who published the first volume of the *Principles of Geology* in 1830.

Lyell advocated what came to be known as *uniformitarianism* (the term was actually coined by William Whewell in a review of Lyell's book). There are two aspects to uniformitarianism, which, as Stephen Jay Gould has pointed out, Lyell conflated.[6] The first aspect, what Europeans call *actualism* ("actual causes"), is methodological. This is the principle that there is uniformity in the laws and the processes at work in nature. This kind of uniformity is assumed by scientific methodology. In other words, if a natural process is discovered today, it is assumed to have existed in the past and will continue to exist in the future. The second aspect is a substantive claim that nature works only through those geological forces observable today—the slow, gradual processes of erosion, sedimentation, and volcanism. Extinctions, which had so bothered Cuvier, became a non-problem. Over the vast stretches of geologic time, individual species would come and go. What appeared to be catastrophic breaks between geologic eras Lyell explained away as "gaps in the fossil record" (which, as David Raup comments, is a classic case of allowing theory to determine what is fact).[7] By conflating these two aspects of his theory, however, Lyell was able to make his approach seem the only way to be scientific, and uniformitarianism became orthodoxy in the earth sciences.

Charles Darwin took the *Principles of Geology* with him on *HMS Beagle* and quickly became an enthusiastic convert. Darwin grounded his theory of evolution firmly upon uniformitarian principles. For Darwin, extinction was not much more of a problem than it was for Lyell. It was a slow, gradual process as an individual species lost out in the "battle for life." He dismissed the appearance of sudden mass extinctions in the fossil record as illusory: "With respect to the apparently sudden extermination of whole families of orders, as of Trilobites at the close of the palæozoic period and of Ammonites at the close of the secondary period, we must remember . . . the probable wide intervals of time between our consecutive formations; and in these intervals there may have been much slow extermination." Natural selection meant the survival of the fittest, and if a species died out, it was because it lost in competition with those that were more fit. He continued: "New species become superior to their predecessors for they have to beat in the struggle for life all the older forms, with which they come into close competition. . . . So that by this fundamental test of victory in the battle for life, as well as by the standard of the specialization of organs, modern forms ought, on the theory of natural selection, to stand higher than ancient forms."[8] Because life was a constant struggle for existence, each generation of survivors would be superior to those that came before. Thus evolution was a record of progress.

Implicit in the idea of evolution as progress was a theodicy. In the eighteenth and early nineteenth centuries, natural theologians such as William Paley had argued that nature provided proof of God. The fitness of organisms (wings are perfect for flying, the complexity of the eye, etc.) was evidence for design, and design required a designer. Darwin knew this theology but rejected it, in large part because he saw nature as far less benign, as he expressed in 1856: "What a book a devil's chaplain might write on the clumsy, wasteful, blundering, low, and horribly cruel works of nature!"[9] But might not all the suffering entailed in natural selection be justified by the end result? As Darwin concluded:

"Thus from the war of nature, from famine and death, the most exalted object that we are capable of conceiving, namely, the production of the higher animals, directly follows."[10] The problem with this, as David Raup says, is that "if we accept that turnover in species is merely nature's way, just as nature has given humans a limited life span, then there is nothing in species extinction worthy of wonder."[11] And if the end of the process is us, well, who are we to complain if the dinosaurs had to die?

In Darwin, this theodicy remained implicit, but those who came later would develop it.[12] Incidental suffering or death did not matter if, on the whole, life became stronger for it. Darwin lived in an age of brutal capitalism and imperial conquest, and people (the ruling classes, at least) were quite prepared to see the sacrifice of the "unfit" as necessary for the greater good. In the words of the U.S. industrialist Andrew Carnegie: "The law of competition, be it benign or not, is here; we cannot evade it; no substitutes for it have been found; and while the law may be sometimes hard for the individual, it is best for the race, because it ensures the survival of the fittest in every department."[13] Social Darwinism— and its religious counterpart, the gospel of wealth—made the theory of evolution into an apology for war, class exploitation, racism, and patriarchy.

Among earth scientists, the combined authority of uniformitarianism and evolution-as-progress bestowed an ethos of conservatism. Even ideas that did not threaten the principle of uniformitarianism, such as continental glaciation (ice ages) and continental drift (today called plate tectonics) took decades to become widely accepted. Extinction remained a nonissue, which the modern synthesis between Darwinism and genetics did nothing to change.[14] Dinosaurs were seen as huge, sluggish, stupid, swamp-loving reptiles that could not compete. There were numerous fanciful speculations on the reasons for their demise, but no serious research. There were, of course, the occasional maverick scientists who suggested catastrophic events (even that extinctions might be caused by impacts), but as a rule they were ignored.

In the 1960s things began to change, for reasons that were as much cultural and political as scientific. Apocalyptic thinking was fostered by political events as the cold war intensified, climaxing in the terrifying Cuban missile crisis of 1962. This was reinforced by a series of bestselling novels and movies, such as *Alas, Babylon*, *On the Beach*, and *Fail-Safe*, which brought home to the public the reality of nuclear war. Doomsday cults and eschatological sects flourished, while end-of-the-world religious tracts such as Hal Lindsay's *The Late Great Planet Earth* became bestsellers. Catastrophic thinking was "in the air."

Three scientific events were to set the stage for the return of catastrophism. First, in the 1970s Stephen Jay Gould and Niles Eldredge proposed the theory of punctuated equilibrium. They argued that the fossil record did not support uniformitarian doctrine, and that evolution was characterized by short periods of rapid speciation, followed by long periods of stability. Their theory was not universally accepted and sparked a fierce and ongoing debate over the rate of evolutionary change. Some scientists began to recognize that mass extinctions were real and not just an artifact of "gaps in the fossil record." Second, space probes began sending back close-up pictures of other planets. For the first time, geologists had more than one world to study. What they saw on every other body in the inner solar system was heavy impact cratering, and some began asking why the Earth would be exempt. Third, the 1970s and 1980s saw the "dinosaur renaissance." Paleontologists such as John Ostrom and Robert Bakker argued that the conventional wisdom about dinosaurs was wrong; they were in fact fast, agile, and warm-blooded, and the direct ancestors of birds.[15] Canadian paleontologist Dale Russell raised the question of their extinction. Dinosaurs had been the dominant form of terrestrial life for 160 million years and had survived numerous climatic changes and fluctuations in sea level. So why did they all suddenly die 65 million years ago at the end of the Cretaceous period? Russell argued that only an extraterrestrial event such as a supernova explosion could account for their extinction.[16]

The Alvarez Hypothesis

Walter Alvarez had the same problem as Georges Cuvier, although he did not realize it at the time.[17] In the late 1970s, Alvarez, a geologist at the University of California at Berkeley, was studying magnetic reversals in the rocks of the mountains near Gubbio, Italy, where limestone strata cross the boundary between the Cretaceous and Tertiary periods (abbreviated as the K/T boundary). Right at the boundary was a centimeter-thick layer of clay. How long had that layer taken to form? Alvarez discussed the problem with his father, Luis, a Nobel Prize–winning physicist, who suggested that they use the element iridium as a measure. Iridium is part of the platinum group of metals that is very rare in the Earth's crust but is common in meteorites. Since the Earth is constantly bombarded by meteors that burn up in the atmosphere, their dust should deposit a steady, albeit tiny, amount of iridium that could act as a clock. In 1977 samples were sent to Berkeley for analysis, with the expectation of finding about 0.1 ppb (parts per billion) of iridium. Instead they discovered 9 ppb in a "spike" right at the boundary. What could cause it? Three years later, after numerous false starts and blind alleys, they published their conclusion: sixty-five million years ago the Earth had been struck by an asteroid that had killed the dinosaurs and most other forms of life on the planet.

The Alvarez hypothesis touched off an enormous controversy that lasted nearly twenty years. One of the reasons that it was so contentious is that it conflated two distinct claims: first, that the Earth was struck by a comet or asteroid sixty-five million years ago, and second, that this impact caused a mass extinction at the end of the Cretaceous period. One could logically accept the first claim and reject the second, although few people on either side did.

The debate was unusual in a number of ways. First was its size. For a scientific controversy, this was a huge debate, with more than twenty-four hundred books and articles published by 1999. Second, unlike most scientific arguments, it crossed disciplinary boundaries, involving geologists, paleontologists, astronomers, biologists, and physicists. New institutions quickly evolved to accommodate the cross-disciplinary nature of the questions, particularly the three "Snowbird" conferences (named after the ski resort in Utah where the first two were held). Third, the popular media reported the debate to an extraordinary degree, almost completely from the standpoint of the impact hypothesis. The dinosaur renaissance had made dinosaurs big business. For example, the opening of the Royal Tyrell Museum changed Drumheller, Alberta, from a sleepy town into a tourist destination for more than two million people a year—and that was before *Jurassic Park*! Couple this public fascination with dinosaurs to several decades of apocalyptic thinking, and it is easy to see why the popular media would create a bandwagon for the Alvarez hypothesis.

Finally, the debate was characterized by exceptional acrimony and bitterness. As William Glen reports in his extensive study of the debate, scientists were quick to choose sides, even if they had little information themselves, and once having declared for or against the hypothesis, few changed their minds.[18] Some geologists and paleontologists were outraged that outsiders would trespass across their disciplinary boundaries. Paleontologist Robert Bakker told a reporter:

> The arrogance of these people is simply unbelievable. They know next to nothing about how real animals evolve, live and become extinct. But despite their ignorance, the geochemists feel that all you have to do is crank up some fancy machine and you've revolutionized science. The real reasons for the dinosaur extinctions have to do with temperature and sea-level changes, the spread of diseases by migration and other complex events. In effect, they're saying this: "we high-tech people have all the answers, and you paleontologists are just primitive rockhounds."[19]

Much of the nastiness in the controversy originated with the leaders on both sides. Luis Alvarez can be fairly described as aggressive and abrasive.

Opponents who refused to accept his data were dismissed as incompetent. Discussing the opposition to his theory, he said: "I don't like to say bad things about paleontologists, but they're really not very good scientists. They're more like stamp collectors."[20] The opposition was led by geologist Charles Officer of Dartmouth College, who charged that the Alvarez hypothesis was "some kind of scam," and, to the extent it diverted resources from elsewhere, "the Alvarez hypothesis has been not merely pathological science but dangerous to boot."[21] So bitter were his personal attacks that one reviewer of his book commented: "The authors characterize Luis Alvarez as little more than the devil incarnate, one of the most extraordinary character assassinations of a recently deceased person that I have ever read."[22] (We should note in fairness that, while significant, this level of acrimony was still the exception and largely confined to North America.)[23]

Debate over whether or not the impact occurred closed after the Chicxulub structure in northern Yucatan, Mexico, was confirmed as the impact crater in the early 1990s, and the impact of comet Shoemaker-Levy 9 on Jupiter in 1994 demonstrated that impacts still occur in the solar system and that they release enormous amounts of energy (although a few holdouts, including Charles Officer, still deny the evidence). The claim that the impact caused a mass extinction was more difficult to establish. Evidence for a catastrophic mass extinction at the end of the Cretaceous has steadily mounted, but many details remain unclear, as does the role of massive volcanic activity that was also going on at that time. To understand the complexities of this debate, we will have to look at how science is practiced.

The Practice of Science in the Debate

The controversy bears little resemblance to textbook descriptions of how science operates as discussed in chapter 3. Throughout this book we have described science as a practice. In order to understand the debate we will have to demonstrate what that involves.

French sociologist Bruno Latour has proposed a model for the practice of science using the circulatory system as a metaphor to describe the activities of a typical scientific discipline.[24] While there is considerable merit in Latour's model, there are a few limitations in applying it to this situation. He describes "normal science" in a single discipline, while we are dealing with a multidisciplinary controversy. However, if we keep the components of Latour's model (somewhat simplified) but change his metaphor, we think it can be expanded to cover the debate over the Alvarez hypothesis. In keeping with our extended metaphor, we can describe the practice of science as itself a web (see fig. 8.1).

There are five components to the model. Radiating out from the hub

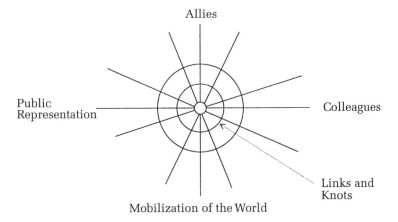

Figure 8.1 Science as a Practice

are four groups of threads. To Latour, the *mobilization of the world* involves all the means used to bring nonhuman nature into the argument. In this study, that means rocks, fossils, and the instruments used to analyze them. *Colleagues* are other scientists. *Allies* are groups outside of the controversy that are enrolled in support. These include funding agencies, nonscientific groups, scientists who are not part of the debate, and, in this one instance, a very timely comet. *Public representation* includes the institutions of popular science, such as museums, and the media, both scientific and popular. Tying the radial threads together are the circular threads, what Latour calls *links and knots*. These are the concepts, theories, and hypotheses that tie together all the other threads. Without the radial threads the web lacks substance and strength. Without the circular threads it would come apart—they are what make it a web.

Latour does not discuss what we call the outer links, but we think they add an important element. These represent the cultural, political, and scientific "background" we have just discussed. The inner links close to the hub tie the web together more tightly than do the outer ones, which make necessary connections between radial threads but are too loose and distant from the center to hold the web together. So, for example, that catastrophic thinking was "in the air" helps us to understand how the theories of both Cuvier (who lived through the French Revolution) and Alvarez were thought to be plausible.[25] But on the other hand, this "background" was not strong enough to influence their contemporaries Jean-Baptiste Lamark or Charles Officer.

While we will look at component threads as a group for analytical purposes, we have to remember that the actual weaving is both simultaneous (various threads spun at the same time) and sequential (as important threads were added later). Thus Luis and Walter Alvarez and their team and supporters were like a spider busy spinning and tying together threads to make a web. Adding new radial threads made the web stronger and firmer, while more circular threads tied it together more firmly. At the same time, their opponents were trying to cut the threads and sometimes trying to appropriate them for their own rival web.

Mobilization of the World

Luis and Walter Alvarez began spinning their web with only three wispy strands of iridium—the one from Gubbio, another from Denmark, and a third independently discovered by Dutch geologist Jan Smits in Spain. Tying down their hypothesis would require a "footprint" of an impact, a series of markers by which anyone could determine if an impact had occurred.

The iridium anomaly was their first marker. Establishing it would require much more fieldwork and the development of a new neutron activation machine (done by Luis Alvarez himself) that could mass-produce iridium analyses.[26] By the time of the first Snowbird conference in 1981, iridium anomalies had been discovered at thirty-six additional sites, and by the late nineties the number had risen to more than one hundred.

Opponents of the impact hypothesis tried to cut the thread by developing an alternative explanation for the iridium. In the mid–1980s Charles Officer and Charles Drake suggested that hot-spot volcanoes, which presumably originate in the Earth's mantle where iridium is thought to be abundant, could have produced the anomaly. When Vincent Courtillot, the eminent French volcanologist, dated the Deccan Traps in India (massive basaltic lava flows 1,500 feet thick) to the K/T boundary, it seemed that an alternative explanation had been found.[27] But further analysis showed the iridium of the anomaly to be two orders of magnitude greater than that produced by volcanoes. The iridium thread held.

More threads were soon added. A layer of soot found at the boundary was interpreted as the result of mass fires, and a "fern spike" of spores just above it indicated widespread disruption of plant life. Minerals associated with known impacts, such as stishovite, spinel, and tektites, were found. The most decisive discovery was the presence at the boundary of shocked quartz. These microscopic deformations of quartz crystals can be produced by only two known events—nuclear weapons tests and meteorite impact. Here was a marker that was familiar and convincing to geologists and that, as Courtillot admitted, is not produced by volcanoes.[28]

By the time of the second Snowbird conference in 1988, many threads had been added to the web and tied down. The evidence for an impact was strong if not yet overwhelming, but evidence that it had caused a mass extinction was more equivocal. In particular was "the ghastly three meter gap," as paleontologist William Clemens called it, between the last known dinosaur fossil and the boundary (and an even larger gap for ammonite fossils, coiled-shelled relatives of the squid that had also gone extinct). The "killing mechanisms" claimed by the Alvarez hypothesis could, their opponents maintained, also be produced by volcanoes, and the massive Deccan Traps stood as an alternative.[29] There were still features of the boundary layer in many places that could not be explained (for instance, in places it seemed as if there had been more than one impact). And most of all, where was the crater?

Colleagues

From the beginning, the controversy was an interdisciplinary debate, and both sides had the problem of recruiting and retaining colleagues from other academic fields. The Snowbird conferences were one means of doing that, since they were organized to discuss the issues of the debate rather than the wide range of topics normally discussed at the usual discipline-specific meetings. On both sides interdisciplinary work teams evolved, but, as William Glen points out, invariably all members of a team were from the same side of the debate.[30]

There were two key variables in determining which camp a scientist would join. The first was the influence of a magister, a trusted academic leader. Most scientists knew little about the issues of the debate beyond their own field. Unlike the textbook image of the dispassionate scientist carefully weighing all the data before making a decision, many joined the debate based on the authority of a magister. As Glen reports: "It is clear that the leadership of the various debates bearing on the K/T mass extinction was in the hands of only one or a very few magisters, to whom the community members deferred and to whom, all too frequently, they turned to form and reform their opinions on evolving issues" (81). This could cut two ways. There has been a long history, from Lord Kelvin on, of prominent physicists pontificating on the earth sciences—and being totally wrong. Luis Alvarez was up against the long-held suspicion of many geologists and paleontologists for outside magisters.

The second variable was the discipline, or in many cases subdiscipline, to which the scientist belonged. Physicists, geochemists, astronomers, and planetary geologists tended to favor the Alvarez hypothesis. These were people who were often familiar with meteorites, and, as Glen comments, "resistance to the hypothesis seemed inverse to familiarity with impacting studies" (51). Geologists were skeptical. Paleontologists were divided. Vertebrate paleontologists, with a few notable exceptions such as Dale Russell, were strongly opposed. Micropaleontologists, with a few notable exceptions such as Gerta Keller, were strongly in favor. Invertebrate paleontologists were divided, with a few prominent members such as Stephen Jay Gould and David Raup strong supporters but with ammonite specialist Peter Ward opposed. Officer's and Drake's rival volcanism hypothesis was greatly weakened when most volcanologists refused to support it, but few of them supported Alvarez either.

Each camp used a different rhetorical strategy to try to win over colleagues. Faced with the burden of proof, the Alvarez camp followed a strategy of strict actualism. Glen notes, "however radical or catastrophic their hypothesis, from the outset the impactors have mainly invoked canonical standards and knowledge in advancing their several lines of evidence" (55). This strategy was to pay dividends. "[Bruce] Bohor's seemingly miraculous find of shocked quartz, evidence that was familiar to and well understood by the geologic community, went far in attracting the attention of many who had initially viewed the 'black box' iridium of 'alien' nuclear chemists as somehow dismissible" (47). Colleagues were tied into the web when convinced by the epistemic culture, that is, the norms and evidentiary standards, of their own discipline.

A second strategy was to attack the principle of uniformitarianism. Historical and philosophical discussion is common among supporters of the Alvarez hypothesis, who argue that Lyell's and Darwin's principle had become the dead hand of orthodoxy. In doing so, they tried to appropriate to themselves the myth of the heroic scientist standing alone against authority (see chapter 3). It was not a strategy that won them any friends. Very few of their opponents ever invoked Lyell or Darwin.[31]

By contrast, the other side was a group only to the extent that they were united in opposition to the Alvarez hypothesis. Opponents brought forward various arguments, many of which were contradictory. Some denied the existence of any mass extinctions; others agreed that mass extinctions had occurred but argued that they were gradual processes of climate and sea level change; still others were as catastrophic as Alvarez but saw volcanoes as the culprit. The one common strategy of the opposition was to insist on ever higher standards of evidence, which led David Raup to comment: "That the burden of proof should be with the new (and revolutionary) theory is reasonable, but the standards that have been demanded are far higher than is normal in science, and far higher than is practiced by most of its participants."[32] One of the causes of acrimony in the debate was the demand by some opponents for higher standards from the Alvarez camp than they themselves practiced.[33]

Allies

The strongest allies Luis and Walter Alvarez had were H-bombs. What they were hypothesizing was so far beyond human experience that before 1953 it would have been very difficult even to describe a measure to which an impact could be compared. Thermonuclear weapons gave them a basis for such a comparison. Throughout the literature, the force of the impact is measured in equivalent megatons of nuclear weapons (actually, in millions of megatons). But the connection does not end there. Early in the 1980s Carl Sagan and others used the Alvarez hypothesis to argue that a nuclear war might also trigger an extinction-level event, which came to be called nuclear winter. As a result, studies undertaken by various scientific groups sought a threshold of environmental damage that might trigger extinction.[34] These studies enhanced the understanding of "killing mechanisms" that might have been part of an impact as well. They also added a political dimension to the debate, as scientists' attitudes toward the arms race and the Strategic Defense Initiative (SDI) were drawn into the arguments.

Other allies were more usual for the practice of science, the public and private funding agencies. Particularly important here was the Lunar and Planetary Institute, which was the major financial support for the Snowbird conferences and which, while officially neutral, was implicitly an ally of Alvarez in that it took the hypothesis seriously enough to fund conferences about it.

One tactic in a scientific dispute is to deny rivals money to do research. Some on both sides charged that their opponents were using their positions in university departments and on the review boards of funding agencies to block research grants.[35] It is easier to prevent a thread from being spun than to cut it out of a web later.

Public Representations

It is hard to imagine either the scope or intensity of the controversy if it had not been about dinosaurs. Trilobites and ammonites may have been interesting creatures that also suffered mass extinction (the ammonites at the same time as the dinosaurs), but their disappearance does not stir much emotion among either scientists or the public. Dinosaurs, on the other hand, inspire passion. That level of feeling was both created by and reflected in the public representations of the debate. And because the debate was interdisciplinary, public representations played a larger than usual part in the controversy.

Dinosaurs were key to sparking interest both in other scientists and in the public. Autobiographical accounts from scientists in many fields indicate that they first became interested in science itself through their childhood fascination with dinosaurs. In this they did not differ from the general public, who, as sociologist Elizabeth Clemens reports, had been conditioned by museums and popular science presentations (particularly children's science literature) to practically identify dinosaurs (and one or two other groups of animals such as mammoths) with prehistory and evolution.[36] The Alvarez hypothesis appealed both to scientists from a variety of disciplines and to the public because they "already knew" about dinosaurs. As Clemens concludes:

> Popular science influences scientific debate at the level of both cognition and material interests. To the extent that the general scientific community "already knows" that a particular question is interesting or significant, interdisciplinary conversation—if not necessarily research—is more likely to develop. To the extent that the general public, and particularly those non-scientific elites who control resources, already knows that a question is reasonable and important, it will be easier to secure funding for that line of research. Consequently, structures of popular interest can create asymmetries even within a single research effort.[37]

One of these asymmetries was with paleontologists, whose professional training forced them to "unlearn" what popular science had taught them about evolution and extinction. They were therefore conditioned not to be receptive to the Alvarez hypothesis, which many saw as simplistic and unprofessional.

Other asymmetries appeared in the media. Because the impact hypothesis was dramatic, the popular media were attracted to it at once. Coverage was extensive and, with the notable exception of the *New York Times*, mostly favorable. Many simply presented the hypothesis as fact. Coverage in the scientific media was somewhat unusual. A disproportionate number of reports and articles about the debate appeared in the general science magazines *Science* and *Nature*, rather than in specialized disciplinary journals. Given the interdisciplinary nature of the discussions, this is perhaps not too surprising. With the huge volume of literature, and the inherent difficulty in mastering technical material outside one's own field, many scientists relied upon general science journals and even the popular media for much of their information.

How the combatants viewed the media depended on how they were being reported on that day. By and large, the Alvarez camp was much more successful in tying the institutions of popular science, the media, and the general science press into their web. This led Officer to complain of bias in the media, particularly on the part of *Science*.[38]

Links, Knots, and Closure

Luis and Walter Alvarez began with meager evidence and a bold assertion. If scientific concepts are what tie together the web of scientific practice, at first the impact hypothesis was a granny knot. The Alvarez team was successful because it was eventually able to tie together a large assortment of rocks, colleagues from several disciplines, nuclear winter, funding agencies, and the popular and scientific media into a web that held in spite of buffeting by the opposition. The Alvarez opponents failed because they were unable to tie together sufficient threads of their own.

The first link—the first of the circular threads in the web—was the original statement of the hypothesis in 1980. The iridium spike provided prima facie evidence for an impact, but that the impact had caused a mass extinction was conjecture. The fossil record at the time apparently showed a gradual dwindling out of species across the K/T boundary. An important link to tie fossils into the hypothesis was presented in a paper by Philip Signor and Jere Lipps at the first Snowbird conference in 1981.[39] The Signor-Lipps effect, as it came to be known, demonstrated that sampling effects could make a mass extinction appear gradual. It works something like this. Moose are less common than gophers. If we assume that a moose was fossilized, say, every one thousand years and a gopher every one hundred years, and that both species became extinct at the same time, moose would seem to disappear from the fossil record before gophers. Therefore the supposed decline in diversity of dinosaurs and ammonites just before the end of the Cretaceous could be accounted for as an artifact of sampling.

As more and more radial threads were tied in, the linking knots of the hypothesis became stronger and tighter and the challenge facing opponents more difficult. As soot and the fern spike and shocked quartz and the other markers were each added to the web (or, to put it in more traditional language, as the hypothesis was able to encompass a broader range of empirical data), each became stronger through its association with the others, and the connections between them became more difficult to contest. As more colleagues and allies were recruited, the hypothesis grew from the opinion of half a dozen individuals to the considered judgment of scores of scientists and the record of international conferences.

By the time of the second Snowbird conference in 1988, those favoring the Alvarez hypothesis were clearly in the majority. But several unsolved problems prevented debate from closing. Even taking the Signor-Lipps effect into account, there appeared to be significant gaps between the impact boundary and the last ammonites and dinosaurs. In a number of places the K/T boundary appeared to show more than one impact. And particularly vexing was the absence of a crater. By 1990, some were suggesting that the hypothesis needed modification. Maybe there was more than one impact. Maybe the extinctions were in steps instead of all at once. And what role did the Deccan volcanic eruptions play? The knots were beginning to loosen.

The publication of the Alvarez hypothesis inspired a worldwide search for the impact crater. There were good reasons not to expect to find it. In sixty-five million years it could have been eroded away or buried under later sediment, or the meteorite could have struck in the ocean. In 1984 it was suggested that the Manson structure in northwestern Iowa could be an impact crater. A team of scientists was formed to study it, and preliminary reports indicated that it was indeed a buried impact crater of about the right age. Some believed that the crater had been found, but the evidence didn't hold up.[40] At thirty-seven kilometers in diameter, it is much too small to have generated the K/T mass extinction. By the early nineties, chemical analysis showed the Manson rocks to be different from many of the K/T boundary markers, and more reliable dating indicated that the crater was nearly ten million years too old. The Manson thread broke.

Then in 1991 several threads were added that tightened the knots again. Peter Ward, one of the world's foremost ammonite specialists, had opposed the Alvarez hypothesis. His own work on the cliffs near Zumaya, Spain, had shown a gap of more than nine meters between the last ammonite and the K/T boundary. Provoked by Alvarez, he returned to the cliffs and found a few poorly preserved shells just below the boundary. Were ammonites absent because they were all dead, or had they simply gone elsewhere? Ward moved down the coast to another area and, as he reports: "I was overjoyed to find a score of ammonites within the last meter of Cretaceous rock during the first hour at Hendaye. In fact, I found more ammonites here than any other fossils."[41] Ammonites had lived right up to the K/T boundary, and Peter Ward became one of the few scientists in the controversy to change sides.

A similar three-meter gap existed for dinosaurs, and many paleontologists argued that dinosaurs were declining in diversity before they slowly disappeared. To find out for sure, Peter Sheehan of the Milwaukee Public Museum organized teams of volunteers who collectively spent fifteen thousand hours of fieldwork scouring the Hell Creek formation in western North Dakota and eastern Montana. In 1991 he reported his findings: "The results indicate that there is no statistically meaningful drop in the ecological diversity of dinosaurs through the Hell Creek formation. . . . Although Hell Creek dinosaurs have long been invoked as documenting a gradual extinction, our data from the Hell Creek are compatible with abrupt extinction scenarios."[42] The dinosaur gap had also been closed. A team of Indian scientists tightened the knot even more at the third Snowbird conference in 1994. They reported finding the K/T boundary in the third intertrappean (layers of sedimentary rock between the layers of basaltic lava in the Deccan Traps). Dinosaur fossils, including eggshells, were found just below the boundary.[43] Not only was this further evidence that dinosaurs had lived right to the end of the Cretaceous, but also the Deccan Traps had to be ruled out as the immediate cause of their extinction.

Finally, in 1991 Canadian geologist Alan Hildebrand, together with several geologists from PEMEX, the Mexican oil company, reported the discovery of an enormous impact structure (at least 175 km in diameter) buried in northern Yucatan, Mexico, which they called Chicxulub. By the third Snowbird conference the evidence was pouring in: The K/T impact crater had been found. The last threads were tied into place.

A few months after that conference a final ally arrived to close the debate over impact. In July 1994, comet Shoemaker-Levy 9, which had broken into fragments, slammed into Jupiter with a total force estimated as several million megatons. For the first time in human experience, scientists witnessed what the impact of a comet could do.

So what happened at the end of the Cretaceous? Current reconstruction is that an object (most likely a comet) about ten kilometers in diameter struck just off the coast.[44] Coming in at an angle of thirty to sixty degrees from the southeast, the object exploded on impact with the force of one hundred million megatons. Ejecta were blown out of the crater on different trajectories, which accounted for the appearance of multiple layers at some sites. The shock wave flattened trees up to 1,000 km away, huge tsunamis ravaged the coasts, a magnitude-thirteen earthquake was triggered, and a heat pulse ignited forests up to 5,000 km away. As red-hot ejecta fell back to Earth, fires spread all over the planet. A dust cloud blocked out sunlight, dropping temperatures and killing plants and plankton in the sea—an impact winter. Because the basement rock in the Yucatan was rich in sulfur, acid rain finished what the cold and darkness had begun, and the food chain collapsed. As the skies cleared, the cold was replaced by heat as gases released by the impact produced a greenhouse effect. By the time it was over, approximately 70 percent of the species on Earth were dead.

Death from Above or Death from Below?

As debate over the existence of an impact at the K/T boundary ended, debate over its significance intensified. Was it an isolated event, a random occurrence in Earth history? Or is the Earth regularly bombarded, causing a cycle of mass extinctions? The end of the Cretaceous was not the only mass extinction, nor was it the largest. Scientists have identified five major mass extinctions and perhaps as many as twenty lesser ones over the past 500 million years. The largest of these, at the end of the Permian period 250 million years ago, killed 90 to 95 percent of the species on Earth. Although claims that mass extinctions fall into a periodic cycle are disputed, it does appear they happen regularly. Two theories attempt to explain why.

Some maintain that the Earth is regularly bombarded from space. Geologists have identified more than one hundred impact craters, at least twenty of which are larger than thirty-five kilometers in diameter (Chicxulub is the third largest).[45] Some of these, together with iridium anomalies, shocked quartz, and other elements of an impact footprint have been associated with mass extinctions, including three of the five major ones (the late Devonian, end-Triassic, and K/T). Charles Frankel summarizes: "Out of 25 mass extinctions tentatively identified in the fossil record, six are associated with significant evidence of impact. . . . Seven other mass extinctions are associated with lesser iridium anomalies. . . . That between a quarter and a half of all mass extinctions in the fossil record appear to be connected with impacts is remarkable, especially since research in the field has just begun."[46] To these scientists, Earth history is punctuated by death from the skies.

Others are not convinced. Vincent Courtillot, who has long opposed the Alvarez hypothesis, admits that the evidence for an impact-caused mass extinction at the K/T boundary is compelling, although he maintains it came as a coup de grâce to a biosphere that was already severely stressed by the eruption of the Deccan Traps. But, he says, there is no unequivocal evidence that an impact caused any other mass extinction. Instead, he finds a close correlation between basaltic flood volcanism and extinction. "Among the 12 traps younger than 300 Ma [million years ago], at least nine can be associated with a major extinction. Seven of the ten principal extinctions can be associated with an episode of massive basaltic volcanism."[47] Most dramatic are the gigantic Siberian Traps that coincide with the extinction at the end of the Permian period. For Courtillot and his supporters, Earth history is punctuated by death from the mantle.

Which of these hypotheses will eventually triumph remains to be seen. Some scientists are trying to combine them into a grand unified theory of Earth systems, in which impacts trigger basaltic flood volcanism and both cause mass extinctions, although so far without a great deal of success.[48] However the debate comes out, though, it is clear that the gradualist uniformitarianism of Lyell and Darwin is being supplanted by a much more catastrophic view of the history of the Earth. It may very well be, as David Raup suggests, that we have chosen to live on an unsafe planet. [49]

Aut Logos Aut Cosmos?

What does it mean to live on an unsafe planet? Ian Barbour observed, "our understanding of God's relation to nature always reflects our view of nature."[50] The Alvarez hypothesis forces us to reevaluate a number of the assumptions found in the science-religion dialogue.

The first issue it forces us to rethink is the meaning of evolution. For Darwin, evolution through natural selection meant "survival of the fittest." As we have seen, Darwin believed that extinction came at the end of a long struggle between species in which the inferior was eliminated by the more fit. Scientists today are less ready to see "nature red in fang and claw" than Darwin was, but the idea of "fitness" has persisted, now defined as differential reproductive success (that is, more surviving offspring). For example, Ursula Goodenough writes: "Genomes that create organisms with sufficient reproductive success to have viable offspring are able to continue into the future; genomes that fail, fail. Reproductive success is governed by many variables, but key adaptations have included the evolution of awareness, valuation, and purpose."[51] The only problem with this, as David Raup notes, is that there are no empirical tests for "fitness," and "the only evidence for the inferiority of victims of extinction is the fact of their extinction—a circular argument."[52] In an Earth history punctuated by catastrophes, survival goes not to the fittest but to the luckiest. When the fire comes by, awareness, valuation, and purpose may count for a lot less than how low a species lives on the food chain. For example, were dinosaurs less fit than, say, mammals? No. Mammals and dinosaurs coexisted for most of the Mesozoic era in which dinosaurs were clearly the dominant terrestrial vertebrates. They were larger, faster, stronger, and smarter than the mammals of their day. They enjoyed great reproductive success for 160 million years. Yet, when the catastrophe came, our ancestors were lucky. Half of the mammal species died alongside the dinosaurs, but enough breeding pairs were left among the others, hiding in their burrows and eating seeds and insects and carrion, to repopulate the suddenly vacant niches as the biosphere recovered. Paleontologist Kenneth Hsü reflects:

> The law of the survival of the fittest may be, therefore, a tautology in which fitness is defined by the fact of survival, not by independent criteria that would form the basis for prediction. . . . If most extinctions are caused by catastrophes, then chance, not superiority, presides over who shall live and who shall die.

Indeed, the whole course of evolution may be governed by chance, and not reflect at all the slow march from inferior to superior forms so beloved of Victorians, and so deeply embedded in Western thought.[53]

Evolution may not be the history of gradual progress that Darwin thought it was.

This reopens the question of theodicy. Darwin's theodicy—that death and suffering are incidental to evolutionary progress—is common in the science-religion dialogue. Extinction is a nonissue. Ian Barbour is typical: "Competition and death are intrinsic to an evolutionary process. Pain is an inescapable concomitant of greater sensitivity and awareness, and it provides a valuable warning against external danger." Michael Ruse is even more explicit: "Physical evil exists, and Darwinism explains why God had no choice but to allow it to occur. He wanted to produce designlike effects—without producing these He would not have organisms, including humankind—and natural selection is the only option open. Natural selection has costs—physical pain—but these are costs that must be paid." Keith Ward is one of the very few who even mentions mass extinction: "The dinosaurs . . . were selected by the ecosystem as good perceivers and agents, but for various reasons they proved to be an evolutionary dead end. . . . Then the ecosystem selected a new set of mutating organisms, which ended in *Homo sapiens*." Dinosaurs were selected out, and, however improbably, we were selected in. Even John Haught, whose profound meditation *God After Darwin* is one of the few books to take the question of theodicy seriously, relates a story of evolutionary progress without catastrophic interruptions.[54] At its root, all of this is still Whig history. Evolutionary progress produced human consciousness—us—so all the pain and death must be worthwhile. It is an extremely human-centered view of nature. Mass extinction, however, challenges the basis of Darwin's theodicy.

Every theodicy is a story that attempts to create meaning in a limit situation, a situation that is inherently meaningless. Darwin's theodicy has been successful for so long because it has allowed people to make sense out of what John Polkinghorne calls "natural evil." Polkinghorne distinguishes between moral and natural evil (called physical evil by some). Moral evil is the result of the choices made by humans, what in traditional theological language is called sin. Natural evil is that which arises out of the working of the world itself; disease and storm and drought and earthquake. Mass extinction is an extreme form of natural evil. Of course, the two may be connected, as when human actions place people at greater risk of natural disaster.[55]

Polkinghorne sets out the criteria that any theodicy must meet: "It is to suggest that the world's suffering is not gratuitous but a necessary contribution to some greater good that could only be realized in this mysterious way. The problem of evil is to be met by setting it within that wider context in which it can dissolve into fulfillment."[56] So moral evil is explained by stories of the Fall and the apocalypse, of slavery and liberation, of sin and redemption, of forgiveness and reconciliation. Natural evil, however, is more difficult to explain.

Most religions respond to limit situations through symbol and myth, not through investigations into nature. Much of the science-religion dialogue differs in that it claims that evidence of God's revelation can be found in the "book of nature" as well as the "book of Scripture." For example, natural theology and Intelligent Design theories try to justify natural evil (to the extent they discuss it at all) by appealing to some grand design in nature, but these approaches end up making the Creator into a monster. The God who designed beauty and complexity must therefore also be the author of suffering and death. Others, such as deism, postulate a remote Creator who, having made the world, now stands aside and lets it run according to its own laws. God made the world. One of its properties is to quake. But this God is callous, indifferent to the suffering inflicted upon the creation. Darwin's theodicy avoided this contradiction by not invoking a creator, but he still sought to justify suffering and death through the immanent fulfillment of progress. To do this, however, he had to deny the existence of catastrophes in Earth history because the randomness and sheer scale of mass extinction events mock any notion of progress. The Alvarez hypothesis falsifies Darwin's theodicy.

Polkinghorne's own solution is what he calls the free-will defense applied to nature. "In his great act of creation I believe God allows the physical world to be itself," he says. "That world is endowed in its fundamental constitution with an anthropic potentiality that makes it capable of fruitful evolution. The exploration and realization of that potentiality is achieved by the universe through the continual interplay of chance and necessity within its unfolding process."[57] This approach avoids making God into a bloody-handed puppet master, but in the end it is only a very sophisticated version of Darwin's theodicy. How can one square any "anthropic potentiality" with death on the scale of a mass extinction?

Perhaps there is no theodicy that is compatible with the discoveries of science. There was always a tension in the Hebrew Scriptures between the God of the Exodus, a God of history who liberates and redeems, and the nature deities of Israel's neighbors. The German philosopher Ernst Bloch expressed the tension inherent in biblical religion as "aut Logos aut Cosmos," either the Word or the Creation.[58] It is a tension, not an absolute break or division. Although some religions, such as Manicheanism and Gnosticism, opt for dualism and solve the problem by declaring nature to be evil, biblical religion begins by declaring the Creation to be good. What Barbour calls "integrationist" approaches have a particular difficulty in that they are committed to harmonizing science and religion, which requires removing the tension between Word and Creation. That may prove to be an insurmountable obstacle.

In the end, all we are left with are symbols. At the end of his reflection on evil, Polkinghorne concludes: "In the lonely figure hanging in the darkness and dereliction of Calvary the Christian believes that he sees God opening his arms to embrace the bitterness of the strange world he has made."[59] In the face of moral and natural evil, with suffering and death, be it of a single child or of a mass extinction, we have only the symbol of a crucified God.

Mystery and Objectivity

9 The Science Wars

There are more things in heaven and earth, Horatio,
Than are dreamt of in your philosophy.

—Shakespeare

Mystery, that which is unknown, is the final category of religious thought, according to Weber. Somewhat ironically, Weber was also one of the originators of the idea of a value-free objective science. What is the relationship between mystery and objectivity, and does it mean that conflict between science and religion is inevitable? The so-called science wars answered that it does and raised in dramatic form many questions that also lie at the heart of the science-religion dialogue. Using the science wars as a foil, in this final section we argue that there is a necessary tension between the poles of mystery and objectivity. Truth is found in the tension between them, and is lost when the tension is abandoned for one pole or the other. The social sciences can bring a crucial means of understanding and retaining this tension to the science-religion dialogue.

At several points throughout this book, we have touched on the science wars, which received a significant level of attention in academic circles and in the popular media throughout the 1990s. While we would agree with many others that the science wars appear to be petering out, an analysis of this controversy will set the stage for our comments on objectivity and mystery. There are a number of good reasons for doing such an analysis. First, the science wars represent an extreme form of the conflict perspective, and therefore they provide a mechanism for clarifying those issues that are at the heart of the controversy, while at the same time they help to demonstrate the absurdity of absolutist positions. Second, the science wars show how the popular media can sometimes distort and sustain discourse through their defense of those whom they think represent the majority view, and through their often relentless and misguided attacks on those whom they perceive as challengers to the status quo. Third, the science wars help to point out the inherent social dangers of the sort of naïve realism that is characteristic of too much scientific thought.

From our perspective, objectivity and mystery are in some ways at opposite ends of a spectrum of understanding. We call something objective when we no longer associate a high level of anxiety with the meaning that we attach to that thing. For example, most of us have a high level of comfort operating in our daily lives, secure that most of what we will encounter while walking or driving a car can be explained by Newtonian physics. At the other end of the spectrum, we call something a mystery when there is a high level of anxiety attached to its meaning. So, for example, when it comes to our salvation, we are anxious and uncertain, and whether it is because our knowledge is deficient or because it is beyond knowing, the fact remains that salvation is a mystery. At the heart of the science wars is an attempt to use objectivity to repress mystery. The form this takes is an obsession with the purported dangers of relativism.

The science wars emerged in an environment where support for the construction of large-scale scientific research facilities was coming under constant attack by government, industry, and academic institutions. The international space station program underwent, and continues to be subjected to, a series of downsizing modifications that in the opinion of many will render it little more than a showpiece, rather than the monument to scientific accomplishment and collaboration it was meant to be. In the United States, the cancellation of the superconducting supercollider was condemned by some as a move back to the Dark Ages. The event was supposedly a clear sign that contemporary U.S. society had little appreciation of the need for scientists to carry out fundamental research, coupled of course with the need for members of that society to provide billions of dollars in support of such research. Scientists felt threatened. For centuries, they had improved the quality and quantity of human life on the planet, conquering superstition, and harnessing nature. Or had they? Aided by the media, and claiming both the moral and intellectual high ground, certain members of the scientific community embarked on a campaign to demonstrate that they in fact had.

We will trace the conduct of the science wars through four major events (skipping some of the smaller skirmishes). The science wars began when biologist Paul Gross and mathematician Norman Levitt published *Higher Superstition* in 1994, and the wars spread after a New York Academy of Sciences conference in 1995.[1] The most intense conflict was during the Sokal affair of 1997–1999. Things were already quieting down when Levitt came out with his own book in 1999.

Gross and Levitt began the science wars by accusing an "academic left," made up of postmodernists, feminists, multiculturalists, and radical environmentalists, of seeking to undermine the foundations of science. They argue that these initiatives are characterized by "open hostility" not just toward the content of scientific knowledge, but "toward the assumption, which one might have supposed universal among educated people, that scientific knowledge is reasonably reliable and rests on a sound methodology" (2). This statement appears bold, if not uninformed, in light of the material that we have presented throughout this book regarding a number of ongoing and unresolved debates over various aspects of science. Among other things, we have shown that there is no clear consensus, even among scientists, on how to demarcate (on the basis of methodology or otherwise) science from nonscience, just as there is no clear, single understanding of the relationship between theory and evidence. Gross and Levitt go on to warn that the greatest danger arising from these initiatives is not with respect to science itself, but rather that "what is threatened is the capability of the larger culture, which embraces the mass media as well as the more serious processes of education, to interact fruitfully with the sciences, to draw insight from scientific advances, and, above all, to evaluate science intelligently" (4). So, not only do the authors present and defend a monolithic and largely taken-for-granted conception of science, but also they are of the opinion that science is, for the most part, immune from the attacks, or constructive criticism, of those in the academy who do not share this view. For Gross and Levitt, it is the public that is at greatest risk. What the authors appear to suggest is that, in order for the public to evaluate and benefit from the work done by scientists, and at the same time to protect themselves from the antiscience rhetoric of the left, they must accept the scientists' definition of what science is.

Gross and Levitt construct their argument around the analysis of what they have determined to be four distinct but related efforts to assess science from within the broader category of cultural studies: social (cultural) constructivist, postmodernist, feminist, and radical environmentalist. These areas are distinct in that they each reflect certain "doctrinal idiosyncrasies" (for example, sexism on the part of feminists), but they are related inasmuch as they all represent some form of radical relativism, with respect to the ontological, epistemological, and methodological foundations of modern Western science. So, for example, Gross and Levitt select the work of sociologists and historians of science Stanley Aronowitz, Bruno Latour, Steve Shapin, and Simon Schaffer to represent the social constructivist perspective. They believe these scholars are attempting to demonstrate how social and political factors, particularly as they relate to the struggle over material and human resources, turn science into a power game, in which references to reason and evidence are merely rhetorical tools. In an effort to turn the tables and point out the "value-laden" nature of social constructivism, Gross and Levitt conclude that "the central ambition of the cultural constructivist program—to explain the deepest and most enduring insights of science as a corollary of social assumptions and ideological agenda—is futile and perverse. The chances are excellent, however, that one can account for the intellectual phenomenon of cultural constructivism *itself* in precisely such terms" (69; emphasis in original). Here, we find a restatement of the traditional view of what constitutes the legitimate purview of the sociology of science, namely, the investigation of the social aspects of science (context of discovery), but not of the internal workings of science (context of justification).

For their analysis of postmodernism, Gross and Levitt select philosopher Steven Best, Andrew Ross (coeditor of *Social Text*, who coined the term *science wars*), and literary critic N. Katherine Hayles. Postmodernist scholars are accused of treating "science as metaphor," and of playing a sort of "intellectual hooky," thinly disguised as philosophy. According to Gross and Levitt, most postmodernists hold that "'reality' is chimerical or at best inaccessible to human cognition, and that all human awareness is a creature and a prisoner of the language games that encode it, (thus) it is a short step to the belief that mastery over words, over terminology and lexicon, is mastery over the world" (74). The catch is that, in the authors' opinion, postmodernists rarely make the effort to understand the meanings of the words they use in their critiques of those that use them. In other words, before some term used by physicists, say, can be used in some other context, it is incumbent upon the borrower first to discover what physicists mean by that term. For example, both Best and Hayles are accused of totally distorting what physicists and mathematicians understand by "chaos theory," and its related vocabulary of nonlinearity, fractal geometry, and so on, thus reverting to the "magical, emblematic thinking of pre-modern (rather than postmodern) times" (105). Postmodernists, freed from the ideological encumbrances of scientists, claim to see more "meaning" in these words than even the scientists are aware of. "Virtually all of them claim to discern important intellectual themes and political motifs in past and current science, themes and motifs that are quite invisible to the scientists themselves. These supposed insights rest, as we have seen, on a technical competence so shallow and incomplete as to be analytically worthless. Their arrogance, then, is comparable to that of "'creation scientists' in addressing evolutionary biology, or to that of Galileo's persecutors within the Inquisition in their response to his cosmology" (106). Again, as with their critique of the social constructivists, Gross and Levitt are supporting an internalist conception of science that is assumed to be true, and that cannot be proven to be false except on its own terms.

With respect to feminism (represented by Sandra Harding, Helen Longino, and others), the argument is basically the same. Gross and Levitt state: "What begins as an epistemological inquiry into science ends as familiar anti-science tricked out in the ambient clichés of the business—science 'harnessed to the making of money and the waging of war'—the old moral one-up *woman*ship, and the call to political action. It ends with the universal complaint of religious zealots, utopians, and totalizers generally" (148; emphasis in the original). All members of the "academic left" are viewed as "totalizers," whom Gross and Levitt define as those with "the impulse to bring the entire range of human phenomena within the rubric of a favored doctrinal system" (225). Science, for Gross and Levitt, is not doctrine, for it is based on logical reasoning and the rules of evidence. Similarly, the "actions" of science are superior to the "talk" of other disciplines. As they conclude with respect to so-called radical environmentalists (represented primarily by Carolyn Merchant), "it is self-evident that a 1 percent improvement in the efficiency of photovoltaic cells, say, is, in environmental terms, worth substantially more than all the utopian eco-babble ever published" (178).

The remainder of Gross and Levitt's text is devoted to the reiteration of similar arguments, with evidence of the social constructivist and relativistic distortion of the scientific "reality" associated with such phenomena as the AIDS epidemic, the animal rights movement, and Afrocentrism (multiculturalism) in science education. In a chapter titled "Why Do the People Imagine a Vain Thing?," the authors' critique turns away from objective analysis toward the kind of zealotry they rail against throughout their text. In blatant support of the "intellectual hegemony of Western science," they state: "No other civilization bears a like gem. Thus science becomes an irresistible target for those whose sense of their own heritage has become an intolerable moral burden" (220). Gross and Levitt conclude their book by returning to an examination of the consequences of the science wars. Here, they highlight the destructive nature of the failure to respect academic colleagues, regardless of their discipline, the (re)creation of a schism in the academy, the debasement of science education at all levels, and what they refer to as the "inanition" (to make inane) of public discourse (248). By way of an illustration of inanition, and as a closing comment on *Higher Superstition*, we offer this "thought experiment" by the authors.

> If, taking a fanciful hypothesis, the humanities department of
> MIT (a bastion, by the way of left-wing rectitude) were to walk
> out in a huff, the scientific faculty could, at need and with
> enough release time, patch together a humanities curriculum,
> to be taught by the scientists themselves. It would have obvi-
> ous gaps and rough spots, to be sure, and it might with some
> regularity prove inane; but on the whole it would be, we imag-
> ine, no worse than operative. What the opposite situation—a
> walkout by the scientists—would produce, as the humanities de-
> partment tried to cope with the demand for science education,
> we leave to the reader's imagination. (243)

The blatant arrogance and closed-mindedness reflected in this sort of
comment is unbelievable in the contemporary world.

The second major event of the science wars was a conference held
by the New York Academy of Sciences in 1995 on the issues raised by
Gross and Levitt. They, along with Martin Lewis, edited the conference
papers into a volume called *The Flight from Science and Reason*.[2] In
this book, more than forty authors reiterated the threats first articulated
by Gross and Levitt to the biological and physical sciences from the hu-
manities, from the environmental movement, from shifting attitudes in
healthcare, and from within the education system. Of particular interest to us is the fact that four chapters were devoted to the threats to science posed by religion. Even though these chapters contain familiar
rhetoric against biblical fundamentalism and so-called creation science,
at least one author appeared to make a concession to the importance and
validity of a religious perspective. Eugenie Scott suggested that scientists accept the fact that most Americans choose to believe in God and
want to retain their faith.[3] This faith, she said, does not prevent them
from understanding and accepting scientific explanations for such phenomena as evolution. Further, she recommended that scientists refrain
from making theological pronouncements and accept to some extent that
metaphysical discussions do not lend themselves to the same methodological rigor as science.

The third major event in the science wars occurred when physicist
Alan Sokal published an article, "Transgressing the Boundaries," in a
special issue of the cultural studies journal *Social Text* devoted to responses to Gross and Levitt's book.[4] The article, which presented a "hermeneutics of quantum gravity," was accepted as a serious and legitimate
contribution to the cultural studies of science, but Sokal had purposely
duped the editors. In an interview in which he describes how he wrote
the article, Sokal says: "I structured the article around the silliest quotations about mathematics and physics from the most prominent aca-

demics, and I invented an argument praising them and linking them together. All this was very easy to carry off, because my article wasn't
obliged to respect any standards of evidence or logic."[5] Sokal's intention was to provide support for Gross and Levitt's evaluation of the cultural studies of science by demonstrating that cultural studies journals,
lacking any rigorous criteria with which to judge sound scientific work,
would publish any "article liberally salted with nonsense if (a) it sounded
good and (b) it flattered the editors' ideological preconceptions."[6]

Sokal admitted to his "hoax" in "A Physicist Experiments with Cultural Studies," published in *Lingua Franca*. However, he echoes much
of the sentiment regarding "science bashing" expressed by Gross and
Levitt. Explaining why he turned to parody and satire for his critique,
he claims that those involved in the cultural studies of science "have
by now become a self-perpetuating academic subculture that typically
ignores (or disdains) reasoned criticism from the outside," so a powerful blow needed to be struck.[7]

The responses to Sokal's "experiment" were swift and widespread,
and another iteration of the science wars was under way. Scientists and
their supposed critics (historians, philosophers, anthropologists, and
sociologists) became engaged in a conflict of words over the integrity
and substance of each other's disciplines. Along the way, far too much
effort was expended on both sides on rhetorical and philosophical arguments designed to defend turf and ward off attack. As a consequence,
science and science studies both suffered, inside and outside of the
academy, as the proponents anxiously pursued "taking in each other's
washing."[8]

A recent study by Stephen Hilgartner attempts to put the "Sokal affair" in context. Hilgartner suggests that not only can Sokal's experiment
be viewed as a direct contribution to the social study of science, but that
it fits very specifically into a set of studies aimed at determining how
journals assess the credibility of submissions, and, even more specifically, into a subset of studies that have employed deception as part of
their method.[9] Hilgartner compares Sokal's efforts to those of William
Epstein, a social worker who conducted a major study of bias in the peer
review process in social work journals.[10] Sokal's piece comes off as quite
unimpressive, especially when judged by his own standards, namely,
evidence and logic. In other words, Sokal's efforts appear less objective,
less scientific. Whereas Epstein set out to test the distinct hypothesis
that confirmational bias exists among social work journals, Sokal refers
more vaguely to such elements as intellectual laziness and weak scholarship as characterizing the editorial practices of cultural studies journals. Similarly, Epstein employed a sample of 146 peer-reviewed journals
compared to Sokal's sample of one journal with no peer review process.

Epstein submitted two versions of an article, one with positive results and one with negative results, to randomly selected groups of journals, and then analyzed the results statistically. Sokal carried out none of these steps, but rather drew what Hilgartner refers to as a "voilà" conclusion (that is, I pulled it off; therefore, I was right).

Hilgartner then goes on to explore the very different reception that the two articles received among academics and in the public forum. Epstein was severely criticized by the social work profession for his deception, to the point of almost being thrown out of his professional association, and the press also responded negatively to his seemingly flagrant abuse of professional ethics. When the results of his study were published in *Science, Technology, and Human Values*, they were accompanied by thirty pages of commentary on the ethical implications of his work by five separate scholars. On the other hand, not only did Sokal's articles receive far greater attention in all venues, but also his conclusions were by and large accepted as a highly accurate and worthy critique of cultural studies in general, and of science studies more particularly, by the mass media and in many scholarly circles.

Given the obvious methodological inferiority of Sokal's efforts compared to Epstein's, Hilgartner offers a number of possible explanations that might account for the vastly different reception these articles received. For example, he suggests that physics, arguably the most scientific of sciences, enjoys a much higher status than either social work or cultural studies, and therefore Sokal, as a physicist, was ipso facto more credible. Similarly, he indicates that the institutional resources available to the intended targets of these studies were vastly different. The editors of the social work journals had the backing of a national association with professional codes and ethics committees to defend themselves against Epstein, who had clearly violated their trust. On the other hand, the cultural studies community is relatively diverse and fragmented, and so *Social Text*, as a single journal, was not in much of a position to mount a defense against Sokal. As a third element, Hilgartner observes that the timing of Sokal's experiment fit nicely into the present fascination in the media with the so-called decline of the universities. What Hilgartner is suggesting is that members of various groups responded to these articles on the basis of the meaning that the articles had for them. While this may appear to be an inane truism, it points to the fact that there is much to be learned from exploring the contexts and processes being engaged in, in these disputes, rather than limiting analysis to the content and products. As has been demonstrated throughout the last several chapters, neither science nor science studies is monolithic, and, therefore, it is unreasonable to expect that clear monolithic pro-science and antiscience positions can be identified among the protagonists. At the same time, we would suggest that while it appears as though the science wars are being waged on a philosophical or metaphysical battlefield, the real issue has much more to do with the actual practice of science and the social study of that practice.

The final major event of the science wars that we will analyze is the publication of Norman Levitt's book *Prometheus Bedeviled*. In an apparent effort to keep the science wars alive, Levitt attempts to demonstrate how the major institutions that constitute contemporary society continually distort and misrepresent science, with the inevitable result that the vast majority of people neither understand nor appreciate what science has done for them. For Levitt, this is the ultimate paradox. How is it possible that in a society largely constructed by science, science becomes the enemy? His answer is that most people are ignorant, lazy, apathetic, and for the most part more willing to accept irrational explanations in support of their own views and aspirations than they are to acknowledge the objective truths of science. Levitt's remedy is for us to "give science a social authority commensurate with its astonishing success in living up to its own ambitions. The corollary is that we have to ignore or reject its rivals."[11]

Levitt's book is of interest because of his direct attack on religion. He makes explicit here what had been implicit in the earlier skirmishes, the view that science and religion are of necessity opposed to each other. Levitt, a declared atheist, gives no quarter. Religion and science are enemies. "Religion had to be annulled and diluted as doctrine, or divested of its political power and shunted to a subsidiary social position, for either democratic politics or science to thrive." He mocks the churches, ridicules the anthropic principle, argues that "evolutionary theory, presented soberly and honestly, subverts the foundational view of morality," and declares that science reveals the universe "as altogether without purpose or design." Science is a purely monistic and reductionistic process. "Science, bluntly, has no room for human values, purposes, ethics, or hopes." And science is the only road to objective truth, for as he states, "in cases of conflict, a reasonably well-established scientific conclusion trumps any challenger."[12]

For Levitt, any tension between objectivity and mystery is abolished and only objectivity remains. As for the great mysteries of life that have been the core of religion, concern with them is only for the weak: "Bluntly, human existence is an accident, with no ultimate purpose. I believe this, as do most of my close friends. We're reasonably comfortable with this conclusion. But it would be fatuous to pretend that it does not inflict pain and psychic dislocation on millions, possibly billions, of people. Science is clearly the primary sponsor and authority for this view of things."[13] Levitt and the others thus state the issues clearly and starkly. For them, science and religion are incompatible, and no dialogue is possible.

What is the importance of the science wars, and what can we learn from the experience? We think the episode has two implications, one for the social study of science and another for the science-religion dialogue.

Reflecting on the impact of Gross and Levitt's book and his own experiment, Sokal states that the issue at the heart of the science wars is "the nature of truth, reason, and objectivity."[14] Similarly, Jardine and Frasca-Spada observe that the science wars have provoked "a renewed and public engagement with scientists on central issues concerning the nature of scientific truth and rationality, and the unity and autonomy of science."[15] In other words, representatives from both sides of these debates identify a philosophical battlefield where the ontology, epistemology, and methodology of science are open to question. According to Gross and Levitt, the vast majority of scientists hold with some form of logical positivism (with a few Popperian addenda), while those on the academic left favor some version of radical (that is, ontological, epistemological, and methodological) relativism.[16] As the material presented in our earlier chapters indicates, not only are philosophical debates about the nature of science ongoing and largely unresolvable, at least by purely philosophical means, it is grossly inaccurate to characterize the philosophical positions of scientists, and those that study science, as simplistically as Gross and Levitt's comments would imply. Consequently, the absence of an adequate foundation (or shared constellation of meanings) upon which to carry out constructive debate over the nature of science has regrettably led to specious posturing and ad hominem attacks. Jardine and Frasca-Spada provide the following two statements to illustrate this phenomenon, the first by biologist Lewis Wolpert and the second by sociologist of science Bruno Latour.

> You might expect that the sociologists and philosophers would have helped to illuminate the nature of science. The great disappointment is that not only have they failed to illuminate it, but they have actually obfuscated it. . . . Why are the sociologists of science doing this? I can only give a sociological explanation. It's little more than envy. For me science has been remarkably successful in providing us with an understanding of the world.

> A small number of theoretical physicists deprived of the fat budgets of the cold war, seek a new menace against which they heroically offer the protection of their *esprit*. . . . France, in their eyes, has become another Colombia, a country of dealers who

produce hard drugs—derridium, lacanium, to which American
doctoral students have no more resistance than to crack.[17]

The upshot of this situation, at least with respect to social studies
of science, is that the time has come to abandon philosophical debates
about the nature of science, and return to, or perhaps begin to undertake, the genuine and, we would suggest, largely unexplored social study
of science. In a recent statement, Sokal warns:

> Science Studies' epistemological conceits are a diversion from
> the important matters that motivated Science Studies in the first
> place: namely, the social, economic and political roles of sci-
> ence and technology. To be sure those conceits are not an acci-
> dent; they have a history, which can be subjected to sociological
> study. But Science Studies practitioners are not obliged to per-
> sist in a misguided epistemology; they can give it up, and go
> on with the serious task of studying science. Perhaps, from the
> perspective of a few years from now, today's so-called "Science
> Wars" will turn out to have marked such a turning point.[18]

Apart from the obvious "physician heal thyself" remark that this
statement elicits, Sokal is on the right track in one important respect.
The social study of science is not about trying to solve philosophical
issues about what science essentially is or should be. Rather, it is about
trying to capture what science actually is, that is, how it is carried out
on a day-to-day basis. However, this will only happen through the open
exploration of daily practice, by interacting with working scientists, in
what Herbert Blumer calls a "naturalistic" investigation, an "investigation that is directed to a given empirical world in its natural, ongoing
character instead of to a simulation of such a world, or to an abstraction from it (as in the case of laboratory experimentation), or to a substitute for the world in the form of a preset image of it."[19] This statement
holds for both physicists and sociologists. Studying subatomic particles
requires a method that respects the nature of quarks and leptons. Studying
the scientists that carry out this research requires a method that respects
the (human) nature of those scientists. This is a key insight of interpretive social science.

Many approaches to science start out from the position that there
is a philosophically consistent set of propositions that defines what science should be; or that some set of institutional norms exists that con-
strains the behavior of scientists; or, as some postmodernists would have
it, that science is all just language games. Starting out in any of these
ways inevitably leads to arguments over competing ideologies, with the

result that empirical investigations of what goes on in science are generally dismissed as inherently biased, or they are just not done. Alternatively, interpretive social science would have us start from the position that there is no a priori foundation for science, and that we should explore, instead, the ways that meanings are constructed, maintained, and altered by those engaged in doing science. The science wars would quickly fade if the protagonists abandoned philosophizing and mud slinging and returned to engaging in the activities that constitute the realms of human endeavor through which they intersubjectively, rather than objectively, construct their identities and accomplish their goals. For those in the social study of science, this means studying science socially.

The implications of the science wars for the science-religion dialogue are a little different. Because of widespread favorable media coverage, many people assumed that Gross, Levitt, and Sokal spoke for science. The issues they identified became the agenda for debate, especially their fear of relativism. Indeed, because many religionists are equally opposed to relativism, there was even some sympathy for their point of view on the part of some in the dialogue. It is perhaps one of the great ironies of the science wars, and one that many scientists do not realize, that people of faith share their conviction regarding the existence and pursuit of truth. Because their attack upon religion was implicit, at least until Levitt's most recent book, the full implications of what they had to say were not always recognized.

10 Naturalism, Science, and Religion

The scientist does not study nature because it is useful; he studies it because he delights in it, and he delights in it because it is beautiful. If nature were not beautiful, it would not be worth knowing, and if nature were not worth knowing, life would not be worth living.

—Henri Poincaré, *Science and Method*

One problem with the science wars is that they mystify science. The science wars, however, do raise some important issues for the science-religion dialogue. Alan Sokal and Norman Levitt, discussed at length in the previous chapter, represent an extreme conflict position in the context of what in chapter 4 we called metaphysical naturalism. This understanding of science leaves no place for religion. As we will demonstrate, metaphysical naturalism is an inadequate approach to science. An examination of how scientists, in particular physicists, approach the creation and validation of scientific knowledge will show that there is a relationship between the different ways of knowing reality and that there is nothing in science that necessarily excludes religion.

The Aims of Modern Science

Why scientists believe what they believe is as important as what they believe. The enterprise of modern science attempts to understand nature through posing and answering specific questions. This enterprise involves the creation of new hypotheses, the accumulation of evidence, the setting of standards of proof, and the validation of ideas through the institutional consensus of public knowledge.

Science is a human activity, and scientific work is a human construction that pragmatically attempts to be as objective as possible while balancing various human, traditional, institutional, and cultural forces that inevitably impact the enterprise. But ironically, the doing of science is more an art than a science, and scientific knowledge is always a work in progress involving this matrix of internal and external factors.

How one views reality is intimately related to the kinds of questions one is seeking to answer. These questions always reflect one's temperament, background, training, and culture. We will see that scientists are no exception, for they are constantly making choices about what to study, what instruments to use, and what theories to apply in their inquiries. And the answers they receive to questions posed to nature always require interpretation.

In essence, modern science involves a dialogue between scientists and nature. Hypotheses created in the minds of the scientists are used as vehicles to predict answers to the questions which scientists ask nature through controlled experiments. Modern science differs from earlier forms of science in its choice of questions and its attempt to interact objectively with an external world. This is also reflected in a shift in goals from descriptions of nature to the prediction of future events in natural systems. The significance and importance of this shift cannot be overstated: the laws of nature, which are based on things we have observed and measured, allow us to know in the future about things we have not observed or measured.

The development of modern science was aided by two historical shifts in human attitude and perspective. By restricting the scope of questions to be answered and problems to be solved, it was possible to develop an understanding that was qualitatively different from earlier understandings. In chapter 5 we outlined some of the ways in which this change in perspective came about. Science as we know it today was born on the day that people stopped asking why a particular stone fell upon a certain workman on a specific day and started asking how stones fall in general. From a prescientific perspective, it would have been natural to personalize this event and ask what this person did to cause the stone to fall on him. The scientific viewpoint rejects the idea that every event that occurs is unique and is directly caused by our personal relationship with the gods, God, or the stars. In the scientific way of thinking, events on Earth are not caused by actions in the heavens or the spirit world. With this change in perspective, science became decoupled from religion and began to ask different questions and expect different answers. In general, scientists are concerned not with why things happen, but with how they happen. This reflects the pragmatic frame of mind of most scientists and the adoption of utility as the primary criterion in science for determining understanding, truth, and value.

The second change involved an ethos shift during the Scientific Revolution of the seventeenth century from general philosophical questions to specific problems that can be solved in detail.[1] For modern science, it is only through the specific that the general can be identified and elucidated. This approach to science as problem solving has evolved to become the guiding aim of modern science.

Scientific Questions, Evidence, and Validation

What is the justification for the credence, belief, and trust in the accepted facts, conclusions, and pronouncements of the scientific community? How do we know for sure that the mass of an electron equals 9.11×10^{-31} kg or whether electrons really exist at all? Physics is not an exact science, but it is a quantitatively experimental science that always must deal with uncertainties. Though there are always alternative reasons for things happening in the natural world, the important question is, what is the best or most likely reason? The justification of scientific knowledge ultimately is that it is based on the criteria and standards developed and accepted by the scientific community.

It is important to remember that the enterprise of modern science involves three distinct aspects: first, the creation of hypotheses; second, the verification or falsification of hypotheses; and third, the validation and acceptance of a hypothesis by the scientific community. The creation of hypotheses involves a combination of persistence, talent, intuition, imagination, timing, and luck. It is very difficult to come up with plausible new hypotheses that are substantive, useful, and testable, and the process of how good hypotheses occur to scientists is very difficult to explain. In fact, most scientists go through their careers without coming up with a single important hypothesis that later became confirmed.

The verification of any scientific idea usually involves the careful and critical correlation of interdependent work of many scientists from many different labs in many countries. The scientists involved in the verification process often bring along auxiliary baggage that creates conflict with other scientists. Often it is difficult to determine whether scientific conflicts are conflicts over substantive data, interpretations, and issues or whether the conflicts are really personality clashes or differences in traditions or values.

Ideally, scientists should attempt to falsify or disprove their proposed hypotheses, that is, challenge the appropriateness and validity of their own ideas and understanding. In reality this rarely happens; instead most scientists try to confirm the validity of their ideas. The falsification of hypotheses by third parties is a process more likely to occur when there are rival hypotheses that are inconsistent with each other in a profound way within a larger theory. Ultimately one of the hypotheses will have to exit the intellectual stage, leaving the survivor as the "best" or most appropriate hypothesis under the given circumstances and evidence.

The final aspect of the scientific enterprise is validation by the scientific community. This is a communal activity involving the hierarchy and the political dynamics within the appropriate scientific field. The British physicist John Ziman has developed a very useful perspective and understanding of the enterprise of modern science that is based on the concept that science is public knowledge.[2] The growth of science then becomes the process of developing a consensus of this public knowledge by the scientific community. Individual and institutional communications, networks of trust, and institutional dynamics play pivotal roles in how scientific knowledge progresses through validation. An example of the complex dynamics of this process was demonstrated in chapter 8, which dealt with the controversy over the extinction of the dinosaurs.

Models and Theory

Newtonian mechanics was the first closed system of mathematical physics; in fact, it can be thought of as a branch of experimental mathematics. Its structure naturally led to the decoupling of the general laws of nature and the specific models created for each system of objects being studied. The revolutionary separation by Newton of theory from the specific models used to study various systems of nature is a feature that has continuously been used in physics.[3] Interestingly, Newtonian theory was really Platonic in nature in that it dealt with ideal concepts and principles that, even in principle, were neither directly observable nor testable.[4]

In the Newtonian system, as in the Euclidean system of geometry upon which Newton modeled his work, a theory involving concepts and principles is constructed to be logically true, while the approximations (and shortcomings) always come in the models. In practice, one assumes the theory to be true; it is then applied to specific cases in nature through the models for those systems. In the Newtonian view of physics, theory represents an ideal facsimile or verisimilitude of the structure and behavior of nature, while the physical models represent an actual sampling of nature.

The testing of Newtonian mechanics is always done within the context of a model of some specific system, which always includes a set of assumptions and simplifications. Each model has its own set of assumptions and simplifications and is therefore unique. The model approach of Newtonian mechanics and the controlled experimental testing of hypotheses combine to naturally suggest a selection of problems to be studied by physicists. It is profitable to attack specific problems that are, at least in theory, quantitatively solvable using mathematical techniques. These problems are usually relatively simple problems that are idealized and treated as a series of successive approximations to reality.

In order to solve any physical problem, one must be able to set up a model that is realistic enough to be relevant while at the same time simple enough to be solved mathematically. The first step in this process, and probably the most important one, is choosing what is essential and what details can be left out of the model. As William James once remarked with profound insight: "As the art of reading (after a certain stage in one's education) is the art of skipping, so the art of being wise is the art of knowing what to overlook."[5]

Physicists are not interested in the truth, the whole truth, and nothing but the truth. In fact, if we could know everything about the world, we would be overwhelmed and understand nothing. For example, if we could actually see atoms, the nearly infinite number of atoms impinging on our senses would cause us not to be able to see beyond the thin layer of atoms next to our eyes, and we would be effectively blind. Too much information can be disabling; it is important to be selective in what to use and how to use it. Ultimately these important choices are intuitive, based on experience and imagination, and reflect the talents and judgments of the individual scientists.

One cannot do controlled experiments without breaking down the relevant system into its smallest components. The way physicists study nature is similar to the operation of CT scans, where carefully chosen two-dimensional slices can be used to reconstruct the whole three-dimensional organism. This reconstruction involves the solution of the inverse problem that attempts to determine what the whole entity actually is from what carefully selected segments appear to be. Physicists understand their sample systems through a series of successive approximation models. They identify and eliminate all possible complicating factors in order to construct the simplest possible model that can still realistically describe the essential features of the system. After this simplified model is analyzed and understood, complicating factors (complexities) are added to the model one at a time in order to make it more realistic and more closely correspond to the real system that they are modeling.

Platonism, Realism, Truth, and Objectivity

In essence, theoretical physicists create a parallel universe in mental space that is a conceptual template in which empirical facts can be correlated and analyzed, and that also can be used as a computational tool to crank out answers to questions posed to nature through controlled experiments. This Platonic conceptual universe is an acceptable facsimile of nature if, and only if, it can correctly predict answers to future questions submitted to nature by empirical testing. Ideally, the conceptual framework of a theory will suggest significant questions to pose to nature which have never been asked.

Objectivity and Quantum Mechanics

The scientist is strongly coupled to nature through the questioning process, which uses various ideal conceptual models of nature and whatever instrumentation is employed to ask the questions. This view of modern science as inquiry was significantly extended and modified during the 1920s by the development of quantum mechanics, which suggested a change in what was considered possible to know about nature. The fundamental outcome of the "quantum crisis" in early-twentieth-century physics was the realization that "whatever fundamental units the world is put together from, they are more delicate, more fugitive, more startling than we catch in the butterfly net of our senses."[6] Werner Heisenberg discussed the significance of this change: "Natural science does not simply describe and explain nature; it is a part of the interplay between nature and ourselves; it describes nature as exposed to our method of questioning."[7] An important corollary to Heisenberg's observation is that strict objectivity, at least at the quantum level, does not and cannot exist.[8] Nature and the scientist are coupled through the experimental process and become more coupled as the questioning becomes more intimate. Modern twentieth-century physics is essentially a questioning process that says less about the nature of nature and more about what we can ask and say about nature.

It should be emphasized that the observer-system dilemma in quantum mechanics is not incompatible with the traditional aim of objectivity in science. Classically, the strong version of objectivity is viewed as the separation of the observer from the system he or she is studying.[9] The weak version of objectivity represents the dispassionate approach a scientist takes toward her or his work. Instead of aiming for complete objectivity, scientists today generally strive for the best objectivity possible under the circumstances.

Practically viewed, then, one can speak of degrees of objectivity. This involves a deliberate attempt to be impartial and dispassionate in one's research and to be detached from the outcome of that work. Certainly one should strive to avoid injecting one's politics, religious views, ambition, or personal conflicts into scientific observations, analyses, interpretations, and pronouncements. Thus, the contemporary view of objectivity is less a condition and more a pragmatic attitude toward one's work.

Varieties of Scientific Truth

There is a major caveat for this philosophical discussion that also applies to many other general analyses and discussions about "science" and "scientists." The problem is simply that there is no generic science or generic scientists. When people talk about "science" or "scientists," they are referring to a generalized ideal that does not exist.

Scientists are really astronomers, physicists, chemists, biologists, geologists, and so on, and these different kinds of scientist view and deal with the natural world in profoundly different ways. The division of labor in the scientific enterprise also affects the different perspectives typical of theoreticians and experimentalists. Theoretical physicists, for example, tend to see, understand, and appreciate the universe in vastly different ways than do observational astronomers.

It is possible to gain some general insight into the mindset of scientists by comparing the perceived relationship between nature and science typical of theoretical physicists with that typical of observational astronomers. The theoreticians tend to see the nature/science reality in terms of a trinity consisting of nature, theory (which is necessarily idealized), and models. The models for the particular systems being studied act as intermediaries between nature and scientific theories. Theory is usually treated in the same fashion as Newton treated his theory in the *Principia*, that is, as an axiomatic, deductive system patterned after Euclid's geometry. After the individual concepts and principles have been adequately tested and verified and successfully incorporated into a general theory, these components are assumed to be true as they are applied to various models.

Is this conceptual world real? The answer depends on one's relationship to it. As physicist John Barrow points out: "Most scientists and mathematicians operate as if Platonism is true, regardless of whether they believe it is. That is, they work as though there were an unknown realm of truth to be discovered."[10] If the importance of something is measured in terms of what it causes one to do, then to most scientists this imaginary world seems real because they act upon the belief that it is real.

Observational astronomers are probably closer to other scientific disciplines in their view of the relationship between nature and science than are theoretical physicists. Astronomers tend to be empirical model builders who view nature/science as a doublet consisting of nature and their empirically constructed models that are continually being revised. Astronomers pragmatically take the concepts and principles from physics, chemistry, and geology as needed to build the appropriate models that correlate the information that their instruments have yielded them. Few astronomers believe their models are real or that they will survive to be actively used in research fifty years into the future.

The Scientific View of Reality and Its Limitations

The scientific view of reality has been successful and influential far beyond the scientific laboratories. In fact, our modern society is based upon the fruits of scientific perspectives and research.

But this worldview has limitations that should be acknowledged and understood in order to prevent abuses and unrealistic expectations. The limitations of the scientific viewpoint and approach can be grouped into three categories: epistemological, systematic, and cultural.[11]

The two major epistemological features of modern science are the questioning of nature through controlled experiments and the mathematical modeling of the systems of nature being studied. Controlled experiments are the best-known method of testing scientific hypotheses, but there are a number of limitations that influence the interpretation and meaning of the experimental results. First, all data are theory laden, that is, they are embedded within some theoretical framework. Second, hypotheses always involve a set of associated assumptions, and third and finally, hypotheses are almost never tested individually. In most cases, a group of hypotheses and their associated assumptions are tested as a unit that requires an interpretative analysis. And, of course, there may be some truths about nature that are not discernable through controlled experiments.

Constructing the laws of nature in mathematical terms and using mathematical models are very powerful approaches for examining patterns, relationships, and interrelationships among observed phenomena. Though extremely powerful as a system and as an analytic tool, the mathematical approach to understanding nature shares the limitations of the system of mathematics being applied.[12]

Science has been very successful at uncovering and elucidating relationships among natural phenomena, especially phenomena connected through causal relationships. In a real sense, this ability to predict the future behavior of nature is the strength of science.[13] But as was discovered and analyzed by David Hume, this edifice of knowledge is built on soft ground.[14] The only reason we can say with confidence that the sun will rise tomorrow is that from past experience it always has risen. The scientist's ability to predict the future of natural events depends on inferences from the past and present that are projected into the future. Bertrand Russell pointed out that a similar problem exists with the validity of induction.[15] Scientific predictions are based on past experiences, and it is impossible to know definitely whether scientific principles applied to a new system will be valid for that system until they are tested.[16] The problems of causality and induction are examples of the general paradox of human understanding, in that it is always easy to believe more than you can prove or know for sure. The laws of nature themselves place some limits on what is measurable and what is knowable. Heisenberg's uncertainty principle, in particular, places a restriction on our access to the microscopic world.[17] Whether this restriction reflects the limitations of our knowing or whether it represents a basic reality of nature has been an issue of debate for more than sixty years. At the quantum level, we have reached a level of nature that is impossible to perceive in terms of simple classical ideas, models, and experiences.

Science, Religion, and the Webs of Reality

Based on our study of how science works, it is clear that science is an interpretive activity requiring human choices at each step of the various processes. These choices are resolved through a combination of intelligence, tradition, communal interactions, and contingency. This interpretive aspect of science is the key to understanding how science relates to other ways of knowing. We argue that the scientific view is certainly very important, but that other approaches to reality also need to be included in our lives and in our understanding of the universe.

Hidden within the conflict over objectivity and realism are the important issues of boundaries and authority. Ultimately this has to do with who gets a voice in determining what is acceptable knowledge and what is the official understanding of the reality that this knowledge implies. On one level these issues reflect a contest for power within society. This relates to our argument for a more open process of inclusion among the relevant players in the science-religion debate. The question of boundaries can be viewed as a struggle between an elitist vision of reality decided by a small number of experts, and a more democratic process of determining who gets a say in the outcome. And as with most issues, it is the extremists who define the arguments, but it is the moderates who live peacefully with each other.

Certainly one extreme view involves the belief that science is the only way to truth. Actually this attitude has a long history going back to the empiricism of John Locke, who viewed sensory experience as the primary source of knowledge and the justification of the truth of propositions. In the early nineteenth century, Auguste Comte proposed positivism as a system of philosophy based on accepting as true knowledge only personal experiences and empirical information of natural phenomena. Reality consisted only of this defined world of empirical facts and logic and mathematics. This belief system became the basis of a later philosophical movement called logical positivism that rejected all metaphysics and believed that all human understanding eventually would be in the form of science. This movement was ideological and promoted an agenda that was material, antimetaphysical, and secular (antitheological). So we see that there was an earlier effort to reduce the ways of knowing to those that could be put on a strict logical basis using empirical data.

But is science the only method to obtain truth, the only valued way of knowing? Certainly this claim is ultimately an ideological dogma and not a scientific or philosophical position. This ideology is also associated with the views of scientific materialism, scientism, and metaphysical naturalism. Materialism is the belief that matter is the basis of all of reality, while scientific materialism is associated with the metaphysical belief that a scientific explanation of matter is a sufficient basis for explaining all of reality. Scientism, which is similar to scientific materialism, is the claim that the only truth is scientific truth and that the only path to knowledge is the path of science. For our purposes, the attitude of scientism has its origins with a later development of positivism by a group of German and Austrian philosophers in the 1920s, referred to as the logical positivists. This school was greatly influenced by developments in formal logic, and it played a dominant role in the philosophy of science for the following half century. Though logical positivism has since lost its dominant position, issues in the philosophy of science are still often framed in terms of a response to logical positivism. Usually scientism is expressed as the belief that the methods of science can and should be used in all fields of investigation. (It should be pointed out that *scientism* is considered a pejorative term and is almost always applied by critics of science to certain scientists who are viewed as promoting a dominating role for science in society.)

One hotly debated issue in the interdisciplinary study of science and religion is the distinction between methodological naturalism and metaphysical naturalism.[18] The use of methodological naturalism restricts explanations of natural phenomena to natural processes and rejects any supernatural influences. Metaphysical naturalism goes one step further and categorically claims that supernatural phenomena and influences do not exist. The adoption of this metaphysical principle by some scientists implies the explicit rejection of a soul, a spirit world, any supernatural influences in the universe, and any God who can directly interact with the universe. The implications of this belief for religion are obvious and draconian.

Any scientist who insists on imposing metaphysical naturalism is guilty of scientism. This involves usurping the boundary between science and religion and claiming all of reality for science. In essence, this would be a form of atheism imposed by fiat and a reconciliation of science and religion by eliminating religion as it is known by most people. This consequence implies that the role of naturalism in science is a fair topic for both scientists and believers to examine and debate. Thoughtful pleas against the excesses of scientism have recently been made by the respected environmental farmer, poet, and essayist Wendell Berry and by the dean of religion writers, Huston Smith.[19] They eloquently argue that any claim of "one way" is hollow and diminishes all of us.

According to Chet Raymo, one useful way to avoid domination by one side or the other is to look at the science-religion debate in terms of skeptics and true believers.[20] True believers are people who believe that their way of knowing is the only way. They have a tendency not to listen to or care about alternative viewpoints and to believe that they are sure they know the truth. This confidence of having superior knowledge creates an inability to live with ambiguity and a need to impose a single belief or restrictions on others.

It is very tempting to claim the right to draw the boundaries between science and the other constituents of society. But it is also very dangerous to claim the power that is implied in that right. The boundaries between different human enterprises should be freely negotiated among the various interested parties and not forced from above by an intellectual elite. But in either science or religion, it is the true believers who have a need to draw sharp boundaries and define what other people are allowed to do and to believe.

At the other extreme of boundary drawing is the desire to integrate science and religion. One of the alternative methods of integration involves restructuring religion to be consistent with the philosophical foundations of science. This approach seems popular today and can be seen in the various versions of process theology, among others. These theologies seem to be built upon a foundation of modern science and tend to associate God with a universe that is growing in complexity and potential. As in the case of scientism, the integration of science and religion reduces the possibilities of ways of knowing and the ways of relating in the world.

A respect for other viewpoints does not include mergers by elite intellectuals to create a forced harmony. All the players, including ordinary scientists and the believers in the pews, should be allowed to participate in drawing the boundaries and deciding on the functions allocated to the different enterprises. Reality is too important to be left to the elites.

One way to encourage the sharing of reality is not to view reality as a single flat plane to be either divided up or taken over. It would be better to view reality as a multifaceted entity that requires multiple maps to fully understand its nature and purpose.[21] These maps should not be viewed as competing alternatives, but as complementary understandings seen through different filters constructed from different experiences, traditions, values, and goals. In essence, these maps represent different layers of meaning that correspond to the different dimensions in which humans understand and relate to the universe.

Science is a wonderful and powerful way of knowing and understanding the universe, but it is only one of many ways of relating to and appreciating it. We have argued that it is possible to recognize and honor science without taking away from the other approaches that humans have taken to relate and enrich their lives.[22] One does not need to know any acoustics to appreciate beautiful music, but having knowledge of acoustics could further add to its appreciation. The beauty and appreciation of a flower, as Richard P. Feynman passionately maintained, can be viewed and understood from multiple human lenses and perspectives that complement each other.[23]

Reality is a complex web with many strands, and our future will be only as interesting and robust as the number of strands we allow in the web. The universe, including humans and their societies, is an amazingly rich source of content, meaning, and opportunity. Adopting a position of pluralism would allow this richness to be appreciated, shared, and developed in a way that will make our lives even richer. The various ways of knowing and appreciating our world should complement each other instead of competing in a winner-take-all contest for reality.

11 | History and Hermeneutics

I read history a little as a duty; but it tells me nothing that does not either vex or weary me. The quarrels of popes and kings, with wars and pestilences in every page; the men all so good for nothing, and hardly any women at all, it is very tiresome; and yet I often think it odd that it should be so dull, for a great deal of it must be invention.
—Jane Austen, *Northanger Abbey*

Catherine Morland, Jane Austen's character quoted in the epigraph, may have shocked nineteenth-century readers with her view of history. Today, the idea that written history is "a great deal of invention" would be commonplace, at least in some academic circles. This is because over the past half-century, notions of historical objectivity have been more or less thoroughly dismantled.

In this book, we are arguing that a similar process has been occurring in the natural sciences. In chapter 9 we detailed the sort of defensive postures that have been taken in some scientific quarters when claims to objectivity in science have been challenged. We will see that these attitudes have arisen in debates within the social sciences as well. In chapter 10 we suggested that a more nuanced view of the practice of science is possible and used the example of physics to illustrate how a scientist works. In this chapter, we engage in a similar exercise and examine how historians work. There are some interesting parallels. The last chapter made two important points: first, that while working scientists often adopt a pragmatic realist position, the search for objectivity is more an attitude than a real condition; and second, that since the development of quantum theory, scientists have become much more comfortable with a view of science as a dialectical activity, one in which the scientist becomes a participant in nature, rather than a mere observer. The adoption of a pragmatic realism on the one hand, and the simultaneous recognition of the role of the scholar as participant on the other, are concepts that historians, like scientists, have learned to balance.

It has become commonplace to understand written history as a product both of the past and of the mind of the historian working to understand the past. Historians look at the evidence from the past (usually in the form of written documents) and create a narrative structure into which the facts gleaned from the documents are fitted. Any historian worthy of the title will try to be as faithful to the sources as possible. In so doing, historians work on the assumption that there is something real to find out. Yet, all historians recognize that they need to do more than merely list the events of the past. They also seek to make sense of the past by setting priorities, organizing, analyzing, and synthesizing the "facts." The ideas and attitudes informing this exercise are not imbedded in the past itself but are those of the individual historian, who is as much a product of time and place as anyone else. The resulting history, therefore, is a conversation between the past and the present. It is this dialectical nature of history writing that has led to generations of debate regarding the issue of objectivity and relativism.

The social sciences have evolved from purportedly scientific disciplines to self-consciously interpretive ones. Along the way, attempts were made to find a middle path through the opposing poles of objectivity and relativism. An examination of how historians have dealt with, and continue to deal with, the question of objectivity has relevance for understanding current debates in science studies and in science-religion discussion. The sorts of issues social scientists faced throughout the past century are now being discussed among the natural scientists. By looking at the evolution of the objectivity question in the writing of the social sciences in general, and of history in particular, we find parallels with current debates in the natural sciences.

The last century has witnessed many attempts to make history and the other social sciences "scientific." Pioneers of the social sciences in the nineteenth and early twentieth centuries dreamed of making the study of human behavior scientific and discovering the laws that governed it. For example, in 1942 Carl Hempel published an essay titled "The Function of General Laws in History" in which he articulated ways in which history could be understood in a systematic manner.[1] Ultimately, this project was doomed to failure, and most social scientists have abandoned this as a goal. In many ways, the same challenges they faced throughout the philosophical evolution of the twentieth century are now being directed toward practitioners of the natural sciences. Therefore, this chapter will trace the most important philosophical trends that have informed the writing of history over the past half century as a way to illustrate how the issue of objectivity has been understood.

History as Discovery

Although natural scientists are apt to emphasize the differences rather than the similarities with social scientists, we might begin by looking at the working assumptions of historians in the past. We will see that both scientists and historians have generally gone about their work from a realist perspective. Both work to understand something that is "out there"; that is, both are driven by a curiosity to know something outside their own skins. For the scientists, it is the natural world, and for the historians, it is the past. In each case, there is a sense that something is waiting to be discovered, analyzed, and understood. Historians would generally agree that some events occurred in the past, and others did not. Like geologists studying a sedimentary rock, historians peer into a past considered by most people to be "real" in some sense. Even if the past is less tangible than a fossil, we can acknowledge that it is something external to the mind of the historian.

The philosophical basis of such an approach is an appeal to a correspondence theory of truth. In other words, historical description is true insofar as it accurately reflects reality. What this means is that, practically speaking, the value of a piece of history is determined by whether it conforms to what is already known about the past through the available evidence. Historians, with a few notable exceptions, make a distinction between history, which tries to conform to the events of the past, and fiction, which does not need to. Historians may, and do, disagree on the relative significance of the facts ascertained from one set of documents as opposed to the next. Nevertheless, the facts and the evidence are the measuring sticks. In 1946, the English historian Robin Collingwood described the good historian as a detective whose task it is to follow the clues to find out the facts of the case.[2] One of the most quoted examples of this attitude is the dictum of the nineteenth-century German historian Leopold von Ranke that the goal of history is to relate "what actually happened." This goal inspired generations of historians, driven to get things right.

This philosophical stance meant historians have occasionally been driven by the desire not just to get the facts right, but to get them all. There have been periodic dreams of learning all the history there is to learn. We find this dream encapsulated in the words of Lord Acton in 1896, as he set out to edit the *Cambridge Modern History*: "It is a unique opportunity of recording, in the way most useful to the greatest number, the fullness of knowledge that the nineteenth century is about to bequeath. . . . By the judicious division of labour we should be able to do it, and to bring home to every man the last document, and the ripest conclusions of international research."[3] This goal of universal knowledge reemerged in a different guise among the *Annales* historians in

France, who spoke of *histoire totale* and saw themselves writing comprehensive, global histories that would cover all facets of human experience. The multivolume and copiously detailed works of the French historian Fernand Braudel—on the Mediterranean and the history of European material culture—are the best examples of the extent to which this kind of energy and drive can lead.[4] The rise of interest in quantitative method and the use of computers in the 1970s furthered this optimistic (if hubristic) desire, as they seemed to offer new opportunities for collecting and analyzing ever-larger quantities of material.

History as Creation

It ought to be clear from the preceding examples that much historical inquiry has been informed by philosophical realism and guided by the desire to discover the past. With this view of history, the historian's task becomes that of adding more facts to the already existing pile. At the same time, however, a contrary trend has emerged. Throughout the last half of the twentieth century, historians became increasingly accustomed to the notion that their histories were conditioned by who they were and by when and where they were writing. The seminal point in this development was the 1931 address delivered by then-president of the American Historical Association, Carl Becker, entitled "Everyman His Own Historian," in which he argued that every generation writes its own history. What is implied in this statement is that every historian's writing is conditioned by the concerns of his or her generation.[5]

It may be humbling to young graduate students to realize that their work, no matter how stunning, will not stand forever; after all, we all hunger for immortality. The fact remains, however, that even the most brilliant historical writers of the nineteenth century—Macaulay, Burckhardt, Michelet—are read now for their style rather than substance, if they are read at all. To read them today is to learn more about the nineteenth century than about the periods that these men studied. This realization is instilled in historians at an early stage of their professional development and serves to engender an attitude of humility. Historians are trained to expect that their ideas will be debated and challenged, not only by those working with different documents or using a different set of analytical tools, but by future generations, who may find that the questions of their forerunners have become irrelevant and who will develop new questions and assumptions to guide their study of the past.

Change in Historical Interpretation

If we recognize that interpretations change over time, we then have to examine the issue of how they are overturned, modified, and rejected. First, at the most basic level, it does sometimes occur that new facts come to light that modify existing knowledge of the past. One example from English history will serve. For decades, historians had assumed English people in the sixteenth century married young and had large families, as is generally the case in preindustrial societies. However, the evidence from extensive research in the 1970s, based primarily on early modern wills, contradicted this assumption. In fact, the average age of marriage was in the late twenties for both men and women. Once this new evidence had come to light, historians began examining other aspects of English social history with fresh eyes. In the same way that scientists imagine coming up with a brilliant new theory that will overturn current understandings, historians dream of finding the documents that will lead to a dramatic reevaluation of conventional historical interpretation. However, as has been pointed out with regard to science in the previous chapter, such breakthroughs are rare. From a realist perspective, this is the most important way in which historical interpretations are overthrown, and it is parallel to the process identified by Thomas Kuhn in his seminal work, *The Structure of Scientific Revolutions.*

However, those who emphasize the role of interpretation in history have found other mechanisms at work. More commonly, history changes because historians bring new assumptions and attitudes to their study of the past. This was convincingly illustrated by Carl Degler in an essay written in 1976 entitled "Why Historians Change their Minds." Degler examined the vicissitudes throughout the twentieth century in historical interpretations of U.S. slavery, demonstrating that what influenced the written histories of slaves and slave owners was not the documents themselves but the shifting cultural attitudes toward race in general and slavery in particular. What had changed most dramatically from the beginning of the twentieth century on was not the documents available, nor even how they were read, but the assumptions about race and race relations that successive generations of historians brought to their research. For Degler then, historical interpretation changes because cultural assumptions and expectations change.[6]

Others took their analysis even further. In 1988, Peter Novick published a provocative book on the politics of the historical profession. In *That Noble Dream: The "Objectivity Question" and the American Historical Profession*, Novick examined discrimination within the historical profession and demonstrated that underneath a great many historiographical disagreements lay more basic issues of politics and territoriality. He argued that proponents of traditional history opposed the growth of social history because it was practiced by a new class of historians. He found tangible evidence for this claim in some of the debates taking place within the profession.[7]

The most interesting aspect of Novick's work for our purposes is that he argued that traditionalists, for the most part white Anglo-Saxon males, opposed plurality in the profession and defended their dominance of the field in the name of objectivity. The attitude Novick identified was clearly demonstrated by Gertrude Himmelfarb. In her book *The New History and the Old,* she contrasted the "old" political history with the "new" social history, phrasing her critique of social history as a philosophical issue:

> For it is not only political history that the social historian de-
> nies or belittles. It is reason itself: the reason embodied in the
> polity, in the constitutions and laws that permit men to order
> their affairs in a rational manner . . . it is the reason transmit-
> ted to the present by way of constitutions and laws. . . . And it
> is the reason inherent in the historical enterprise itself, in the
> search for an objective truth that always eludes the individual
> historian but that always . . . informs and inspires his work. This
> rationality is now consciously denied or unconsciously under-
> mined by every form of the new history.[8]

Revealing about this excerpt is Himmelfarb's equating the old history with the search for objective truth, whereas the new historians ask questions of the past "for which the evidence is sparse and unreliable and to which the answers are necessarily speculative, subjective, and dubious."[9] For Himmelfarb, it is not a question of a new generation of historians asking new questions and developing new analytical tools, but the dismantling of truth itself by those who reject reason. The debates over the issue of what constitutes real history have at times been as vociferous as the science wars. In both cases, claims are made to objectivity when political or territorial issues are at stake. Perhaps it is a common human trait for individuals to appeal to objectivity when they feel their views are threatened.

The expansion of the historical profession did appear to some as a descent into chaos, where there would no longer be consensus on what history was, or on how to do it. However, others have seen the expansion of the profession in less pessimistic terms. One group that has welcomed this dismantling of barriers—both political and methodological—have been the feminist scholars. Joan Wallach Scott, a prominent historian of gender, admitted that "there is no single standard by which we can identify 'true' historical knowledge" but then concluded that this is not a problem.[10] She called for a multiplicity of perspectives as all contributing to the collective historical knowledge. The rise of social history, and in particular women's history, has led to a breakdown of consensus, perhaps, but a breakdown of barriers as well.

Feminist historians, in particular, have been at the forefront of developing new methodologies. The comparative absence of women in the historical record meant historians of women had to develop ways of reading the existing sources in innovative ways to uncover the history of women. A parallel development in feminist critiques of scientific methodology is worth noting. The knowledge claimed by realists, they charge, is disembodied, abstract, asocial, and ahistorical—a god's-eye view of the world. Realism obscures the social, cultural, class, ethnic, and gender relations in which scientists are situated and which inevitably shape their knowledge. For example, feminists point to all the attempts, from Aristotle to Darwin to evolutionary psychology, to portray patriarchy as "natural." Nor is androcentric thinking confined to biology. As Sandra Harding argues:

> Physics, chemistry, and abstract thought in every realm (including philosophy) can be deeply sexist or androcentric even when no humans at all appear in their domain of inquiry. Evidently, abstract thought is not quite as abstract as most have assumed. Perhaps even excessive preferences for the abstract themselves undercut the point of abstraction: these preferences, like all others, can be historically located.[11]

Feminists go on to demonstrate the difference the standpoint of women can make to a supposedly objective science. For example, a significant number of women have entered the field of primatology in the past thirty years and by considering the "female monkey's point of view" have revolutionized our understanding of the lives of monkeys and apes.[12]

The Postmodern Challenge

One step beyond the political is the postmodern. The last several decades have been characterized by a sense that the historical profession is in crisis, due to challenges, perceived or real, by postmodern literary theorists and philosophers. Claims that there is no reality outside of the text, and that all reality is conditioned by the language in which it is described, have left historians scrambling to defend what they do and how they work. It is impossible here to summarize this extensive debate, but a short summary is pertinent.

First, we find those who look at the rhetorical structures used in history writing. A major influence in this sphere has been Hayden White, who has pointed out to historians that the narratives in which they frame the facts of history are governed by the same literary tropes and conventions as fictional narratives.[13] He argues that the mere selection of facts, not to mention their ordering and framing into a narrative structure, is itself a creative and an interpretive act. Historians have known this for a long time. But White goes further in his analysis. For him, it is not a question of framing the facts into a narrative but of determining the facts by the narrative. In other words, it is no longer a question of conforming the narrative to some real past. There is no meaning inherent in the past waiting to be discovered; rather, whatever meaning we find in the world is what we impose on it. To his mind, history is not about the recovery of the past in any objective sense.

One implication of White's work is that there is no real distinction between history and fiction. This attitude is articulated by, among others, Dominick LaCapra, who argues that the conventional distinction between history and fiction is illusory, because fiction uses facts and history fictionalizes facts in telling its story.[14] This blurring of the distinction has led to the creation of rather mischievous pieces of writing. For example, the historian Donald Akenson produced a biography of a nineteenth-century Canadian politician written from the perspective that the politician had actually been a woman disguised as a man. His argument rests on some clever sleuthing, but the biography itself is admittedly fictional. Akenson dismisses as irrelevant the question of whether the politician had historically been a woman: "Was John White really a woman? That is a question from male history and an inherently, if unconsciously, hostile one." He suggests the process of writing biography ought to be a "self-conscious exercise of imagination" and that "stories of individual human lives might better be called speculative history or historians' fiction."[15] His rationale for this claim is that the only alternative is to be unself-consciously subjective. In other words, objectivity is not even part of the equation.

Postmodern critics also attempt to dismantle the dichotomy that historians tend to draw between a text and its context. Many historians tend to see historical insights as measured in terms of the extent to which they conform to their historical context. However, the critics of this position argue that there is no context. Drawing on the insights of Michel Foucault and Jacques Derrida, F. R. Ankersmit argues that because our understanding of texts is always based on other texts, there is nothing to use as a measuring stick. There is no context.

Many of the conclusions reached by postmodern critics of history leave historians somewhat rattled. Hayden White goes so far as to assert that "events are real not because they occurred but because . . . they were remembered."[16] The conclusion reached by Ankersmit is that "at the level of the historical text and of historical interpretation, we cannot appropriately use the words truth and falsity."[17] The blurring of history and fiction attempted by Akenson and others leaves many working historians wondering what to do next. In many cases, the extreme relativism demonstrated by these conclusions has led historians to reject this perspective outright.

Historians' Reactions

An analysis of the varieties of historical interpretation is certainly something that historians are comfortable with. Students are taught they can arrive at conclusions that disagree with those of their professor, and as long as they can substantiate them, they will pass the course. That said, for almost everyone there is a line that will not be crossed. For many people, the Holocaust is such a line. To argue that all of history is subjective is to deny the reality of human suffering. In the end, it is often for moral reasons historians reiterate the need to continue the task of sorting fact from fiction. The cultural historian Robert Darnton had this in mind when he asked: "What is our science in the face of great events like wars and revolutions? What is our sophistication in the light of the lives that never made the news, that never had obituaries? To visit the dead, the historian needs something more than methodology. . . . No matter how skeptical we may be about the life to come, we cannot but feel humbled before all the lives that have gone."[18] In the face of both human suffering and human accomplishment, and in the face of holocaust denial, historians remain, in spite of postmodern trends, driven by the need to "get things right." Whether people have been killed or not, whether injustices have occurred—these are questions that still matter.

The Narrow Path

A great deal of ink has been spilled over the last thirty years as historians have reacted to postmodern influences. It would be a mistake to suggest anything approaching consensus on the impact of postmodern skepticism on the practice of history. The debates continue. Most fall into one of two categories. Many historians simply shrug their shoulders and return to the archives. On a daily basis, historians generally try to work to the best of their abilities to write the best history possible, by which is still meant an accurate representation of the facts. Even those historians whose approach is self-consciously influenced by postmodern concepts and methods tend to rely on basic rules governing the need for and use of evidence. In a sense, most historians share with natural scientists the adoption of a pragmatic realism. The difference lies in the fact that even as historians strive for objectivity, they are perhaps more aware than ever that it is an unattainable goal.

Other historians have tried to incorporate some of the most significant insights from the "linguistic turn," as it is called, into their research methods. Certainly, postmodern ideas have influenced notions of subjectivity, of the significance of text, and of the impossibility of working outside language. Because historians work primarily with language, they need to be particularly sensitive to issues related to the ambiguity embedded in it. Most working historians try to find a middle ground between objective reality and their own subjectivity.

One of the most promising avenues is a hermeneutic approach, a concept introduced earlier in this work. To understand hermeneutics we might look at the words of the philosopher Richard Rorty. Rorty argues, rather than looking at knowledge as representative of reality, we ought to consider it more as acquaintance.[19] For example, the French language uses two verbs for the English "to know," *savoir,* which suggests factual knowledge, and *connaître,* which implies understanding and acquaintance. For Rorty, knowledge of the world is rather like knowledge of an individual; it is built on an increasing awareness of who that person is. Thus, Rorty's definition of knowledge avoids an emphasis on objective truth but at the same time avoids the skepticism prevalent in radical postmodernism. Recognizing one's subjectivity is an essential part of the process of coming to understand and to learn something. This hermeneutic approach is appealing to historians because it reflects the way historians view and practice their craft. It allows a historian to work with both text and context, to move between the past and the present, in order to increase the understanding of both.

In what sense, then, is this relevant for understanding the issue of objectivity in relation to religion-science dialogue or in the use of the social sciences to understand the natural sciences? It is this: Historians continue to find out what happened in the past while acknowledging at the same time that both their findings and their conclusions are contingent. Furthermore, recognizing the role of the historian's subjectivity can become an integral component of the development of a historical narrative. Becoming self-conscious leads to becoming self-critical. The historical profession has benefited from the challenges to its claims to objectivity. To recognize one's subjectivity instills healthy doses of skepticism and of humility, both of which are useful components of any intellectual enterprise.

It will certainly be objected that important differences between the practice of history and of the natural sciences have been overlooked. As we have seen, history is explicitly a conversation between the past and the present, with the historian as mediator. Historians disagree on the ways in which the present should influence the interpretation of the past, but their answers are ones of degree. In the natural sciences, on the other hand, the voice of the individual scientist supposedly is not part of the end product. Scientific results are thought to be independent of the individual who identified them, and scientific experiments are considered accurate if they can be replicated by others. Each generation writes its own history. This is easy to grasp. The possibility that each generation writes its own science seems much less obvious. However, as we saw in chapter 8, this may be often more the case with science than is assumed.

However, what matters is that the discipline of history manages to survive in spite of the fact that it is seen as subjective. Some of the most vibrant breakthroughs occur when historians remove themselves from the categories of analysis that have become commonplace and ask themselves if those categories have any real meaning, as we have seen historians doing with the concept of the Scientific Revolution. This is a healthy intellectual exercise. In the same way, science will not necessarily disintegrate simply because a sociologist looks at the politics behind the granting of funds. Barry Allen makes this point succinctly: "Showing an important discovery (quarks, microbes) to be 'socially constructed' is not supposed to make us skeptical about quarks or microbes. It is instead a standing invitation to rethink the idea that science is a bastion of objective knowledge, or the scientist a guardian 'of the most important truths about the world,' truths which the laity should receive with 'pious reverence.'"[20] It appears that the natural scientists are now facing challenges that the social scientists, including historians, faced in the last century. But it is a sign of health and vigor if practitioners within a discipline can meet these challenges and respond to them in a way that leads to greater self-reflection and understanding on the part of their fellow practitioners and those examining their discipline.

The Possibility for Dialogue

Where does all this leave the science-religion dialogue? Both sides of this argument—realism and relativism—create problems. The problem with realism is that it does not leave much room for dialogue. We have seen that on occasion, both natural and social scientists have tried to build barriers to keep people out, based on exclusive truth claims. If this position is adopted, religion-science dialogue becomes impossible. At best, "objective" science talks, and "subjective" religion listens. Religion has little more to do than adapt its beliefs to the scientific findings of the day. Relativism creates difficulties of its own, not least because the various positions have little in common except their opposition to realism. The idea that knowledge is relative to identity can be carried too far. At its worst, it can become a reflection theory, in which a person's ideas are no more than the mirror image of her or his social group. But if nothing transcends identity, there is no basis for dialogue. Neither religion nor science can get beyond being just another viewpoint.

Fortunately, there is no need to accept either extreme. We can go beyond the false dichotomy of objectivism and relativism by focusing on a hermeneutical approach. The difficulty is to find an understanding of language that can encompass both subject and object. To begin with, there is no access to "reality" that is not mediated by language. The history of the Alvarez hypothesis demonstrates that scientists do not speak with the unmediated voice of nature. For nearly twenty years scientists argued (frequently without even much civility), each side claiming to have nature in its corner. What was at dispute were the facts, but the different sides could not agree on what the facts were or even what the standards of evaluation were, the means of determining whether a purported fact was relevant or not. What realists overlook is that all language is metaphorical (including their own) and that empirical observation can never be separated from the language in which it is imbedded. As Bruce Gregory explains: "The observations with which physicists compare their predictions are not some mute expression of the world. They are symbolic and gain their meaning and value in a system of interpretation. No experiment . . . has any meaning at all until it is interpreted by theory."[21] Both the natural sciences and the social sciences are very much human activities, governed and conditioned by the language with which we communicate them.

12 | The Centrality of Dialogue

It seems clear we cannot distinguish reality as such from our symbolizations of it. Being human we can only think in symbols, only make sense of any experience in symbols.

—Robert Bellah, *Beyond Belief*

The ancient Greek philosopher Archimedes is supposed to have said that he could move the world with a lever, if only he had a place to stand. The search for a philosophical Archimedean point is a quest for certainty, for objectivity, for knowledge that is beyond society, history, or individual subjectivity. What constitutes an Archimedean point has varied from philosophy to philosophy over the centuries, but in our time the claim is made for science.

The sacred is mysterious. Various scholars describe the sacred as that which is set apart and forbidden, as the ineffable, the wholly other.[1] It is the awe-inspiring and fascinating mystery, which exerts a terrible power. The sacred creates its own time and space outside the normal bounds of society and rationality. And mystery, as Weber noted, is one of the fundamental characteristics of religion.

As practical beings, who must live in the material world, humans want objectivity. As spiritual beings who need meaning as much as bread, humans require mystery. Truth is found in the necessary tension between the poles of mystery and objectivity, and truth is lost when the tension is abandoned. Yet imbalance is all too characteristic of our times. Those who see a necessary conflict between science and religion try to escape the tension by fleeing to one pole or the other. Those who compartmentalize science and religion try to ignore the tension. Those who work to integrate science and religion try to resolve the tension. We believe that only through dialogue can the tension be retained and a constructive balance be achieved between science and religion.

This chapter is about two different ways of knowing. One is the quest for certainty, which is exemplified by the science wars. The other is truth as dialogue.

The Quest for Certainty

Although the truth may be found in the tension between objectivity and mystery, it is often an uncomfortable position. It is frequently ambiguous and gives rise to discussions that rarely provide clear-cut answers. Many try to escape the tension by trying to find some absolute basis for knowledge. The science wars are exemplars of the quest for certainty.

This quest reflects three perennial issues that go to the root of Western culture. First, there have always been those who try to escape the inherent tension between objectivity and mystery by seeking an anchor, an Archimedean point, and fear all will be lost without it. Behind much of this fear is what philosopher Richard Bernstein called the "Cartesian anxiety." Arising with Descartes, he says, this is "a grand and seductive Either/Or. *Either* there is some support for our being, a fixed foundation for our knowledge, *or* we cannot escape the forces of darkness that envelop us with madness, with intellectual and moral chaos."[2] The science wars are an expression of this anxiety.

Second, the quest for certainty is deeply suspicious of dialogue. Those who seek certainty have frequently seen themselves as engaged in an argument between philosophy (or science) and rhetoric, which is usually portrayed as a contest between the truth and mere opinion. What is true is seen as objectively real, while everything else is only ephemeral language. As Levitt puts it: "Science matters greatly because it tells us how the world works, whereas the work of humanists and many social thinkers matters hardly at all because it only tells us how their minds work."[3] The individual who knows the objective truth, the argument goes, can stand alone against the opinions of both the crowd and those in power. This attitude is not new. Ian Hacking comments that these issues replicate the philosophical debate between realists and nominalists that extends back to medieval times.[4] Bruno Latour traces the origin even further back, to the debate between Socrates and the sophist Callicles in Plato's *Gorgias*.[5] Kary Smout documents how the same argument has appeared over the past century in the debates between evolutionists and creationists.[6] In part it is manifest in the idea of science as salvation discussed in chapter 1 and in the myth of the heroic scientist examined in chapter 3. What all these have in common is the rejection of dialogue. Honest debate is premised on the notion that all positions are commensurate and have something to say. If one is certain of the truth, however, dialogue is irrelevant, because error lacks legitimacy. Thus Levitt says of his opponents: "The willingness of the credulous to refuse the wisdom (and the presumptive consolations) of the scientific view may often be a . . . subtle affair in which the roles of fool and knave (if there is knavishness at all) can be strangely confounded."[7] Those who are certain may challenge people who think differently, but nothing is to be gained by engaging in discussion with them.

Third, the science wars embody the ancient Western spirit of sectarianism. Like members of any other sect, these defenders of science claim that they have a monopoly on truth and that outside the church (science) there is no salvation; they campaign to purify the community of what they see as corruption and laxness. This places them in the odd company of those sectarians who put forth religious dogma as an expression of objective reality. Recent examples would include, for instance, creation science, whose practitioners argue that the first chapter of Genesis is a full and adequate account of the origin of the world. Ironically, fundamentalist science and fundamentalist religion end up being mirror images of each other.

The problem with the quest for certainty, in any of these forms, is that it wants to take people out of the process of knowing. Sokal, Levitt, and company pretend that scientists possess a disembodied knowledge, a god's-eye view of the world. Just as religious fundamentalists claim to be mere conduits for the voice of God, so scientific fundamentalists declare that they speak with the unmediated voice of nature. But as we have seen in previous chapters, this is a mystified view of science, one that all too often cloaks an agenda.[8] Thus the quest for certainty is built upon an illusion. In claiming a fixed foundation for knowledge, it rejects dialogue. And all too often, as in the science wars, what begins as an appeal to reason ends up as an appeal to authority.

The Question of Relativism

If one side of the Cartesian anxiety is the quest for certainty, the other is the fear of relativism. The evil of relativism is ostensibly the issue that drives the science wars. Unfortunately, probably more nonsense has been written about relativism in the past twenty years than about any other issue in the philosophy of science. All too often, relativism has become a term of abuse used to knock down straw men in an argument. Relativism is a term too often applied to all of science studies, a sin of even an otherwise careful scholar like Ian Barbour.[9] On the other side, relativism is a good way to proclaim oneself an intellectual "bad boy" (or girl), and trumpeting one's supposed relativism is a device used by some to gain notoriety.[10]

In the previous chapter, we saw how the social sciences may offer guidance to the natural sciences in confronting this question in a more constructive manner. We want to continue the discussion here, but on a different tack. In some ways, the debate over relativism parallels the debate over reductionism. We use Ian Barbour's answer to the problem of reductionism as a guide for working through the question of relativism.

Scientists are often accused of reductionism, of trying to "explain away" phenomena by reducing them to underlying mechanical forces. Ian Barbour presents a very useful way of thinking through the problem. Rather than see reductionism as a single phenomenon, Barbour argues that there are three kinds, which can be organized into a hierarchy of levels. First is *methodological reductionism,* which is "a research strategy: the study of lower levels to better understand relationships at higher levels." Epistemology comes from the Greek word "to know," so *epistemological reductionism* is "a relation between theories, the claim that laws and theories at one level of analysis can be derived from laws and theories at lower levels." At the highest level, *ontological reductionism* is "a claim about the kinds of reality and the kinds of causality that exist in the world."[11] Here the most basic level of material reality is seen as "the real." Each of these different levels has to be evaluated separately, and very different consequences flow from each.

We think that the same three levels can be made to apply to discussions about relativism. *Methodological relativism* is a research strategy. It is most frequently expressed in the concept of symmetry. Most simply put, symmetry is the principle that an investigator should not assume the answer before she or he begins, that is, one should not treat the *explandum* (that which needs to be explained) as the *explanans* (the cause or reason).

For example, a key issue in the study of science is the question of how scientific controversies are ended, or closed. We cannot assume that nature is the reason that a scientific debate closed (the explanans) if nature is the explandum (that which needs to be explained). The Alvarez hypothesis is a good illustration. A realist account of the controversy might go like this: "Alvarez was right and Officer was wrong because Alvarez discovered the way nature is." Now, nature may very well be the way Alvarez said it was, but assuming that tells us nothing about the practice of science and covers up many uncertainties. It certainly would not tell us why the controversy went on for nearly twenty years. If we want to understand science, we have to treat the winners and losers in a controversy equally (that is, symmetrically), and not let the fact that we may know how it comes out bias our study. Symmetry is no more than applying the methods of science to the study of science itself.

Epistemological relativism claims that there is more than one way to know the world, or, in our context, scientific knowledge is relative to the social location or identity of the knower. Men and women, for instance, may very well perceive the world differently, because of their different life experiences. There is a wide variety of opinions on this issue within science studies itself, and we have to be careful not to make one author speak for the whole discipline.

Those caught up in the Cartesian anxiety (from either side) argue for an epistemology that is asymmetrical, as Bruno Latour observes.[12] In keeping with traditional Western dualism, both realists and relativists see nature and society as polarized. For realists, nature is the source of truth and society is the source of error. To the extent that society impinges upon the study of nature (and honest realists acknowledge that it does), that study is biased. So realists hold pure objectivity as a goal, even if it is not always attained. But it does provide them with a foundation, and they charge science studies with a dangerous relativism. For their part, many in science studies see society as the source of knowledge, including our knowledge of nature. For them, all knowledge is local and shaped by the culture (and for some, by the individual or group experiences) of the knower. Both approaches are asymmetrical in that they focus on one side of the nature-society polarity to the exclusion of the other.

The problem with asymmetrical epistemologies is that they are very good at generating the kind of polemics typical of the science wars but do not provide much of a basis for dialogue. We will have to work toward an epistemology that is symmetrical. This means abandoning the polarity between nature and society and approaching both equally as sources of knowledge.

Ontology refers to being, so if epistemological relativism says there are many ways to know, *ontological relativism* says there are many realities. Ontological relativism is the mirror image of ontological reductionism.[13] The problem with any statement about "the way things are" is how do you know—Kant's old problem of can we ever know "the thing in itself." Thus it is very difficult to clearly separate ontological from epistemological questions.

As we have seen, those who claim the material world is the only reality have no use for religion and see little point in dialogue. They believe there is only one truth and they know what it is, so there is no point in a discussion with those who believe otherwise. Seeking a middle ground, Ian Barbour says: "I have defended *ontological pluralism*, a multileveled view of reality in which differing (epistemological) levels of analysis are taken to refer to differing (ontological) levels of events and processes in the world."[14] Barbour might be quite surprised therefore to find himself standing alongside many practitioners of science studies.

The problem remains, though, about how many "realities" can be encompassed within pluralism before it dissolves into relativistic chaos.

Christians, Jews, and Muslims, for instance, all maintain that there is only one God, and therefore ultimately only one truth, even if the more liberal among them will grant that there may be many paths to God. Most scientists would maintain there is a reality that can be understood, even if what we think of as the material universe may not be all there is. Few from either science or religion are willing to accede to the idea that reality is mere chaos or illusion. If we wish to engage in dialogue, we have to reject single vision, but finding balance may not be easy.

A Dialogical Approach

The alternative to the quest for certainty is an understanding of the truth as emerging out of dialogue. Real science is not some royal road to absolute truth but a practice engaged in by a community. Where the quest for certainty is dismissive of language, we have to explore its nuances. If, as we contend, truth emerges out of the tension between objectivity and mystery, we will have to demonstrate the basis for dialogue.

Interpretive social science posits the world as a symbolic reality. In the words of sociologist Richard Brown: "All social reality is symbolic, and there is no reality that is not experienced through the social matrix of discourse. . . . [R]ather than there being a single reality of which non-scientific accounts are erroneous representations, there are multiple ways of construing realities, each of which is privileged for the reality so construed."[15] Or as the German philosopher Jürgen Habermas says, we attribute "epistemic authority to the community of those who cooperate and speak with one another."[16] Two questions emerge from these statements. First, what in the nature of symbols creates the "social matrix of discourse"? And second, what is involved in "multiple ways of construing realities" that might help us understand the tension between objectivity and mystery? We will build upon the work of the Austrian phenomenologist Alfred Schutz. His theories on the nature of symbols and multiple realities demonstrate the centrality of dialogue and ground our approach to the science-religion debate.

If "there is no reality that is not experienced through the social matrix of discourse," what are the building blocks of discourse? This first question deals with the nature of symbols. Alfred Schutz argued that all symbols consist of a triadic relationship (see fig. 12.1).[17] First, there is the signifier, the sign or symbol itself. This can be anything accessible to our senses—a word, an object, an image, music, and so on. Second, there is the signified, that to which the signifier points, its meaning. Third, there is an interpreter. All three elements are necessary if a symbol is to convey meaning. Obviously, the signifier is necessary or there is no symbol. Absence of the signified would be like hearing a word

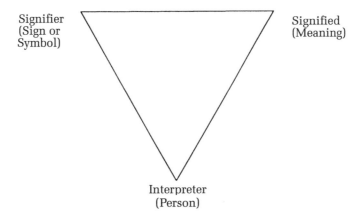

Signifier
(Sign or
Symbol)

Signified
(Meaning)

Interpreter
(Person)

Figure 12.1 Schutz's Model of Symbolic Relationships

in a language we do not understand, or seeing a curious object the purpose of which we do not know. We perceive that something is there (the signifier), but we do not know its meaning. But the interpreter is just as necessary, or the symbol stands mute. There is no such thing as meaning independent of people; they are an intrinsic part of the symbolic relationship.

This has two implications for our study. The first is that Schutz's understanding of symbols breaks down the dichotomy between subject and object. Symbols are objectively real, that is, they exist before we do and apart from us, and we cannot make them mean whatever we please, but at the same time our subjectivity as interpreters is part of every symbol. While the subjective element is inherently part of every symbolic structure, symbols are more than subjective. So symbols are neither subjective nor objective, but relational.[18] Interpretation of symbols is therefore an attempt to find neither an underlying objective reality nor relativistic subjectivity but instead it is an attempt to communicate and understand. It is inherently dialogical.

Second, the quest for certainty is foreclosed. It is precisely because our experience is structured through the symbols of our culture that our understanding is limited. Symbols are finite and ambiguous. As rich and complex as the web of interpretations for a symbol may be, no single symbol can structure all of experience, although those who dogmatize doctrine and belief often forget this. Symbols may be so basic to the structuring of our experience that we do not see them as symbols at all and take them for unmediated reality—a failing common to both science and religion.

While symbols structure experience into a consistent conceptual system, it is a system that arises out of a particular culture at a particular time, indeed out of a particular class and gender. For example, Lakoff and Johnson describe the structural metaphors "Labor is a resource" and "Time is a resource" found in our language. Both metaphors are so basic to industrial society that they are rarely seen as metaphors, yet they reify the experience of time and labor. They "permit labor and time to be quantified—that is, measured, conceived of as being progressively 'used up,' and assigned monetary values; they also allow us to view time and labor as things that can be 'used' for various ends."[19] Our language thus turns a human relationship into a thing, and the people involved become things as well. Marx could not have described alienation better.

Symbols are inherently finite and ambiguous and therefore must be interpreted. We thus have a situation where something—an object, a word, an image, and the like—stands for, represents, or evokes something else, but only in a relationship with a person, group, or society that interprets and invests meaning in that relationship. The structure of symbols shows that ambiguity is no unfortunate aberration or prescientific imprecision. The subjectivity, and hence relativity, of interpretation is an intrinsic element of the symbolic that no social or natural science, however brilliantly reductionistic, can eliminate. Every symbolic structure is first confronted as a text to be interpreted. But the variety of intents and methodologies brought to each text means that no single interpretation has the last word. No symbolic structure is ever exhausted of meaning. But without interpretation, and hence dialogue, symbols stand mute.

Multiple Realities

According to Schutz, reality is divided into multiple spheres of meaning, each of which constitutes a separate reality. The world our bodies inhabit is the paramount reality. This is the world of everyday life—the world of getting up in the morning, having breakfast, going to work. It is paramount because we occupy it at every moment and it impinges upon us continuously. (If you doubt this, just try concentrating on reading this with a bad toothache, or a cat yowling to go outside.) The everyday world is both pragmatic and intersubjective. It is the place where we meet and communicate with other people. Indeed, it is the only place where communication can go on.

Surrounding this paramount reality are a large number of other spheres of meaning, such as the worlds of dreams, of art, of religion, or of science. Schutz calls these "finite provinces of meaning," because "it is the meaning of our experiences and not the ontological structure of the objects that constitutes reality. Hence we call a certain set of our experiences a finite province of meaning if all of them show a specific cognitive style and are—*with respect to this style*—not only consistent in themselves but also compatible with one another."[20] Each of these spheres of meaning is mediated into everyday life through symbols.

Each sphere has its own peculiarities. The sphere we call scientific theory requires those entering it to bracket their own subjective points of view. Having done so, "the scientist enters a preconstituted world of scientific contemplation handed down to him by the historical tradition of his science. Henceforth, he will participate in a universe of discourse embracing the results obtained by others, problems stated by others, solutions suggested by others, methods worked out by others."[21] In other words, scientists temporarily set aside their own identity and enter into the epistemic culture of their discipline. For example, Jane Doe brackets her identity as mother, university professor, and cat fancier and becomes Jane Doe, biochemist. But she does not decide what constitutes biochemistry—that is a given of history, traditions, tacit knowledge, norms, and practices of the discipline. Indeed, to the extent that she is a biochemist, biochemistry defines her.

Thinking about science this way has several advantages. First, it shows that science is a fully social activity—there is no god's-eye view of the world here. But each sphere of meaning is a domain of external reality. Each is a practice with its own epistemic culture and authority. Individual scientists submit to the discipline of their practice (which is why they are called disciplines, after all) and in doing so transcend their own identity—but only temporarily. They are always called back to the preeminent reality of the everyday world, from which they may enter another sphere of meaning. So, to continue our example, when Jane Doe, biochemist, leaves her lab, she returns to being Jane Doe, mother, teacher, and cat lover. On Sunday when she attends mass, she enters into yet another sphere of meaning, religion.

Second, each of these spheres is a finite province of meaning. This means, while any particular sphere will be internally consistent, each differs from the others. What appears to be reality within one sphere of meaning "would appear as merely fictitious, inconsistent and incompatible" within another.[22] From within the sphere of biochemistry, Roman Catholicism makes little sense, and vice versa. But as sociologist Richard Brown cautions, these "various symbol systems do not warrant an absolute and universal priority for any one over the others. Each is more or less appropriate for certain purposes with reference to certain domains."[23] Thus to proclaim one sphere to be the only reality or to privilege only one form of knowing is a sign of both arrogance and shallowness. Science and religion are different provinces of meaning, and one cannot be substituted for the other.

Finally, the relationship between all these spheres of meaning is dialectical. Schutz maintains that "the finite provinces of meaning are not separated states of mental life. . . . They are merely names for different tensions of one and the same consciousness, and it is the same life, the mundane life, unbroken from birth to death, which is attended to in different modifications."[24] They are different moments in the consciousness of every one of us. This is crucial. We move from the everyday world to the sphere of science (or religion) and then back to the everyday world. When Jane Doe is practicing biochemistry, she is not engaging in Roman Catholicism. When she is taking the sacrament, she is not practicing biochemistry. But neither her science nor her religion is a reified entity, some "thing" existing "out there."[25] They are moments in her life. The tension between objectivity and mystery, between science and religion, is first and foremost a tension within all of us.

As we have seen, different people will try to cope with these tensions in different ways. None of these attempts is particularly satisfactory. Those with a low tolerance toward ambiguity will engage in a quest for certainty and try to escape to objectivity, but limit situations will impinge upon all our lives sooner or later. Tragedy, illness, or death will eventually bring even the most unyielding realist face to face with the unknown. Others will try to escape by immersing themselves in the realms of mystery, but they can do so only by pretending to ignore the modern world. This leads to inauthenticity, as with those who, for instance, denounce science and technology from their Web pages. Yet others will try to escape by building walls between the spheres and compartmentalizing their lives. This is possible, but only at the cost of living a blinkered existence, afraid to ask too many questions lest the walls be breached. Only through dialogue can the tension be retained and a constructive balance achieved between science and religion.

In summary, reality is constituted of a number of domains mediated by symbols, grounded in the experience and interpretation of each individual and of the community. When we attend to the sphere of science, we step into the epistemic community of other scientists. When as believers we attend to the sphere of religion, we step into the community of faith. The point is that we do so as one and the same person who lives in the intertwined communities of scientists and believers. The web of reality exists inside every person. Science and religion, objectivity and mystery, are different moments in our own consciousness and in our discourse. The practice of science (of religion, of ethics, and of technology) is by its very nature a dialogue.[26]

Notes

PREFACE

1. John Hedley Brooke, *Science and Religion: Some Historical Perspectives* (Cambridge, U.K.: Cambridge University Press, 1991). Among the philosophers, see Mikael Stenmark, *Rationality in Science, Religion, and Everyday Life: A Critical Evaluation of Four Models of Rationality* (Notre Dame, Ind.: University of Notre Dame Press, 1995), and Willem B. Drees, *Religion, Science, and Naturalism* (Cambridge, U.K.: Cambridge University Press, 1996).
2. See David Bloor, *Knowledge and Social Imagery* (London: Routledge and Kegan Paul, 1976); Barry Barnes, David Bloor, and John Henry, *Scientific Knowledge* (Chicago: University of Chicago Press, 1996); Robert K. Merton, *The Sociology of Science* (Chicago: University of Chicago Press, 1973); Bruno Latour, *Science in Action* (Cambridge, Mass.: Harvard University Press, 1987); Steve Fuller, *Social Epistemology* (Bloomington: Indiana University Press, 1988); Steve Fuller, *Philosophy of Science and Its Discontents*, 2d ed. (New York: Guilford, 1993); Karin Knorr Cetina, *Epistemic Culture* (Cambridge, Mass.: Harvard University Press, 1999); Evelyn Fox Keller, *Reflections on Gender and Science* (New Haven, Conn.: Yale University Press, 1985); Evelyn Fox Keller, *Secrets of Life, Secrets of Death* (New York: Routledge, 1992); Sandra Harding, *The Science Question in Feminism* (Ithaca, N.Y.: Cornell University Press, 1986); Sandra Harding, *Whose Science? Whose Knowledge?* (Ithaca, N.Y.: Cornell University Press, 1991); Donna Haraway, *Simians, Cyborgs, and Women* (New York: Routledge, 1991).
3. Steve Fuller, *Science* (Minneapolis: University of Minnesota Press, 1997).

INTRODUCTION: FINDING A PLACE AT THE TABLE

1. James Gilbert, *Redeeming Culture: American Religion in an Age of Science* (Chicago: University of Chicago Press, 1997), 253–295.
2. Thomas Gieryn, *Cultural Boundaries of Science* (Chicago: University of Chicago Press, 1999).
3. We will primarily use Barbour's most recent elaborations of his model in *Religion and Science: Historical and Contemporary Issues* (San Francisco:

HarperSanFrancisco, 1997), 77–105, and *When Science Meets Religion* (San Francisco: HarperSanFrancisco, 2000).

4. See www.ctns.org.
5. For example: John F. Haught, *Science and Religion* (New York: Paulist Press, 1995); Christopher Southgate et al., *God, Humanity, and the Cosmos* (Edinburgh: T and T Clark, 1999), 9ff.
6. Barbour, *When Science Meets Religion*, 3.
7. In the revised Gifford Lectures, *Religion and Science*, Barbour added three short historical chapters at the beginning that were absent from the original. These chapters are not, however, integrated into his model. He also briefly discusses history in science and religion (137–144) but again, it is not integrated into his model.
8. Ibid., 144–146.
9. Ibid., 147–151.
10. Ian Barbour, "Response to Critiques of *Religion in an Age of Science*," *Zygon* 31, 1 (March 1996): 55.
11. Ian Barbour, *Ethics in an Age of Technology* (San Francisco: HarperSanFrancisco, 1993).
12. This is reinforced in the special issue of *Zygon* devoted to his Gifford Lectures (*Zygon* 31, 1 [March 1996]). Each volume was discussed separately, Barbour responded in separate sections, and no one made the slightest connection between the two.
13. Stephen Jay Gould, *Rocks of Ages: Science and Religion in the Fullness of Life* (New York: Ballantine, 1999), 5.
14. Ibid., 6.
15. Ibid., 61.
16. See, for example, Michael Ruse, "A Separate Peace: Stephen Jay Gould and the Limits of Tolerance," *Science and Spirit* 10, 3 (September/October 1999): 20–22.
17. Gould, *Rocks of Ages,* 65.
18. Stephen Jay Gould, *Leonardo's Mountain of Clams and the Diet of Worms* (New York: Harmony Books, 1998), 274.
19. Gould, *Rocks of Ages*, 65.
20. Ibid., 6.
21. Thomas Gieryn, "Boundaries of Science," in *Handbook of Science and Technology Studies*, ed. Sheila Jsanoff, Gerald Markle, James Petersen, and Trevor Pinch (Thousand Oaks, Calif.: Sage, 1995), 393.
22. Ronald Cole-Turner, "Theology's Future with Science," address to the John Templeton Foundation Toronto Workshop on the Design of Academic Courses in Science and Religion, Victoria College, University of Toronto, 10 July 1998.
23. Ronald Cole-Turner, *Science, Technology, and Mission* (Trinity Press International, in press).
24. Ibid., 23.
25. Cf. Michael Ruse, "Creation Science: The Ultimate Fraud," in *Philosophy of Biology*, ed. Michael Ruse (New York: Prometheus Books, 1998), 329–336.
26. Cf. Brooke, *Science and Religion*.
27. Edward J. Larson, *Summer of the Gods: The Scopes Trial and America's Continuing Debate over Science and Religion* (New York: Basic Books, 1997), 31–59.
28. Gilbert, *Redeeming Culture,* 23–35.
29. Fundamentalism is often portrayed as an exclusively rural and southern phenomenon, but as Ronald Numbers points out, this is a mistake. See Numbers, *Darwin Comes to America* (Cambridge, Mass.: Harvard University Press, 1998).
30. George M. Marsden, *Understanding Fundamentalism and Evangelicalism* (Grand Rapids, Mich.: Eerdmans, 1991), 179.

31. Edward J. Larson and Larry Witham, "Scientists and Religion in America," *Scientific American*, September 1999, 88–93.
32. Gieryn, *Cultural Boundaries of Science*, 1.
33. See George Ritzer, *Classical Sociological Theory* (New York: McGraw-Hill, 1992), 213–259.
34. See Michael Ermarth, *Wilhelm Dilthey: The Critique of Historical Reason* (Chicago: University of Chicago Press, 1978).
35. See Robert Prus, *Symbolic Interaction and Ethnographic Research: Intersubjectivity and the Study of Human Lived Experience* (Albany: State University of New York Press, 1996).
36. Max Weber, *The Protestant Ethic and the Spirit of Capitalism* (New York: Scribner's, 1958).
37. Robert K. Merton, *Science, Technology, and Society in Seventeenth Century England (*New York: Howard Fertig, 1970).
38. Stephen Kalberg, "Max Weber's Types of Rationality: Cornerstones for the Analysis of Rationalization Processes in History," *American Journal of Sociology* 85 (1980): 1145–1179.
39. Max Weber, *Sociology of Religion* (Boston: Beacon Press, 1963).
40. Fuller, *Science.*
41. Ibid., 50.
42. Ibid., 57.
43. See Merton, *Sociology of Science.*

ONE THE SACRED MYTH OF SCIENCE

1. See Kenneth Surin, "Liberation," in *Critical Terms for Religious Studies*, ed. M. C. Taylor (Chicago: University of Chicago Press, 1998), 173–199.
2. See Bryan Appleyard, *Understanding the Present* (London: Pan Books, 1993), 1–16.
3. Weber, *The Protestant Ethic.*
4. Merton, *Science, Technology, and Society.*
5. Bryan Wilson, *Religion in Sociological Perspective* (Oxford, U.K.: Oxford University Press, 1982), 27.
6. E. O. Wilson, *Consilience* (New York: Knopf, 1998), 53.
7. Fuller, *Science*, 61–62.
8. Ibid., 50, 51.
9. Mary Midgley, *Science as Salvation* (London: Routledge, 1992), 156.
10. Cited in ibid., 150.
11. Appleyard, *Understanding the Present*, 224.
12. Stephen Hawking, *A Brief History of Time* (New York: Bantam, 1988), 175.
13. John D. Barrow and Frank J. Tipler, *The Anthropic Cosmological Principle* (Oxford, U.K.: Oxford University Press, 1986).
14. Midgley, *Science as Salvation*, 27.
15. Ibid., 9.
16. Ibid., 10.
17. Weber, *Sociology of Religion*, 187.
18. Mikael Stenmark, "What is Scientism?" *Religious Studies* 33, 1 (1997): 27.
19. Cited in ibid., 27–28.
20. Ibid., 30.
21. Sharon Traweek, *Beamtimes and Lifetimes* (Cambridge, Mass.: Harvard University Press, 1988), 86.
22. Fuller, *Science,* 87–88.
23. Weber, *Sociology of Religion,* 190.
24. Ibid., 194–195.
25. Ibid., 196.0
26. Rodney Stark, "Atheism, Faith, and the Social Scientific Study of Religion," *Journal of Contemporary Religion* 14, 1 (1999): 51–62.

27. Ibid., 47.

28. Stewart Guthrie, *Faces in the Clouds: A New Theory of Religion* (Oxford, U.K.: Oxford University Press, 1993); Midgley, *Science as Salvation*, 147.

29. Steven Weinberg, *Dreams of a Final Theory* (Chicago: University of Chicago Press, 1992), 188.

30. Fuller, *Science,* 10.

31. Cited in Stark, "Atheism, Faith," 48, 51, 57.

32. Ibid., 57–59.

33. See Merton, *Sociology of Science.*

34. See Thomas Kuhn, *The Structure of Scientific Revolutions* (Chicago: University of Chicago Press, 1970).

35. Appleyard, *Understanding the Present,* 228.

36. Midgley, *Science as Salvation,* 37.

TWO   WRITING THE HISTORY OF SCIENCE

1. For example, one could read a recent study entitled *The Scientific Revolution: A Historiographical Inquiry* by H. Floris Cohen (Chicago: University of Chicago Press, 1994).

2. David C. Lindberg and Robert Westman, eds., *Reappraisals of the Scientific Revolution* (Cambridge, U.K.: Cambridge University Press, 1990), and Margaret Osler, ed., *Rethinking the Scientific Revolution* (Cambridge, U.K.: Cambridge University Press, 2000).

3. S. A. Jayawardine, *The Scientific Revolution: An Annotated Bibliography* (West Cornell, Conn.: Locust Hill Press, 1996).

4. Steven Shapin, *The Scientific Revolution* (Chicago: University of Chicago Press, 1996), 1.

5. An important study on this topic is I. Bernard Cohen's *Revolution in Science* (Cambridge, Mass.: Belknap Press, 1985).

6. Barbour, *Religion and Science*, 25.

7. John William Draper, *History of the Conflict Between Religion and Science* (London: Henry S. King, 1875), vi.

8. *Anticlericalism* may be defined as an attitude of antagonism toward the institution of the Church and, in particular, the clergy. The *philosophes* were the leaders of the French Enlightenment. Material in this paragraph is summarized primarily from A. N. Wilson, *God's Funeral* (New York: Norton, 1999), chapters 8 and 9.

9. On the history of geology, see Rachel Laudan, *From Minerology to Geology: The Foundations of a Science, 1650–1830* (Chicago: University of Chicago Press, 1987), and Roy Porter, *The Making of Geology: Earth Science in Britain, 1660–1815* (Cambridge, U.K.: Cambridge University Press, 1977).

10. A discussion of this event opens William Irvine's *Apes, Angels, and Victorians: Darwin, Huxley, and Evolution* (Cleveland, Ohio: World Publishing, 1955). See also Brooke, *Science and Religion*, 41.

11. F. L. Cross, ed. *The Oxford Dictionary of the Christian Church,* 2ᵈ ed. (Oxford, U.K.: Oxford University Press, 1983), 1427.

12. Wilson, *God's Funeral*, 196.

13. Quoted in Cohen, *Scientific Revolution*, 36.

14. One could cite, for example the ideas of John Bagnell Bury, who, in 1902, delivered an address entitled "The Science of History" to a Cambridge audience. See Fritz Stern, ed., *The Varieties of History from Voltaire to the Present* (New York: Vintage Books, 1973), 209–223.

15. Cohen, *Scientific Revolution*, 39.

16. Dorothy Stimson, ed., *Sarton on the History of Science: Essays by George Sarton* (Cambridge, Mass.: Harvard University Press, 1962), 364–366.

17. Ibid., 16.
18. *Dictionary of Scientific Biography* (1973), s.v. George Alfred Léon Sarton, 109.
19. Stimson, *Sarton on the History of Science*, 22.
20. George Sarton, *Six Wings: Men of Science in the Renaissance* (Bloomington: Indiana University Press, 1957), 218.
21. Herbert Butterfield, *The Origins of Modern Science, 1300–1800* (London: G. Bell, 1949), 7.
22. Herbert Butterfield, *The Whig Interpretation of History* (London: G. Bell, 1968).
23. Stimson, *Sarton on the History of Science*, 19–21.
24. *Dictionary of Scientific Biography*, s.v. Pierre-Maurice-Marie Duhem, 232.
25. Stanley L. Jaki, *Uneasy Genius: The Life and Work of Pierre Duhem* (The Hague: Nijhoff, 1984).
26. Stanley L. Jaki, *God and the Cosmologists* (Edinburgh: Scottish Academic Press, 1989), 198.
27. Cohen, *Scientific Revolution*, 528, n.13.
28. Lynn Thorndike, *A History of Magic and Experimental Science*, 8 vols. (New York: Macmillan, 1923–1958).
29. See Allen Debus, "Chemists, Physicians, and Changing Perspectives on the Scientific Revolution," *Isis* 89 (1998): 67.
30. Butterfield, *Origins of Modern Science*, 48.
31. Cited in Colin Russell, "Whigs and Professionals," *Nature,* 26 (April–2 May 1984): 777.
32. *Dictionary of Scientific Biography,* s.v. Alexandre Koyré, 485.
33. Cohen, *Scientific Revolution*, 76–78.
34. Alexandre Koyré, *Galileo Studies*, trans. John Mepham (Hassocks, U.K.: Harvester Press, 1978).
35. Roy Porter, review of *The Scientific Revolution,* by H. Floris Cohen, *Journal of Modern History* 68 (1996): 663.
36. Debus, "Chemists, Physicians," 74.
37. Brian Vickers, "On the Function of Analogy in the Occult," in *Hermeticism and the Renaissance: Intellectual History and the Occult in Early Modern Europe*, ed. Ingrid Merkel and Allen G. Debus (London: Associated University Press, 1988), 289. See also Brian Vickers, "Frances Yates and the Writing of History," *Journal of Modern History* 51 (1979): 287–316.
38. Patrick Curry, "Revisions of Science and Magic," *History of Science* 23 (1985): 303.
39. Margaret Jacob, "Constructing, Deconstructing, and Reconstructing the History of Science," *Journal of British Studies* 36 (1997): 461.
40. Betty Jo Dobbs, *The Janus Face of Genius: The Role of Alchemy in Newton's Thought* (Cambridge, U.K.: Cambridge University Press, 1991).
41. Lawrence Principe, *The Aspiring Adept: Robert Boyle and His Alchemical Quest* (Princeton, N.J.: Princeton University Press, 1998).
42. Jacob, "Constructing," 459.
43. Lindberg and Westman, *Reappraisals of the Scientific Revolution*, xix–xx.
44. William Shea, review of *The Scientific Revolution,* by Steven Shapin, *Nature,* (23 January 1997): 312.
45. Osler, *Rethinking the Scientific Revolution*.
46. Philippians 2:12.

THREE   THE ICONOGRAPHY OF SCIENCE

1. Dorothy Nelkin, *Selling Science: How the Press Covers Science and Technology* (New York: Freeman, 1987), 2.

2. The textbooks are: Burton S. Guttman, *Biology* (Boston: WCB/McGraw Hill, 1999); Ticki Lewis, *Life,* 3d ed. (Boston: WCB/McGraw Hill, 1998); Sylvia S. Mader, *Biology,* 6th ed. (Boston: WCB/McGraw Hill, 1998); Allan J. Tobin and Jennie Dusheck, *Asking About Life* (Fort Worth, Tex.: Harcourt Brace, 1998); and Robert Wallace, Gerald Sanders, and Robert Ferl, *Biology: The Science of Life,* 3d ed. (New York: HarperCollins, 1991).

3. Tobin and Dusheck, *Asking About Life,* vi–vii.

4. The fifth, Guttman, emphasized instead values such as wonder, curiosity, and liberation together with the socially important consequences of biological discoveries. It is perhaps significant that Guttman is aimed at first-year biology majors, since the task of recruitment would be different for those with some prior commitment to the discipline.

5. Tobin and Dusheck, *Asking About Life,* 1.

6. Wallace, Sanders, and Ferl, *Biology,* 2–3.

7. William Atkinson, "The Elusive Genius," *Toronto Globe and Mail,* national ed., 22 March 2000.

8. Fuller, *Science,* 53.

9. Wallace, Sanders, and Ferl, *Biology,* 6–7; Lewis, *Life,* 13.

10. Quoted in Fuller, *Science,* 43.

11. See Bruno Latour, *Pandora's Hope* (Cambridge, Mass.: Harvard University Press, 1999), 216–266.

12. Robert Park, *Voodoo Science: The Road from Foolishness to Fraud* (Oxford, U.K.: Oxford University Press, 2000).

13. Wallace, Sanders, and Ferl, *Biology,* 12.

14. Henry H. Bauer, *Scientific Literacy and the Myth of the Scientific Method* (Urbana: University of Illinois Press, 1992).

15. Harry Collins and Trevor Pinch, *The Golem: What You Should Know About Science,* 2d ed. (Cambridge, U.K.: Cambridge University Press, 1998), 52, 98.

16. Knorr Cetina, *Epistemic Culture;* Diane Vaughan, *The Challenger Launch Decision* (Chicago: University of Chicago Press, 1996); Sal Restivo, *Science, Society, and Values: Towards a Sociology of Objectivity* (Bethlehem, Pa.: Lehigh University Press, 1994), 90–95.

17. Wallace, Sanders, and Ferl, *Biology,* 6; Guttman, *Biology,* 7–9; Mader, *Biology,* 11.

18. Ian Hacking, *The Social Construction of What?* (Cambridge, Mass.: Harvard University Press, 1999).

19. Barbour, *Religion and Science,* 116.

20. Stephen Jay Gould, *Wonderful Life: The Burgess Shale and the Nature of History* (New York: Norton, 1989), 28

21. Charles Darwin, *The Origin of Species* (New York: Modern Library, 1993), 171.

22. Darwin was not the first to use this metaphor, but his usage became canonical. See Michael Ruse, *From Monad to Man: The Concept of Progress in Evolutionary Biology* (Cambridge, Mass.: Harvard University Press, 1996).

23. Gould, *Wonderful Life,* 39, 43.

24. For an opposing interpretation of the Burgess shale, see Simon Conway Morris, *The Crucible of Creation: The Burgess Shale and the Rise of Animals* (Oxford, U.K.: Oxford University Press, 1998).

25. But not all of them. These texts display many of the features Gould complains of, especially copying from one text to another, including the same examples and photographs. See Stephen J. Gould, "The Case of the Creeping Fox Terrier Clone," in *Bully for Brontosaurus* (New York: Norton, 1991), 155–167.

26. Lewis, *Life,* 368; Wallace, Sanders, and Ferl, *Biology,* 386–387; Guttman, *Biology,* 485–486.

FOUR   THE NEWTONIAN REVOLUTION

1. The often-made observation that Newton was born in the same year Galileo died is technically not correct. Galileo died under house arrest at his little estate at Arcetri outside of Florence on 8 January 1642 (in the Gregorian calendar). The problem is that when Newton was born on Christmas Day, England still used the Julian calendar, which was ten days out of sync with the Gregorian calendar used in Catholic countries.
2. John Maynard Keynes, "Newton, the Man," in *Essays in Biography* (New York: Horizon Press, 1951), 311. Keynes's essay was read by Geoffrey Keynes at Trinity College on 17 July 1946 as part of the Newton Tercentenary Celebrations.
3. See, for example, Gale E. Christianson, "The Alchemist," in *Isaac Newton and the Scientific Revolution* (Oxford, U.K.: Oxford University Press, 1996), 66–75.
4. H.B.G. Casimir, "Annus physicalis 1932," *Nature* (2 December 1999): 463. The year 1905 is the year Albert Einstein burst on the scientific scene from obscurity with five papers that transformed the field of physics. These revolutionary contributions involved special relativity, the quantum nature of light, and the Brownian motion of small particles. In 1932, there were four major experimental discoveries by different groups of individuals: the neutron, heavy hydrogen (deuterium), the positron (positive electron), and nuclear reactions induced by accelerated particles.
5. It is a little simplistic (and self-serving) to assign all of Newton's great accomplishments to the single year 1666. Cambridge University's senate voted in October 1665 to close the institution, and Newton did his monumental work over a period beginning at the end of 1665 and extending to 1667.
6. We will focus on Newton's work in mechanics and not deal with his equally important contributions in mathematics and optics. To get an overview of his work in mathematics, see, for example, E. T. Bell, *Men of Mathematics* (New York: Simon and Schuster, 1965), and the book review by I. Bernard Cohen of *The Mathematical Papers of Isaac Newton, Volume I: 1664–1666,* ed. D. T. Whiteside, *Scientific American* (January 1968): 134–144. The role of Newton's work in optics is explored by David Park, *The Fire Within the Eye: A Historical Essay on the Nature and Meaning of Light* (Princeton, N.J.: Princeton University Press, 1997).
7. Albert Einstein, foreword to Isaac Newton, *Opticks* (1730; reprint, based on the 4th ed., New York: Dover, 1952), lix.
8. Cohen, review of *Mathematical Papers,* 134.
9. It should be noted that while Newton's work was immediately embraced in England, it took a generation of Continental scientists to overcome their affinity for Cartesian ideas and their dislike of Newton's idea of action at a distance.
10. See, for example, David Park, *The How and the Why: An Essay on the Origins and Development of Physical Theory* (Princeton, N.J.: Princeton University Press, 1988), 170–223, and I. Bernard Cohen, "Newton's Discovery of Gravity," *Scientific American* (March 1981): 166–179.
11. See, for example, Gerald Holton and Stephen G. Brush, *Introduction to Concepts and Theories in Physical Science,* 2d ed. (Reading, Mass.: Addison-Wesley, 1973), 28, and Butterfield, *Origins of Modern Science.*
12. Butterfield, *Origins of Modern Science,* 3.
13. See, for example, Dietrich Schroeer, "The World as a Clockwork Mechanism," in *Physics and Its Fifth Dimension: Society* (Reading, Mass.: Addison-Wesley, 1972), 90–100, and A. B. Arons, "Newton and the American Political Tradition," *American Journal of Physics,* 43, 3 (1975): 209–213.

14. Alan L. Mackay, ed., *A Dictionary of Scientific Quotations* (Bristol, U.K.: Institute of Physics Publishing, 1991), 13.

15. Quoted in *Biographia Britannica* (London, 1760), 5, 3241; Richard S. Westfall, *Never at Rest: A Biography of Isaac Newton* (Cambridge, U.K.: Cambridge University, 1980).

16. See, for example, F. W. Sears and M. W. Zemansky, *University Physics*, 3d ed. (Reading, Mass.: Addison-Wesley, 1964), and David Halliday and Robert Resnick, *Fundamentals of Physics*, 3d ed. (New York: Wiley, 1988).

17. Quoted in Joseph F. Mulligan, *Introductory College Physics*, 2d ed. (New York: McGraw-Hill, 1991), 119.

18. See, for example, *New Encyclopaedia Britannica*, 15th ed., s.v. "Aristotle and Aristotelianism," and John D. Barrow,"*The World Within the World* (Oxford, U.K.: Oxford University Press, 1988), 48–53.

19. See, for example, Nathan Spielberg and Bryon D. Anderson, *Seven Ideas that Shook the Universe,* 2d ed. (New York: Wiley, 1995), 60–65, and "The Old Physics," in I. Bernard Cohen, *The Birth of a New Physics* (Garden City, N.Y.: Anchor Books, 1960), 22–35.

20. Cited in *Great Treasury of Western Thought*, ed. Mortimer J. Adler and Charles Van Doren (New York: Bowker, 1977), 1179. Also, Isaac Newton, *Sir Isaac Newton's Mathematical Principles of Natural Philosophy and His System of the World*, trans. Andrew Motte, rev. Florian Cajori (1729; Berkeley: University of California Press, 1934), 3: 398.

21. "Nature does nothing in vain." Aristotle quoted in *New Encyclopaedia Britannica*, 15th ed., s.v. "Aristotle and Aristotelianism."

22. Isaac Newton, "A Scheme for Establishing the Royal Society," quoted in H. S. Thayer, *Newton's Philosophy of Nature: Selections from His Writings* (New York: Hafner, 1953), 1, from David Brewster, *Memoirs of the Life, Writings, and Discoveries of Sir Isaac Newton* (1855; New York: Johnson Reprint, 1965), 1:102.

23. See Peter Medawar, *The Limits of Science* (Oxford, U.K.: Oxford University Press, 1984), 16–18, 50–52.

24. Ibid., 16–18.

25. See, for example, Schroeer, "World as a Clockwork Mechanism," 94–98.

26. See "Truth Revealed," in Michael White, *Isaac Newton: The Last Sorcerer* (Reading, Mass.: Helix Books, 1997), 1–5. Typical of the early biographies was William Stukeley's *Memoirs of Sir Isaac Newton's Life* (London: Taylor and Francis, 1936), originally written in the 1720s, and Brewster's *Memoirs of the Life* (1965). In Brewster's two volumes there are just three references to alchemy in the indexes, and he clearly expresses his opinion that it is a great mystery why some of the greatest minds in the age of Newton succumbed to the temptation of alchemy.

27. White, *Isaac Newton,* 3–4.

28. Ibid., 346.

29. See, for example, Christianson, *Isaac Newton,* 82–83, 117–122, 126–137, for a general outline of the famous disputes with Robert Hooke, Astronomer Royal John Flamsteed, and Gottfried Wilhelm Leibniz.

30. Keynes, "Newton, the Man," 323.

31. Christianson, *Isaac Newton,* 69–72.

32. For background on Newton's work in biblical prophecy, see ibid.; White, *Isaac Newton,* 154–162; and "Prophecy and History," in Frank E. Manuel, *The Religion of Isaac Newton* (Oxford, U.K.: Oxford University Press, 1974), 83–104.

33. Christianson, *Isaac Newton,* 72–75. Christianson makes the interesting and perplexing observation that "[from his first religious scribbling, Newton] would go on to write an estimated 1,400,000 words on religion, more than

the alchemy, more than the mathematics, more even than the physics and astronomy that made him immortal."

34. See, for example, Bert Hansen, "The Complementarity of Science and Magic Before the Scientific Revolution," *American Scientist* 74, 2 (1986): 130.

35. Alexander Pope, "An Essay on Man," epistle 1: l. 267–280, in *The Poetical Works of Alexander Pope* (New York: Macmillan, 1927), 199–200.

36. This well-known exchange appears in a number of places; probably the most familiar is the famous popular history of mathematics by Bell, *Men of Mathematics*, 181. The original written source for this famous anecdote is usually given as Augustus de Morgan, *Athenaeum*, no. 1921 (20 August 1865), 247. It should be noted that Bell is notoriously unreliable as a source. For an extensive discussion of the significance of Laplace's comment, see Roger Hahn, "Laplace and the Mechanistic Universe," in David C. Lindberg and Ronald L. Numbers, *God and Nature: Historical Essays on the Encounter Between Christianity and Science* (Berkeley: University of California Press, 1986).

37. It is interesting that physicists concern themselves with the issue of realism and almost never with naturalism; biologists, on the other hand, seem to be concerned with naturalism and never with realism. It should also be noted that human beings have a remarkable capacity for compartmentalizing conflicting beliefs. See, for example, Janet Raloff, "When Science and Beliefs Collide," *Science News* (8 June 1996): 360–361.

38. Albert Einstein, "Religion and Science: Irreconcilable?" *Ideas and Opinions* (New York: Dell, 1954), 59, and Gould, *Rocks of Ages,* 55.

39. Michael Ruse, *Can a Darwinian Be a Christian?* (Cambridge, U.K.: Cambridge University Press, 2001).

FIVE MAGICIANS, REFORMERS, AND SCIENTISTS

1. Cited in John Shinners, ed., *Medieval Popular Religion, 1000–1500: A Reader* (Peterborough, Ontario: Broadview Press, 1997), 286.

2. For more on the nature of demons, see Wayne Shumaker, *Natural Magic and Modern Science: Four Treatises* (Binghamton, N.Y.: Center for Medieval and Early Renaissance Studies, 1989), 7.

3. St. Augustine, *City of God* (Harmondsworth, U.K.: Penguin, 1984), 383.

4. Stuart Clark, "The Rational Witchfinder: Conscience, Demonological Naturalism, and Popular Superstitions," in *Science, Culture, and Popular Belief in Renaissance Europe*, ed. Stephen Pumfrey, Paolo Rossi, and Maurice Slawinski (Manchester, U.K.: Manchester University Press, 1991), 223.

5. Keith Hutchison, "What Happened to Occult Qualities in the Scientific Revolution?" *Isis* 73 (1982): 237.

6. William Eamon, "Technology as Magic in the Late Middle Ages and the Renaissance," *Janus* 70 (1983): 195.

7. Ibid., 182.

8. Walter Scott, ed., *Hermetica* (Boston: Shambala, 1993), 339.

9. See Chaim Wirszubski, *Pico della Mirandola's Encounter with Jewish Mysticism* (Cambridge, Mass.: Harvard University Press, 1989).

10. Moshe Idel, "The Magical and Neoplatonic Interpretations of the Kabbalah in the Renaissance," in *Jewish Thought in the Sixteenth Century*, ed. Bernard Cooperman (Cambridge, Mass.: Harvard University Press, 1983), 197.

11. Frances Yates, "The Hermetic Tradition in Renaissance Science," in *Art, Science, and History in the Renaissance*, ed. Charles S. Singleton (Baltimore, Md.: Johns Hopkins University Press, 1967), 258–259.

12. Quoted in Germana Ernst, "Astrology, Religion, and Politics in Counter-Reformation Rome," in *Science, Culture, and Popular Belief,* ed. Pumfrey et al., 252.

13. David B. Ruderman, "The Italian Renaissance and Jewish Thought," in *Renaissance Humanism: Foundations, Forms, and Legacy*, vol. 2, *Humanism in Italy*, ed. Albert Rabil, Jr. (Philadelphia: University of Pennsylvania Press, 1988), 400.

14. Fischel Lachower and Isaiah Tishby, eds., *The Wisdom of the Zohar: An Anthology of Texts*, trans. David Goldstein (Oxford, U.K.: Oxford University Press, 1989), 2:751–753.

15. Quoted in J. L. Blau, *The Christian Interpretation of the Cabala in the Renaissance* (New York: Columbia University Press, 1944), 68.

16. Henry Cornelius Agrippa of Nettesheim, *Three Books of Occult Philosophy* (London: Gregory Moule, 1651), 352.

17. Hans J. Hillerbrand, ed., *The Oxford Encyclopedia of the Reformation* (Oxford, U.K.: Oxford University Press, 1996), s.v. "alchemy."

18. D. P. Walker, *Spiritual and Demonic Magic: From Ficino to Campanella* (London: Warburg Institute, 1958), 182.

19. Pierre Viret, *The Cauteles, Canon, and Ceremonies of the Most Blasphemous, abhominable, and monstrous popish masse* (London: Thomas Vautrollier for Andrewe Maunsell . . . , 1584), 26–27.

20. Marnix van Sant Aldegonde, Philips van. *The Bee hive of the Romishe church*, trans. George Gilpin the Elder (London: At the Three Cranes in the Vinetree, by Thomas Dawson for John Stell, 1579), 62.

21. Guillaume Postel, "La naturelle raison," Bibliothèque Nationale (Paris), ms.Fonds Français 2115, fol.20v.

22. François Secret, *Les kabbalistes chrétiens de la Renaissance* (Paris: Dunod, 1964), 255–256.

23. Norman P. Tanner, ed., *Decrees of the Ecumenical Councils* (Washington, D.C.: Georgetown University Press, 1990), 2:775.

24. Walker, *Spiritual and Demonic Magic*, 181–182; Shumaker, *Natural Magic and Modern Science*, 84.

25. Shumaker, *Natural Magic and Modern Science*, 79.

26. Jacques Gaffarel, *Unheard of curiosities concerning the talismanical sculpture of the Persians, the horoscope of the patriarkes, and the reading of the stars*, trans. Edmund Chilmead (Worcester, Mass.: Readex Microprint Corp., 1977).

27. William Hine, "Marin Mersenne: Renaissance Naturalism and Renaissance Magic," in *Occult and Scientific Mentalities in the Renaissance*, ed. B. Vickers (Cambridge, U.K.: Cambridge University Press, 1984), 108–109.

28. Hillerbrand, *Oxford Encyclopedia*, s.v. "magic."

29. John Calvine, *An Admonicion against Astrology Judiciall and other curiosities* (London: Roulande Hall, [1561]), Aviii.

30. Philip Melanchthon, *Initia doctrinae physicae* (1549), quoted in *The Occult in Early Modern Europe: A Documentary History*, ed. P. G. Maxwell-Stuart (New York: St. Martin's Press, 1999), 6.

31. Walker, *Spiritual and Demonic Magic*, 175.

32. Ibid., 36.

33. An exremely interesting work on this topic is that of Jonathan Pearl, *The Crime of Crimes: Demonology and Politics in France, 1560–1620* (Waterloo, Ontario: Wilfrid Laurier University Press, 1999).

34. The *Malleus Maleficarum*, in *Witchcraft in Europe, 1100–1700: A Documentary History*, ed. Alan C. Kors and Edward Peters (Philadelphia: University of Pennsylvania Press, 1972), 137.

35. Stuart Clark, "The Scientific Status of Demonology," in *Occult and Scientific Mentalities*, ed. Vickers, 369.

36. Brian P. Levack, *The Witch-Hunt in Early Modern Europe*, 2d ed. (New York: Longman: 1995), 170.

37. Ann Blair, *The Theater of Nature: Jean Bodin and Renaissance Science* (Princeton, N.J.: Princeton University Press, 1997), 151.

38. Thomas Bergin and Jennifer Speake, eds., *The Encyclopedia of the Renaissance* (New York: Facts on File, 1987), s.v. "John Dee."
39. Secret, *Kabbalistes chrétiens*, 300.
40. Yates, "Hermetic Tradition," 272.
41. Moshe Idel, "Differing Conceptions of Kabbalah in the Early Seventeenth Century," in *Jewish Thought in the Seventeenth Century*, ed. Isadore Twersky and Bernard Septimus (Cambridge, Mass.: Harvard University Press, 1987), 160, 162.
42. Frances Yates, *The Occult Philosophy in the Elizabethan Age* (London: Ark, 1983), 172.
43. Yates, "Hermetic Tradition," 271.
44. M. Mersenne, *Traité de l'harmonie universelle où est contenu la musique thérique et pratique des Anciens et Modernes, avec les causes de ses effets* (Paris: Guillaume Baudry, 1627), 421–422.
45. Quoted in Hine, "Marin Mersenne," 172.
46. Quoted in Hutchison, "What Happened to Occult Qualities," 242.
47. Ibid., 245.
48. Hine, "Marin Mersenne," 170.
49. Quoted in Lawrence Stone, *The Past and the Present* (Boston: Routledge and Kegan Paul, 1981), 169.
50. *Catholic Encyclopedia*, s.v. "necromancy" [http://www.newadvent.org/cathen/10735a.htm], accessed 9 November 2001.

SIX   AS IF BY MAGIC

1. Thomas Barfield, ed., *Dictionary of Anthropology* (Oxford, U.K.: Blackwell, 1997), 298. Other issues between science and magic, such as the relationship of magic to the laws of conservation of matter and energy, are beyond the scope of this study.
2. See Peter Berger, *The Sacred Canopy* (New York: Doubleday, 1967), and Weber, *Sociology of Religion*.
3. Rodney M. Coe, "The Magic of Science and the Science of Magic: An Essay on the Process of Healing," *Journal of Health and Social Behavior* 38 (1997): 2.
4. Fuller, *Science*, 56.
5. Ibid., 57.
6. See Edward Hooper, *The River: A Journey to the Source of HIV and AIDS* (Boston: Little, Brown, 1999), 169.
7. R. C. Lewontin, *Biology as Ideology* (Concord, Ontario: Anansi, 1991), 41ff.
8. Susan Sontag, *Illness as Metaphor* (New York: Farrar, Strauss and Giroux, 1978), 58.
9. Hooper, *The River*, 151–169.
10. A recent study disputes Hooper's theory. See Jon Cohen, "Disputed AIDS Theory Dies Its Final Death" *Science* 27 (April 2001): 615.
11. Peter Duesberg, "AIDS Acquisition by Drug Consumption and other Non-Contagious Risk Factors," *Pharmacology and Therapeutics* 55 (1992): 201–277.
12. Kary Mullis, *Dancing Naked in the Mind Field* (New York: Pantheon Books, 1998), 180, 181.
13. See Jon Cohen, "Ground Zero: AIDS Research in Africa," *Science,* June 2000, 2152, and Peter Piot, Michael Bartos, Peter Ghys, Neff Walker, and Bernhard Schwartländer, "The Global Impact of HIV/Aids," *Nature,* 19 April 2001, 968–973.
14. Randolph C. Byrd, "Positive Therapeutic Effects of Intercessory Prayer in a Coronary Care Unit Population," *Southern Medical Journal* 81 (1988): 826–829.

15. C. Cohen, S. Wheeler, D. Scott, B. Edwards, and P. Lusk, "Prayer as Therapy," *Hastings Center Report* 30, 3 (2000): 40.

16. Larry Dossey, *Healing Words: The Power of Prayer and the Practice of Medicine* (New York: HarperCollins, 1993), 200–205.

17. Cohen et al., "Prayer as Therapy," 42.

18. Herbert Benson, *Beyond the Relaxation Response* (New York: Time Books, 1984).

19. See J. K. Kiecolt-Glaser and R. Glaser, "Psychoneuroimmunology: Can Psychological Intervention Modulate Immunity?" *Journal of Consulting and Clinical Psychology* 60 (1992): 569–575.

20. Coe, "Magic of Science," 3.

21. Christina E. Hughes, "Prayer and Healing," *Journal of Holistic Nursing* 15 (1997): 318–324.

22. Walter Weston, *How Prayer Heals: A Scientific Approach* (Charlottesville, Va.: Hampton Roads, 1998).

23. Dossey, *Healing Words,* 189–195.

24. Ibid., xv.

25. Duane A. Matcha, *Medical Sociology* (Needham Heights, Mass.: Allyn and Bacon, 2000).

SEVEN TECHNOLOGY AS MAGIC

1. Mircea Eliade, *The Forge and the Crucible*, trans. Stephen Corrin (Chicago: University of Chicago Press, 1978). See also Carolyn Merchant, *The Death of Nature* (New York: Harper and Row, 1980).

2. Bert Hansen, "The Complementarity of Science and Magic Before the Scientific Revolution," *American Scientist* 74 (1986): 128.

3. Joachim Wach, *Sociology of Religion* (Chicago: University of Chicago Press, 1944), 353.

4. This considerably exaggerates the number of Internet users. A survey by the Angus Reid group estimated that 275 million people worldwide had used the Web at least once between November 1999 and January 2000. Mark Evans, "Canada Second in Internet Use," *Toronto Globe and Mail*, national ed., 13 March 2000. Given the percentage of people who own computers, the Angus Reid estimate seems high.

5. In Hermetic alchemy, the philosopher's stone was a substance of tremendous power that, supposedly, could make silver and gold out of base metals and "had unexampled powers of healing the human body and indeed of perfecting all things in their kind." F. Sherwood Taylor, *The Alchemists* (New York: Arno Press, 1974), 66.

6. Arthur C. Clarke, *Profiles of the Future* (New York: Harper and Row, 1973), 21.

7. In Hansen, "Complementarity of Science," 135.

8. William A. Stahl, *God and the Chip: Religion and the Culture of Technology* (Waterloo, Ontario: Wilfrid Laurier University Press, 1999).

9. In the mid–1630s Holland was caught up in a speculative frenzy for tulip bulbs. At the height of the mania, single bulbs were trading for the modern-day equivalent of thousands of dollars. The bubble burst in 1637, wiping out hundreds of investors. The bubble of 1999 was no different. The NASDAQ index peaked in March 2000 and crashed in April. By November 2000 all the gains made during the bubble had been erased, and by the spring of 2001 the NASDAQ had lost more than 60 percent of its value.

10. David Noble, *The Religion of Technology* (New York: Penguin Books, 1997).

11. Note the many levels of meaning packed into this one phrase. All three activities—saving the Earth, relating to others, and making money—are taken

to be equivalent. It perpetuates the idea that science will solve all our problems, no matter how great they are. This is yet another example of science as salvation (see chapter 1).

12. George Grant, *Technology and Empire* (Toronto, Ontario: House of Anansi, 1969), 27.

13. Paul Ricoeur, *Freud and Philosophy*, trans. D. Savage (New Haven, Conn: Yale University Press, 1970), 27, 543.

14. Eva Allen, John Burke, Mark Welch, and Loren Rieseberg, "How Reliable Is Science Information on the Web?" *Nature*, 16 December 1999, 722

15. Jim Stanford, "Beyond e-Hype," *Briarpatch*, 29, 4 (May 2000): 16.

16. Clifford Stoll, *High Tech Heretic* (New York: Doubleday, 1999), 174.

17. Margaret Wertheim, *The Pearly Gates of Cyberspace* (New York: Norton, 1999), 30.

18. Ibid., 286.

19. Frank Ogden, *Navigating in Cyberspace* (Toronto, Ontario: Macfarlane Walter and Ross, 1995), 137; Ray Kurzweil, *The Age of Spiritual Machines* (New York: Penguin Putnam, 1999); Yoneji Masuda, *The Information Society* (Washington, D.C.: World Future Society, 1980), 154–155.

20 Bill Joy, "Why the Future Doesn't Need Us," *Wired*, April 2000, 242.

21. Stoll, *High Tech Heretic*, 116–118.

22. Ernst Bloch, *The Principle of Hope*, trans. N. Plaice, S. Plaice, and P. Knight (Cambridge, Mass., MIT Press, 1986).

23. Rubem Alves, *Tomorrow's Child: Imagination, Creativity, and the Rebirth of Culture* (New York: Harper and Row, 1972), 81.

24. Wiebe Bijker, *Of Bicycles, Bakelites, and Bulbs: Toward a Theory of Sociotechnical Change* (Cambridge, Mass: MIT Press, 1995).

25. Michael L. Smith, "Selling the Moon: The U.S. Manned Space Program and the Triumph of Commodity Scientism," in *The Culture of Consumption*, ed. R. Fox and T. J. Lears (New York: Pantheon Books, 1983), 179.

26. Theodore Adorno, "The Stars down to Earth: The Los Angeles Times Astrology Column," *Telos* 19 (spring 1974): 84.

27. Thomas Jefferson, "Notes on the State of Virginia," in *The Portable Thomas Jefferson*, ed. M. D. Peterson (New York: Viking Press, 1975), 217.

28. John Ralston Saul, *The Unconscious Civilization* (Toronto, Ontario: House of Anansi, 1995), 76.

29. Robert D. Putnam, *Bowling Alone: The Collapse and Revival of American Community* (New York: Simon and Schuster, 2000).

30. Adorno, "Stars down to Earth," 78.

31. Wertheim, *Pearly Gates of Cyberspace*, 256–257.

32. Ibid., 271.

33. Joy, "Why the Future," 246.

34. Stoll, *High Tech Heretic*, 141–148; "Yeah, You've Got Mail," *Scientific American*, May 2000, 37.

35. Ronald Cole-Turner, *Science, Technology, and Mission* (Trinity Press International, in press), 29.

EIGHT   THE MORAL OF THE DINOSAUR

1. Clifford Geertz, *The Interpretation of Cultures* (New York: Basic Books, 1973), 98–108.

2. Wilfred Owen, "Anthem for Doomed Youth," in *The Collected Poems of Wilfred Owen* (New York: New Directions, 1963), 44.

3. Antoni Hoffman, "Changing Palaeontological Views on Mass Extinction Phenomena," in *Mass Extinctions: Processes and Evidence*, ed. Stephen K. Donovan (New York: Columbia University Press, 1989), 1–18.

4. Georges Cuvier, "Memoir on the Species of Elephants, Both Living and Fossil," in Martin J. S. Rudwick, ed., *Georges Cuvier, Fossil Bones and Geological Catastrophes: New Translations and Interpretations of the Primary Texts* (Chicago: University of Chicago Press, 1997), 18–24.

5. Rudwick, "Conclusions," *Georges Cuvier*, 253–267.

6. Stephen Jay Gould, "Toward the Vindication of Punctuational Change," in *Catastrophes and Earth History*, ed. W. A. Berggren and John Van Couvering (Princeton, N.J.: Princeton University Press, 1984), 9–16.

7. David M. Raup, "The Extinction Debates: A View From the Trenches," in *The Mass-Extinction Debates: How Science Works in a Crisis*, ed. William Glen (Stanford, Calif.: Stanford University Press, 1994), 149.

8. Darwin, *Origin of Species*, 454, 470.

9. Cited in Stephen Jay Gould, *Eight Little Piggies* (London: Penguin Books, 1993), 146.

10. Darwin, *Origin of Species*, 648.

11. David M. Raup, *Extinction: Bad Luck or Bad Genes?* (New York: Norton, 1991), 6.

12. John Brooke and Geoffrey Cantor, *Reconstructing Nature: The Engagement of Science and Religion* (Edinburgh: T and T Clark, 1998), 165–166.

13. Cited in Kenneth J. Hsü, *The Great Dying* (New York: Ballantine Books, 1986), 10.

14. For example, see George Gaylord Simpson, *The Meaning of Evolution,* rev. ed. (New York: Bantam Books, 1967).

15. See, for example, Robert Bakker, *The Dinosaur Heresies* (New York: Morrow, 1986).

16. Dale A. Russell, *A Vanished World: The Dinosaurs of Western Canada* (Ottawa: National Museum of Canada, 1977).

17. For Alvarez's own account, see Walter Alvarez, *T. Rex and the Crater of Doom* (Princeton, N.J.: Princeton University Press, 1997).

18. William Glen, "How Science Works in the Mass Extinction Debates," in *Mass-Extinction Debates*, ed. Glen, 46–50.

19. Cited in Charles Officer and Jake Page, *The Great Dinosaur Extinction Controversy* (Reading, Mass.: Addison-Wesley, 1996), 77–78.

20. Cited in James Powell, *Night Comes to the Cretaceous: Dinosaur Extinction and the Transformation of Modern Geology* (New York: Freeman, 1998), 164.

21. Ibid., 185.

22. Michael J. Benton, "Dusk of the Dinosaurs," *Scientific American*, September 1997, 96.

23. Charles Frankel, *The End of the Dinosaurs* (Cambridge, U.K.: Cambridge University Press, 1999), 52–60.

24. Latour, *Pandora's Hope*, 98–112.

25. For instance, Stephen Jay Gould recounts how his own controversies over punctuated equilibrium "predisposed" him to accept the Alvarez hypothesis. William Glen, "On the Mass Extinction Debates: An Interview With Stephen Jay Gould," in *Mass-Extinction Debates*, ed. Glen, 253–267.

26. Alvarez, *T-Rex*, 102–103.

27. Vincent Courtillot, *Evolutionary Catastrophes: The Science of Mass Extinction,* trans. Joe McClinton (Cambridge, U.K.: Cambridge University Press, 1999).

28. Ibid., 68–69.

29. See, for example, Martin G. Lockley and Alan Rice, eds., *Volcanism and Fossil Biotas*, Special Paper 244 (Boulder, Colo.: Geological Society of America, 1990).

30. Glen, "How Science Works," 82–85. Subsequent citations of this work will appear as page numbers in the text.

31. Raup, "Extinction Debates," 151. For examples of a few of those who did, see John Briggs, "Mass Extinctions: Fact or Fallacy?" in *Mass-Extinction Debates*, ed. Glen, 230–236; Norman D. Newell, "Mass Extinctions—Illusions or Realities?" in *Geological Implications of Impacts of Large Asteroids and Comets on the Earth*, Special Paper 190, from "Conference on Large Body Impacts and Terrestrial Evolution: Geological, Climatological, and Biological Implications held at Snowbird, Utah, October 19–22, 1981" (Boulder, Colo.: Geological Society of America, 1982), 257–263.

32. Raup, "Extinction Debates," 151.

33. Powell, *Night Comes to the Cretaceous*, 74, 216–218.

34. For example, see *Nuclear Winter and Associated Effects*, Report of the Committee on the Environmental Consequences of Nuclear War (Ottawa: Royal Society of Canada, 1984).

35. For example, see Officer and Page, *Great Dinosaur Extinction Controversy*, 79–84.

36. Elisabeth Clemens, "The Impact Hypothesis and Popular Science: Conditions and Consequences of Interdisciplinary Debate," in *Mass-Extinction Debates*, ed. Glen, 93–120.

37. Ibid., 104.

38. Officer and Page, *Great Dinosaur Extinction Controversy*, 90–109.

39. Philip W. Signor III and Jere H. Lipps, "Sampling Bias, Gradual Extinction Patterns, and Catastrophes in the Fossil Record," in *Geological Implications of Impacts*, 291–296.

40. Glen A. Izett, *The Cretaceous/Tertiary Boundary Interval, Raton Basin, Colorado and New Mexico, and Its Content of Shock-Metamorphosed Minerals; Evidence Relevant to the K/T Boundary Impact-Extinction Theory*, Special Paper 249 (Boulder, Colo.: Geological Society of America, 1990). See also Christian Koeberl and Raymond Anderson, eds., *The Manson Impact Structure, Iowa: Anatomy of an Impact Crater*, Special Paper 302 (Boulder, Colo.: Geological Society of America, 1996).

41. Peter Ward, *On Methuselah's Trail: Living Fossils and the Great Extinctions* (New York: Freeman, 1992), 122.

42. Peter M. Sheehan, David E. Fostevsky, Raymond G. Hoffmann, Claudia B. Berghaus, and Diane L. Gabriel, "Sudden Extinction of the Dinosaurs: Latest Cretaceous, Upper Great Plains, U.S.A.," *Science* (8 November 1991): 835–839.

43. N. Bhandari, P. N. Shukla, Z. G. Ghevariya, and M. Sundaram, "K/T Boundary Layer in Deccan Intertrappeans at Anjar, Kutch," in *The Cretaceous-Tertiary Event and Other Catastrophes in Earth History*, ed. Graham Ryder, David Fastovsky, and Stephan Gartner, Special Paper 307 (Boulder, Colo.: Geological Society of America, 1996), 417–424.

44. See Frankel, *End of the Dinosaurs*, 111–140.

45. Ibid., 64–65.

46. Ibid., 164–165.

47. Courtillot, *Evolutionary Catastrophes*, 98.

48. See Powell, *Night Comes to the Cretaceous*, 208ff.

49. Raup, *Extinction*, 195–199.

50. Barbour, *Religion and Science*, 247.

51. Ursula Goodenough, *The Sacred Depths of Nature* (Oxford, U.K.: Oxford University Press, 1998), 170–171.

52. Raup, *Extinction*, 17.

53. Hsü, *The Great Dying*, 21–22.

54. Barbour, *When Science Meets Religion*, 113; Ruse, *Can a Darwinian*, 137; Keith Ward, *God, Faith, and the New Millennium* (Oxford, U.K.: Oneworld Publications, 1998), 118; John Haught, *God After Darwin: A Theology of Evolution* (Boulder, Colo.: Westview Press, 2000).

55. Cf. Timothy C. Weiskel, "In Dust and Ashes: The Environmental Crisis in Religious Perspective," *Harvard Divinity Bulletin* 21, 3 (1992): 11, 19, 23.
56. John Polkinghorne, *Science and Providence* (Boston: New Science Library, 1989), 63.
57. Ibid., 66.
58. Ernst Bloch, *Atheism in Christianity*, trans. J. T. Swann (New York: Herder and Herder, 1972), 196–234.
59. Polkinghorne, *Science and Providence*, 68.

NINE   THE SCIENCE WARS

1. Paul R. Gross and Norman Levitt, *Higher Superstition: The Academic Left and Its Quarrel with Science* (Baltimore, Md.: Johns Hopkins University Press, 1994); subsequent citations of this work appear as page numbers in the text. A previous work, Gerald Holton's *Science and Anti-Science* (Cambridge, Mass.: Harvard University Press, 1993), was the first to draw attention to contemporary threats to science, but Holton's work was a much more specialized defense of logical positivism and did not generate the level of response that Gross and Levitt's book did.
2. Paul Gross, Norman Levitt, and Martin Lewis, eds., *The Flight from Science and Reason* (Baltimore, Md.: Johns Hopkins University Press, 1996).
3. Eugenie C. Scott, "Creationism, Ideology, and Science," in ibid., 505–522.
4. Alan Sokal, "Transgressing the Boundaries: Toward a Transformative Hermeneutics of Quantum Gravity," *Social Text* 14 (1996): 217–257.
5. Cited in Nick Jardine and Marina Frasca-Spada, "Splendours and Miseries of the Science Wars," *Studies in History and Philosophy of Science* 28 (1997): 219.
6. Alan Sokal, "A Physicist Experiments with Cultural Studies," *Lingua Franca*, May/June 1996, 62.
7. Ibid., 64.
8. Herbert Blumer, *Symbolic Interactionism* (Berkeley: University of California Press, 1969), 142.
9. Stephen Hilgartner, "The Sokal Affair in Context," *Science, Technology, and Human Values* 22 (1997): 509. On journals' assessment of submissions, see, for example, Daryl E. Chubin and Edward J. Hackett, *Peerless Science: Peer Review and U.S. Science Policy* (Albany: State University of New York Press, 1990); Lowell L. Hargens, "Variation in Journal Peer Review Systems," *Journal of the American Medical Association* 263 (1990): 1348–1352; and Marcel C. LaFollette, *Stealing into Print* (Berkeley: University of California Press, 1992). On studies that have employed deception, see Michael J. Mahoney, "Publication Prejudices: An Experimental Study of Confirmatory Bias in the Peer Review System," *Cognitive Therapy and Research* 1 (1977): 161–175; Douglas P. Peters and Stephen J. Ceci, "Peer Review Practices of Psychological Journals: The Fate of Published Articles Submitted Again," *Behavioral and Brain Sciences* 5 (1981): 187–255; and William M. Epstein, "Confirmational Response Bias among Social Work Journals," *Science, Technology, and Human Values* 15 (1990): 9–38.
10. Epstein, "Confirmational Response Bias."
11. Norman Levitt, *Prometheus Bedeviled: Science and the Contradictions of Contemporary Culture* (New Brunswick, N.J.: Rutgers University Press, 1999), 307.
12. Ibid., 5, 71, 62, 21, 29.
13. Ibid., 71.
14. Alan Sokal, "A Plea for Reason, Evidence, and Logic," *New Politics* 6 (1997): 126.

15. Jardine and Frasca-Spada, "Splendours and Miseries," 223.

16. Gross and Levitt, *Higher Superstition,* 86. Logical positivism was a philosophy of science in the first half of the twentieth century that argued only strict empirical verification could confirm scientific theories. In the 1950s, the German philosopher of science Karl Popper argued that scientific theories could not be confirmed but only proven false.

17. Jardine and Frasca-Spada, "Splendours and Miseries," 222.

18. Alan Sokal, "What the *Social Text* Affair Does and Does Not Prove," in *A House Built on Sand: Exposing Postmodernist Myths About Science,* ed. Noretta Koertge (New York: Oxford University Press, 1998), 18.

19. Blumer, *Symbolic Interactionism,* 46.

TEN NATURALISM, SCIENCE, AND RELIGION

1. See, for example, Werner Heisenberg, *Physics and Beyond: Encounters and Conversations* (New York: Harper and Row), 207.

2. John Ziman, *Of One Mind: The Collectivization of Science* (New York: Springer Verlag, 1995); J. M. Ziman, *Reliable Knowledge: An Exploration of the Grounds for Belief in Science* (Cambridge, U.K.: Cambridge University Press, 1991).

3. Theory in this context means an interconnected set of concepts and principles that has been extensively tested and that explains a large number of phenomena. The terms *principle* and *law* are basically synonymous, but *law* is often used in the case of a very important or general principle. For example, the law of conservation of energy is a very general and important principle.

4. "Platonic in nature" refers to a nonmaterial, conceptual construct that is considered real and treated as real.

5. William James, *The Principles of Psychology* (New York: Dover, 1950), 2:369.

6. J. Bronowski, *The Ascent of Man* (Boston: Little, Brown, 1973), 364.

7. Werner Heisenberg, *Physics and Philosophy: The Revolution in Modern Science* (New York: Harper, 1958), 81.

8. At the base of this lack of objectivity lies Heisenberg's uncertainty principle, which places restrictions on the knowledge we can obtain from quantum systems. This situation is the starting point for very profound and difficult questions concerning the philosophical basis of quantum mechanics and of the nature of reality. If one accepts quantum mechanics as the correct understanding of the true behavior of the atomic realm of reality, one can choose between two positions. Either this uncertainty reflects a limitation on our ability to know reality, or it reflects the nature of reality itself. Heisenberg felt that his uncertainty principle put limits on what scientists can measure. Anything outside of what is measurable becomes not science but speculation. Niels Bohr, on the other hand, viewed quantum theory as prescribing what is knowable (as opposed to what is measurable). The first position makes the problem an epistemological problem, while the second position makes it an ontological problem. See Jim Baggott, *The Meaning of Quantum Theory* (Oxford, U.K.: Oxford University Press, 1992), 32–33.

9. See, for example, ibid., 80–81, 86–87.

10. John D. Barrow, *Theories of Everything: The Quest for Ultimate Explanation* (Oxford, U.K.: Clarendon Press, 1991), 184.

11. See, for example, John Horgan, *The End of Science* (New York: Broadway Books, 1996), and Tony Rothman and George Sudarshan, *Doubt and Certainty: The Celebrated Academy* (Reading, Mass.: Perseus Books, 1998).

12. An extensive and profitable discussion of the role and limitations of mathematics in science, as well as other limitations of science, is presented in

John D. Barrow, *Impossibility: The Limits of Science and the Science of Limits* (Oxford, U.K.: Oxford University Press, 1998).

13. Science, the philosophy of science, and the history of science are interconnected in numerous ways. The problems of induction, causality, and determinism are extremely complex and touch all of these fields of inquiry. Unfortunately, within the scope of this book, it is not possible to discuss the knotty history of these issues in greater depth. At the minimum, one needs to go back at least to Aristotle to do justice to these problems. Since the paramount issues of realism, truth, and justification are guided in part by one's views and beliefs concerning these "three classical problems," the subtlety and importance of these topics cannot be overemphasized.

14. See, for example, Allan Goddard Lindh, "Did Popper Solve Hume's Problem?" *Nature* (11 November 1993): 105–106.

15. Bertrand Russell, *The Basic Writings of Bertrand Russell, 1903–1959* (New York: Simon and Schuster, 1961), 620–627.

16. Hume's devastating attack on induction has never been satisfactorily answered and may never be totally refuted. No matter how many times the condition A leads to (or causes) the state or observation B, it is not logically possible to infer that the next A will also lead to B. In essence, the induction problem is that although logically A does not imply B, empirically it does correlate to B. This has been a vexing paradox that implies that we know more truth from experience than we can prove with our minds.

17. See, for example, Baggott, *Meaning of Quantum Theory*, 30–33.

18. See, for example, David Ray Griffin, *Religion and Scientific Naturalism: Overcoming the Conflicts* (Albany: State University of New York Press, 2000), and Haught, *God After Darwin*.

19. Wendell Berry, *Life is a Miracle: An Essay Against Modern Superstition* (Washington, D.C.: Counterpoint, 2000); Huston Smith, *Why Religion Matters: The Fate of the Human Spirit in an Age of Disbelief* (New York: HarperSan Francisco, 2001).

20. Chet Raymo, *Skeptics and True Believers: The Exhilarating Connection Between Science and Religion* (New York: Walker, 1998).

21. Southgate et al., *God, Humanity, and the Cosmos*, 15–16.

22. Victor F. Weisskopf, "The Frontiers and Limits of Science," *American Scientist* 65 (1977): 405–411.

23. Richard P. Feynman, *"What Do You Care What Other People Think?" Further Adventures of a Curious Character* (New York: Norton, 1988), 11.

ELEVEN   HISTORY AND HERMENEUTICS

1. Hempel's laws are discussed in David Hackett Fischer, *Historians' Fallacies: Towards a Logic of Historical Thought* (New York: Harper and Row, 1970), 128–130.

2. Robin G. Collingwood, *The Idea of History* (New York: Oxford University Press, 1956), 249–280.

3. Lord Acton, cited in E. H. Carr, *What is History?* (Harmondsworth, U.K.: Penguin, 1961), 7.

4. For more on Braudel, see Peter Burke, *The French Historical Revolution: The Annales School, 1929–89* (Stanford, Calif.: Stanford University Press, 1990), 32–64.

5. Carl Becker, "Everyman His Own Historian," *American Historical Review*, 37 (1932): 221–236.

6. Carl Degler, "Why Historians Change Their Minds," *Pacific Historical Review* 45 (1976): 167–184.

7. Peter Novick, *That Noble Dream: The "Objectivity Question" and the Ameri-*

can Historical Profession (Cambridge, U.K.: Cambridge University Press, 1988).

8. Gertrude Himmelfarb, *The New History and the Old: Critical Essays and Reappraisals* (Cambridge, Mass.: Belknap Press, 1987), 21.
9. Ibid., 22.
10. Joan Wallach Scott, "History in Crisis? The Others' Side of the Story," *American Historical Review* 94 (1989): 681.
11. Harding, *Whose Science? Whose Knowledge?*, 46.
12. See Haraway, *Simians, Cyborgs, and Women.*
13. Hayden White, *The Content of the Form: Narrative Discourse and Historical Representation* (Baltimore, Md.: Johns Hopkins University Press, 1989).
14. Dominick LaCapra, *Rethinking Intellectual History: Texts, Contexts, Language* (Ithaca, N.Y.: Cornell University Press, 1983), 57.
15. Don Akenson, *At Face Value: The Life and Times of Eliza McCormack/John White* (Montreal, Ontario: McGill–Queen's University Press, 1990), xii.
16. White, *Content of the Form*, 20.
17. F. R. Ankersmit, "Reply to Professor Zagorin," *History and Theory* 29 (1990): 282.
18. Robert Darnton, *The Kiss of Lamourette: Reflections in Cultural History* (New York: Norton, 1990), xxi.
19. Richard Rorty, *Philosophy and the Mirror of Nature* (Princeton, N.J.: Princeton University Press, 1979), 318–319.
20. Barry Allen, "What It's All About," *Science*, 9 July 1999, 205.
21. Bruce Gregory, *Inventing Reality: Physics as Language* (New York: Wiley, 1988), 190.

TWELVE   THE CENTRALITY OF DIALOGUE

1. See, for example: Emile Durkheim, *The Elementary Forms of the Religious Life* (New York: Free Press, 1915); Rudolf Otto, *The Idea of the Holy*, 2d ed., trans. John Harvey (Oxford, U.K.: Oxford University Press, 1950); Mircea Eliade, *The Sacred and the Profane*, trans. Willard Trask (New York: Harcourt, Brace and World, 1959).
2. Richard Bernstein, *Beyond Objectivism and Relativism* (Philadelphia: University of Pennsylvania Press, 1983), 18.
3. Levitt, *Prometheus Bedeviled*, 300–301.
4. Hacking, *Social Construction of What?*
5. Latour, *Pandora's Hope*, 216–265.
6. Kary Doyle Smout, *The Creation/Evolution Controversy* (Westport, Conn.: Praeger, 1998).
7. Levitt, *Prometheus Bedeviled*, 80.
8. So Levitt concludes: "I am in favor of authority—authority recognized, empowered, and perhaps even institutionalized. Concomitantly, I implicitly seek to legitimize order and hierarchy as well. The ambient society must recognize the necessity for order, hierarchy, and authority, both within science and in the interactions of science with the wider culture." Ibid., 309.
9. Barbour only discusses the early work of the strong program in the sociology of scientific knowledge. Ian Barbour, *Religion in an Age of Science* (San Francisco: HarperSanFrancisco, 1990), 74–75.
10. For example, see Paul Feyerabend, *Against Method* (London: Verso, 1975).
11. Barbour, *When Science Meets Religion*, 108–109.
12. See Bruno Latour, "One More Turn After the Social Turn . . . " in *The Science Studies Reader*, ed. Mario Biagioli (New York: Routledge, 1999), 276–289.

13. The position Barbour calls ontological reductionism is the same as metaphysical naturalism, discussed in chapter 4. It may also be called monistic materialism or monistic reductionism in the literature. Monism is the belief that there is only one reality.

14. Barbour, *When Science Meets Religion*, 109.

15. Richard Brown, *Society as Text: Essays on Rhetoric, Reason, and Reality* (Chicago: University of Chicago Press, 1987), 86.

16. Jürgen Habermas, *Moral Consciousness and Communicative Action*, trans. Christian Lenhardt and Shierry Nicholsen (Cambridge, Mass.: MIT Press, 1991), 19.

17. Alfred Schutz, *Collected Papers*, vol. 1, *The Problem of Social Reality*, ed. Maurice Natanson (The Hague: Martinus Nijhoff, 1973), 301.

18. Robert N. Bellah, *Beyond Belief* (New York: Harper and Row, 1970), 202.

19. George Lakoff and Mark Johnson, *Metaphors We Live By* (Chicago: University of Chicago Press, 1980), 66.

20. Ibid., 66.

21. Schutz, *Collected Papers*, 230.

22. Ibid., 250.

23. Ibid., 232.

24. Brown, *Society as Text*, 86.

25. Schutz, *Collected Papers*, 258.

26. This is the mistake of Gould's NOMA model of the dialogue (see the introduction). Science and religion are indeed distinct domains, but they overlap continuously.

Selected References

Alvarez, Walter. *T. Rex and the Crater of Doom*. Princeton, N.J.: Princeton University Press, 1997.

Alves, Rubem. *Tomorrow's Child: Imagination, Creativity, and the Rebirth of Culture*. New York: Harper and Row, 1972.

Appleyard, Bryan. *Understanding the Present*. London: Pan Books, 1993.

Bakker, Robert. *The Dinosaur Heresies*. New York: Morrow, 1986.

Barbour, Ian. *When Science Meets Religion*. San Francisco: HarperSanFrancisco, 2000.

———. *Religion and Science: Historical and Contemporary Issues*. San Francisco: HarperSanFrancisco, 1997.

———. *Ethics in an Age of Technology*. San Francisco: HarperSanFrancisco, 1993.

———. *Religion in an Age of Science*. San Francisco: HarperSanFrancisco, 1990.

Barnes, Barry, David Bloor, and John Henry. *Scientific Knowledge*. Chicago: University of Chicago Press, 1996.

Barrow, John D. *The World Within the World*. Oxford, U.K.: Oxford University Press, 1988.

———. *Theories of Everything: The Quest for Ultimate Explanation*. Oxford, U.K.: Clarendon Press, 1991.

Barrow, John D., and Frank J. Tipler. *The Anthropic Cosmological Principle*. Oxford, U.K.: Oxford University Press, 1986.

Bauer, Henry H. *Scientific Literacy and the Myth of the Scientific Method*. Urbana: University of Illinois Press, 1992.

Bellah, Robert. *Beyond Belief*. New York: Harper and Row, 1970.

Berger, Peter. *The Sacred Canopy*. New York: Doubleday, 1967.

Berggren, W. A., and John Van Couvering. *Catastrophes and Earth History*. Princeton, N.J.: Princeton University Press, 1984.

Bernstein, Richard. *Beyond Objectivism and Relativism*. Philadelphia: University of Pennsylvania Press, 1983.

Biagioli, Mario, ed. *The Science Studies Reader*. New York: Routledge, 1999.

Bijker, Wiebe. *Of Bicycles, Bakelites, and Bulbs: Toward a Theory of Sociotechnical Change*. Cambridge: MIT Press, 1995.

Bloch, Ernst. *The Principle of Hope*. Translated by N. Plaice, S. Plaice, and P. Knight. Cambridge: MIT Press, 1986.

————. *Atheism in Christianity.* Translated by J. T. Swann. New York: Herder and Herder, 1972.

Bloor, David. *Knowledge and Social Imagery.* London: Routledge and Kegan Paul, 1976.

Brooke, John Hedley. *Science and Religion: Some Historical Perspectives.* Cambridge, U.K.: Cambridge University Press, 1991.

Brooke, John, and Geoffrey Cantor. *Reconstructing Nature: The Engagement of Science and Religion.* Edinburgh: T and T Clark, 1998.

Brown, Richard. *Society as Text: Essays on Rhetoric, Reason, and Reality.* Chicago: University of Chicago Press, 1987.

Butterfield, Herbert. *The Origins of Modern Science, 1300–1800.* London: G. Bell, 1949.

Christianson, Gale E. *Isaac Newton and the Scientific Revolution.* Oxford, U.K.: Oxford University Press, 1996.

Clarke, Arthur C. *Profiles of the Future.* New York: Harper and Row, 1973.

Cohen, H. Floris. *The Scientific Revolution: A Historiographical Inquiry.* Chicago: University of Chicago Press, 1994.

Cohen, I. Bernard. *Revolution in Science.* Cambridge, Mass.: Belknap Press, 1985.

Collins, Harry, and Trevor Pinch. *The Golem: What You Should Know About Science.* 2d ed. Cambridge, U.K.: Cambridge University Press, 1998.

Conway Morris, Simon. *The Crucible of Creation: The Burgess Shale and the Rise of Animals.* Oxford, U.K.: Oxford University Press, 1998.

Courtillot, Vincent. *Evolutionary Catastrophes: The Science of Mass Extinction.* Translated by Joe McClinton. Cambridge, U.K.: Cambridge University Press, 1999.

Darwin, Charles. *The Origin of Species.* New York: Modern Library, 1993.

Dobbs, Betty Jo. *The Janus Face of Genius: The Role of Alchemy in Newton's Thought.* Cambridge, U.K.: Cambridge University Press, 1991.

Donovan, Stephen K., ed. *Mass Extinctions: Processes and Evidence.* New York: Columbia University Press, 1989.

Draper, John William. *History of the Conflict Between Religion and Science.* London: Henry S. King, 1875.

Drees, Willem B. *Religion, Science, and Naturalism.* Cambridge, U.K.: Cambridge University Press, 1996.

Einstein, Albert. *Ideas and Opinions.* New York: Dell, 1954.

Eliade, Mircea. *The Forge and the Crucible.* Translated by Stephen Corrin. Chicago: University of Chicago Press, 1978.

Ermarth, Michael. *Wilhelm Dilthey: The Critique of Historical Reason.* Chicago: University of Chicago Press, 1978.

Feynman, Richard. *The Character of Physical Law.* Cambridge, Mass.: MIT Press, 1965.

Frankel, Charles. *The End of the Dinosaurs.* Cambridge, U.K.: Cambridge University Press, 1999.

Fuller, Steve. *Science.* Minneapolis: University of Minnesota Press, 1997.

————. *Philosophy of Science and Its Discontents.* 2d ed. New York: Guilford Press, 1993.

————. *Social Epistemology.* Bloomington: Indiana University Press, 1988.

Geertz, Clifford. *The Interpretation of Cultures.* New York: Basic Books, 1973.

Gieryn, Thomas. *Cultural Boundaries of Science.* Chicago: University of Chicago Press, 1999.

Gilbert, James. *Redeeming Culture: American Religion in an Age of Science.* Chicago: University of Chicago Press, 1997.

Glen, William, ed. *The Mass-Extinction Debates: How Science Works in a Crisis.* Stanford, Calif.: Stanford University Press, 1994.

Goodenough, Ursula. *The Sacred Depths of Nature.* Oxford, U.K.: Oxford University Press, 1998.

Gould, Stephen Jay. *Rocks of Ages: Science and Religion in the Fullness of Life.* New York: Ballantine, 1999.

———. *Leonardo's Mountain of Clams and the Diet of Worms.* New York: Harmony Books, 1998.

———. *Bully for Brontosaurus.* New York: Norton, 1991.

———. *Wonderful Life: The Burgess Shale and the Nature of History.* New York: Norton, 1989.

Grant, George. *Technology and Empire.* Toronto: House of Anansi, 1969.

Gregory, Bruce. *Inventing Reality: Physics as Language.* New York: Wiley, 1988.

Griffin, David Ray. *Religion and Scientific Naturalism: Overcoming the Conflicts.* Albany: State University of New York Press, 2000.

Gross, Paul R., and Norman Levitt. *Higher Superstition: The Academic Left and Its Quarrel with Science.* Baltimore, Md.: Johns Hopkins University Press, 1994.

Gross, Paul R., Norman Levitt, and Martin Lewis, eds. *The Flight from Science and Reason.* Baltimore, Md.: Johns Hopkins University Press, 1996.

Guthrie, Stewart. *Faces in the Clouds: A New Theory of Religion.* Oxford, U.K.: Oxford University Press, 1993.

Habermas, Jürgen. *Moral Consciousness and Communicative Action.* Translated by C. Lenhardt and S. W. Nicholsen. Cambridge, Mass.: MIT Press, 1991.

Hacking, Ian. *The Social Construction of What?* Cambridge, Mass.: Harvard University Press, 1999.

Haraway, Donna. *Simians, Cyborgs, and Women.* New York: Routledge, 1991.

Harding, Sandra. *Whose Science? Whose Knowledge?* Ithaca, N.Y.: Cornell University Press, 1991.

———. *The Science Question in Feminism.* Ithaca, N.Y.: Cornell University Press, 1986.

Haught, John. *God After Darwin: A Theology of Evolution.* Boulder, Colo.: Westview Press, 2000.

———. *Science and Religion.* New York: Paulist Press, 1995.

Hawking, Stephen. *A Brief History of Time.* New York: Bantam, 1988.

Himmelfarb, Gertrude. *The New History and the Old: Critical Essays and Reappraisals.* Cambridge, Mass.: Belknap Press, 1987.

Hooper, Edward. *The River: A Journey to the Source of HIV and AIDS.* Boston: Little, Brown, 1999.

Horgan, John. *The End of Science.* New York: Broadway Books, 1996.

Hsü, Kenneth J. *The Great Dying.* New York: Ballantine Books, 1986.

Innis, Harold. *The Bias of Communication.* Toronto: University of Toronto Press, 1951.

Jasanoff, Sheila, Gerald Markle, James Petersen, and Trevor Pinch, eds. *Handbook of Science and Technology Studies.* Thousand Oaks, Calif.: Sage Publications, 1995.

Jayawardine, S. A. *The Scientific Revolution: An Annotated Bibliography.* West Cornell, Conn.: Locust Hill Press, 1996.

Jefferson, Thomas. "Notes on the State of Virginia." In *The Portable Thomas Jefferson.* Edited by M. D. Peterson. New York: Viking Press, 1975.

Keller, Evelyn Fox. *Secrets of Life, Secrets of Death.* New York: Routledge, 1992.

———. *Reflections on Gender and Science.* New Haven, Conn.: Yale University Press, 1985.

Knorr Cetina, Karin. *Epistemic Culture.* Cambridge, Mass.: Harvard University Press, 1999.

Koertge, Noretta, ed. *A House Built on Sand: Exposing Postmodernist Myths About Science.* New York: Oxford University Press, 1998.

Kuhn, Thomas. *The Structure of Scientific Revolutions*. Chicago: University of Chicago Press, 1970.

Kurzweil, Ray. *The Age of Spiritual Machines*. New York: Penguin Putnam, 1999.

Lang, Bernhard. *Sacred Games: A History of Christian Worship*. New Haven, Conn.: Yale University Press, 1997.

Larson, Edward J. *Summer of the Gods: The Scopes Trial and America's Continuing Debate over Science and Religion*. New York: Basic Books, 1997.

Latour, Bruno. *Pandora's Hope*. Cambridge, Mass.: Harvard University Press, 1999.

———. *Science in Action*. Cambridge, Mass.: Harvard University Press, 1987.

Levitt, Norman. *Prometheus Bedeviled*. New Brunswick, N.J.: Rutgers University Press, 1999.

Lewontin, R. C. *Biology as Ideology*. Concord, Ontario: Anansi, 1991.

Lindberg, David C., and Robert Westman, eds. *Reappraisals of the Scientific Revolution*. Cambridge, U.K.: Cambridge University Press, 1990.

Manuel, Frank E. *The Religion of Isaac Newton*. Oxford, U.K.: Oxford University Press, 1974.

Marsden, George. *Understanding Fundamentalism and Evangelicalism*. Grand Rapids, Mich.: Eerdmans, 1991.

Masuda, Yoneji. *The Information Society*. Washington, D.C.: World Future Society, 1980.

Matcha, Duane A. *Medical Sociology*. Needham Heights, Mass.: Allyn and Bacon, 2000.

Medawar, Peter. *The Limits of Science*. Oxford, U.K.: Oxford University Press, 1984.

Merchant, Carolyn. *The Death of Nature*. New York: Harper and Row, 1980.

Merkel, Ingrid, and Allen G. Debus, eds. *Hermeticism and the Renaissance: Intellectual History and the Occult in Early Modern Europe*. London: Associated University Press, 1988.

Merton, Robert K. *The Sociology of Science*. Chicago: University of Chicago Press, 1973.

———. *Science, Technology, and Society in Seventeenth Century England*. New York: Howard Fertig, 1970.

Midgley, Mary. *Science as Salvation*. London: Routledge, 1992.

Mullis, Kary. *Dancing Naked in the Mind Field*. New York: Pantheon Books, 1998.

Nelkin, Dorothy. *Selling Science: How the Press Covers Science and Technology*. New York: Freeman, 1987.

Noble, David. *The Religion of Technology*. New York: Penguin Books, 1997.

Novick, Peter. *That Noble Dream: The "Objectivity Question" and the American Historical Profession*. Cambridge, U.K.: Cambridge University Press, 1988.

Numbers, Ronald. *Darwin Comes to America*. Cambridge, Mass.: Harvard University Press, 1998.

Officer, Charles, and Jake Page. *The Great Dinosaur Extinction Controversy*. Reading, Mass.: Addison-Wesley, 1996.

Ogden, Frank. *Navigating in Cyberspace*. Toronto: Macfarlane Walter and Ross, 1995.

Osler, Margaret, ed. *Rethinking the Scientific Revolution*. Cambridge, U.K.: Cambridge University Press, 2000.

Park, David. *The How and the Why: An Essay on the Origins and Development of Physical Theory*. Princeton, N.J.: Princeton University Press, 1988.

Park, Robert. *Voodoo Science: The Road from Foolishness to Fraud*. Oxford, U.K.: Oxford University Press, 2000.

Polkinghorne, John. *Science and Providence*. Boston: New Science Library, 1989.

Powell, James. *Night Comes to the Cretaceous: Dinosaur Extinction and the Transformation of Modern Geology*. New York: Freeman, 1998.

Principe, Lawrence. *The Aspiring Adept: Robert Boyle and His Alchemical Quest*. Princeton, N.J.: Princeton University Press, 1998.

Prus, Robert. *Symbolic Interaction and Ethnographic Research: Intersubjectivity and the Study of Human Lived Experience.* Albany: State University of New York Press, 1996.

Pumfrey, Stephen, Paolo Rossi, and Maurice Slawinski, eds. *Science, Culture, and Popular Belief in Renaissance Europe.* Manchester, U.K.: Manchester University Press, 1991.

Raup, David. *Extinction: Bad Luck or Bad Genes?* New York: Norton, 1991.

Raymo, Chet. *Skeptics and True Believers: The Exhilarating Connection Between Science and Religion.* New York: Walker, 1998.

Restivo, Sal. *Science, Society, and Values: Towards a Sociology of Objectivity.* Bethlehem, Pa.: Lehigh University Press, 1994.

Ricoeur, Paul. *Freud and Philosophy.* Translated by D. Savage. New Haven, Conn.: Yale University Press, 1970.

Ritzer, George. *Classical Sociological Theory.* New York: McGraw-Hill, 1992.

Rorty, Richard. *Philosophy and the Mirror of Nature.* Princeton, N.J.: Princeton University Press, 1979.

Ruse, Michael. *Can a Darwinian Be a Christian?* Cambridge, U.K.: Cambridge University Press, 2001.

————. *From Monad to Man: The Concept of Progress in Evolutionary Biology.* Cambridge, Mass.: Harvard University Press, 1996.

Saul, John Ralston. *The Unconscious Civilization.* Toronto, Ontario: House of Anansi, 1995.

Schroeer, Dietrich. *Physics and Its Fifth Dimension: Society.* Reading, Mass.: Addison-Wesley, 1972.

Schutz, Alfred. *Collected Papers.* Vol. 1. *The Problem of Social Reality.* Edited by Maurice Natanson. The Hague: Martinus Nijhoff, 1973.

Shapin, Steven. *The Scientific Revolution.* Chicago: University of Chicago Press, 1996.

Shumaker, Wayne. *Natural Magic and Modern Science: Four Treatises.* Binghamton, N.Y.: Medieval and Renaissance Texts and Studies, 1989.

Simpson, George Gaylord. *The Meaning of Evolution.* Rev. ed. New York: Bantam Books, 1967.

Singleton, Charles S., ed. *Art, Science, and History in the Renaissance.* Baltimore, Md.: Johns Hopkins University Press, 1967.

Smith, Huston. *Why Religion Matters: The Fate of the Human Spirit in an Age of Disbelief.* New York: HarperSan Francisco, 2001.

Smout, Kary Doyle. *The Creation/Evolution Controversy.* Westport, Conn.: Praeger, 1998.

Southgate, Christopher, Celia Deane-Drummond, Paul D. Murray, Michael Negus, Lawrence Osborn, Michael Poole, Jacqui Steward, and Fraser Watts. *God, Humanity, and the Cosmos.* Edinburgh: T and T Clark, 1999.

Stahl, William A. *God and the Chip: Religion and the Culture of Technology.* Waterloo, Ontario: Wilfrid Laurier University Press, 1999.

Stenmark, Mikael. *Rationality in Science, Religion, and Everyday Life: A Critical Evaluation of Four Models of Rationality.* Notre Dame, Ind.: University of Notre Dame Press, 1995.

Stoll, Clifford. *High Tech Heretic.* New York: Doubleday, 1999.

Taylor, F. Sherwood. *The Alchemists.* New York: Arno Press, 1974.

Traweek, Sharon. *Beamtimes and Lifetimes.* Cambridge, Mass.: Harvard University Press, 1988.

Trefil, James. *Reading the Mind of God: In Search of the Principle of Universality.* New York: Scribner's, 1989.

Vaughan, Diane. *The Challenger Launch Decision.* Chicago: University of Chicago Press, 1996.

Vickers, B., ed. *Occult and Scientific Mentalities in the Renaissance.* Cambridge, U.K.: Cambridge University Press, 1984.

Wach, Joachim. *Sociology of Religion*. Chicago: University of Chicago Press, 1944.

Walker, D. P. *Spiritual and Demonic Magic: From Ficino to Campanella*. London: Warburg Institute, 1958.

Ward, Keith, *God, Faith, and the New Millennium*. Oxford, U.K.: Oneworld Publications, 1998.

Ward, Peter. *On Methuselah's Trail: Living Fossils and the Great Extinctions*. New York: Freeman, 1992.

Weber, Max. *Sociology of Religion*. Boston: Beacon Press, 1963.

———. *The Protestant Ethic and the Spirit of Capitalism*. New York: Scribner's, 1958.

Wertheim, Margaret. *The Pearly Gates of Cyberspace*. New York: Norton, 1999.

Westfall, Richard S. *Never at Rest: A Biography of Isaac Newton*. Cambridge, U.K.: Cambridge University Press, 1980.

Weston, Walter. *How Prayer Heals: A Scientific Approach*. Charlottesville, Va.: Hampton Roads, 1998.

White, Michael. *Isaac Newton: The Last Sorcerer*. Reading, Mass.: Helix Books, 1997.

Wilson, A. N. *God's Funeral*. New York: Norton, 1999.

Wilson, Bryan. *Religion in Sociological Perspective*. Oxford, U.K.: Oxford University Press, 1982.

Wilson, E. O. *Consilience*. New York: Knopf, 1998.

Yates, Frances. *The Occult Philosophy in the Elizabethan Age*. London: Ark, 1983.

Index

Acton, Lord, 185
actualism, 137, 146
advanced industrial society, 129, 130
Agrippa, Henry Cornelius, 90, 92, 97
AIDS, xi, 101, 105–110, 115–116
Akenson, Donald, 190
alchemy, 47, 77–79, 90–91, 93,
    212n26, 212n33, 216n5. *See also*
    magic
alienation, 202
Allen, Barry, 193
Allen, Eva, 124
allies, in science practice, 143, 147,
    151
Alvarez, Luis, 140, 141–142, 143–144,
    145, 147
Alvarez, Walter, 140, 143–144, 147
Alvarez hypothesis, 140–150, 194,
    198; allies and colleagues in, 143,
    145–146, 147; links and knots in,
    143, 149–150; mobilization in, 143,
    144–145; public representations in,
    143, 147–148; threads in, 143, 144,
    147. *See also* evolution; model
Alves, Rubem, 128
amulets, 94
Andrade, E. N. da C., 73
angels, 87–89, 91
Ankersmit, F. R., 190
Annales historians, 46, 185–186

anthropic cosmological principle, 27,
    29, 136, 155, 167
anthropomorphism, 32
anticlericalism, 40, 208n8
apocalypse, 127, 128, 139, 141
Appleyard, Bryan, 27, 34
Aquinas, Thomas, 89
Archimedian point, 195, 196
Aristotelian worldview, 70, 72–75
Aristotle, 38–39, 74–76, 89, 222n13
Artsimovich, Lev Andreevich, 72
assumptions: about science and
    religion, 2, 4, 14, 23, 26, 31, 54, 64,
    65, 67, 137, 153, 161, 162; default,
    53, 54, 58; of historians, 38–40,
    42–45; and history, 187. *See also*
    methodology
astrology, 4, 90, 91, 95, 100
asymmetry, asymmetrical, 32, 148, 199
atheism, 12, 42, 95, 167, 180
attitudes: 54, 164; and history, 187;
    toward magic, 86, 87; toward
    science, 37, 44; toward technology,
    123
Augustine, Saint, 88, 93
authority, 14, 30, 54, 57, 59, 62, 66,
    70, 72, 99–100, 103, 110, 129, 139,
    145, 146, 167, 179–182, 197,
    223n8; epistemic, 13–14, 200, 203;
    of textbook science, 62, 66–67

About the Authors

WILLIAM A. STAHL is professor of sociology at Luther College, University of Regina, in Regina, Saskatchewan. He is the author of the award-winning *God and the Chip: Religion and the Culture of Technology*.

ROBERT A. CAMPBELL is associate principal for educational resources and informational technology, University of Toronto at Scarborough.

YVONNE PETRY is assistant professor of history at Luther College, University of Regina.

GARY DIVER teaches physics at the University of Regina and was formerly assistant professor of physics at Mary Baldwin College in Staunton, Virginia.